HOMOSEXUALITY AND AMERICAN PSYCHIATRY

HOMOSEXUALITY AND AMERICAN PSYCHIATRY

The Politics of Diagnosis

RONALD BAYER

With a new Afterword on AIDS and Homosexuality

PRINCETON UNIVERSITY PRESS

Princeton, New Jersey

FOR

Jane, Alessandra, and Julian

Published by Princeton University Press, 41 William Street,
Princeton, New Jersey 08540
In the United Kingdom: Princeton University Press,
Chichester, West Sussex
Afterword to the 1987 Edition © 1987 by Princeton University Press
Copyright © 1981 by Basic Books, Inc.
Published by arrangement with Basic Books, Inc., New York, New York
All rights reserved

First Princeton Paperback printing, 1987

9 8 7 6 5 4 3

LCC 86-43142
ISBN 0-691-02837-0 (pbk.)

Princeton University Press books are printed on acid-free paper
and meet the guidelines for permanence and durability of the
Committee on Production Guidelines for Book Longevity of the
Council on Library Resources

Printed in the United States of America

CONTENTS

ACKNOWLEDGMENTS

The idea of doing this book emerged during a postdoctoral year spent at the Hastings Center. Aware of my interest in the relationship between psychiatry and society, Willard Gaylin, the Center's president, suggested that I might find it rewarding to study the 1973 dispute over homosexuality within the American Psychiatric Association. He was right.

In conducting my research I encountered an extraordinary willingness on the part of those who had been involved in this controversy to spend time with me. Without their assistance it would have been impossible to reconstruct the events of that bitter dispute. The frankness of the interviews and the willingness to open personal files were remarkable given the lingering hostility among many of those who figured prominently in the battle. Though I cannot list each informant, I do wish to express my gratitude to the following psychiatrists: Richard Pillard, Kent Robinson, Charles Socarides, John Spiegel, and Robert Spitzer. Frank Kameny and Bruce Voeller, both activists in the struggle for Gay Liberation, were also extremely helpful.

I was fortunate to have the assistance of Jerome Bayer, Carola Mone, and Marna Howarth at various stages of my search for bibliographical and other documentary material.

Dorothy Nelkin of Cornell University generously agreed to read and comment upon my manuscript.

My colleagues at the Hastings Center provided me with encouragement and support at crucial points. Ruth Macklin and Arthur Caplan read portions of an earlier draft of this book and made useful comments. Willard Gaylin helped me in so many ways that I can say without exaggeration that this study would have been impossible without him. And that despite the fact that we have disagreed about some very fundamental issues.

Benjamin Brody encouraged and challenged me. My debt to him is special.

My typists—Barbara Behar, Bonnie Baya, Mary Gualandi, Ellen McAvoy, and Sue Holt—were more tolerant of my texts than they perhaps should have been.

Finally, Jane Alexander, my wife, shared her understanding of the English language with me, spending time and energy to force me to greater clarity and economy. Her good sense was frustrated only by my resistance.

HOMOSEXUALITY
AND
AMERICAN
PSYCHIATRY

INTRODUCTION

In 1973, after several years of bitter dispute, the Board of Trustees of the American Psychiatric Association decided to remove homosexuality from the *Diagnostic and Statistical Manual of Psychiatric Disorders*, its official list of mental diseases. Infuriated by that action, dissident psychiatrists charged the leadership of their association with an unseemly capitulation to the threats and pressures of Gay Liberation groups, and forced the board to submit its decision to a referendum of the full APA membership. And so America's psychiatrists were called to vote upon the question of whether homosexuality ought to be considered a mental disease. The entire process, from the first confrontations organized by gay demonstrators at psychiatric conventions to the referendum demanded by orthodox psychiatrists, seemed to violate the most basic expectations about how questions of science should be resolved. Instead of being engaged in a sober consideration of data, psychiatrists were swept up in a political controversy. The American Psychiatric Association had fallen victim to the disorder of a tumultuous era, when disruptive conflicts threatened to politicize every aspect of American social life. A furious egalitarianism that challenged every instance of authority had compelled psychiatric experts to negotiate the pathological status of homosexuality with homosexuals themselves. The result was not a conclusion based on an approximation of the scientific truth as dictated by reason, but was instead an action demanded by the ideological temper of the times.

To those who viewed the 1973 decision sympathetically, psychiatry had displayed a remarkable capacity to acknowledge the significance of new research findings and to rethink its approach to sexuality. Psychiatry did not capitulate to the pressure of Gay Liberation, but rather revealed an admirable flexibility. Unlike those who were unyieldingly committed to antihomosexual values rooted in the Judeo-Christian past, the leadership of the American Psychiatric Association had demonstrated wisdom, insight, and the strength to break with conventional but scientifically unwarranted beliefs.

Both those psychiatrists who fought to preserve the status of homosexuality as a pathology and those who, in alliance with Gay Liberation groups, wished to remove it from the list of psychiatric disorders understood the profound significance of the battle that had been joined. Each side mobilized the full range of resources it would need to prevail, limited only by the standards of professional decorum. But despite the tactical maneuvers, both sides recognized the very deep and fundamental questions involved: What is normal sexuality? What is the role of sexuality in human existence? Do the brute requirements of species' survival compel an answer to the question of whether homosexuality is a disorder? How should social values influence psychiatry and help to define the concept of mental illness? What is the appropriate scope of a nosology of psychiatric disorders? How should conflicts over such issues be resolved? How should the opposing principles of democracy and authority be brought to bear in such matters? Each side sought to respond to these issues with intellectual rigor consistent with what it considered the standards of "science."

This book presents a political analysis of the psychiatric battle over homosexuality. Such an analysis is not, however, external to the "real issue" of whether homosexuality represents a psychiatric disorder. To assume that there is an answer

to this question that is not ultimately political is to assume
that it is possible to determine, with the appropriate scientific
methodology, whether homosexuality is a disease given in nature. I do not accept that assumption, seeing in it a mistaken
view of the problem. The status of homosexuality is a political
question, representing a historically rooted, socially determined
choice regarding the ends of human sexuality. It requires a
political analysis.

In *The Triumph of the Therapeutic* Phillip Rieff noted that the
rejection of sexual individualism, which divorces pleasure and
procreation, was the "consensual matrix of Christian culture."[1]
That ethos has all but crumbled in the West, subverted by
profound social changes, battered by movements no longer
bound to its influence, and increasingly deserted by the populations over which its strictures once held sway. Not only have
procreation and pleasure been divorced, but the priority of
the former has been displaced by that of the latter. It is in
this context that the struggle on the part of homosexuals for
the social legitimation of their sexual orientation, the striking—
if grudging—willingness of society to grant tolerance to sexual
practices previously held in abhorrence, and ultimately the decision on the part of the American Psychiatric Association to
delete homosexuality from its nomenclature of mental disorders must be understood.

In explaining the hegemonic status of procreative sexuality,
Herbert Marcuse argued in *Eros and Civilization,* his radical reading of Freud, that the demands of the "performance principle"[2]
required that sexuality be limited to genital functions directed
at the opposite sex. Only in that way could the body be desex-
ualized and made available for work. Only heterosexuality
could guarantee the reproduction of labor so necessary for the
conquest of nature.

In a repressive order, which enforces the equation between the normal,
socially useful and good, the manifestations of pleasure for its own
sake must appear as *fleurs du mal.* Against a society which employs

sexuality as a means for a useful end, the perversions uphold sexuality, as an end in itself; they thus place themselves outside the dominion of the performance principle and challenge its foundations.[3]

The potentially seductive character of sexuality unfettered by the performance principle explains not only the existence of powerful taboos against the perversions, and the reliance on the criminal law to repress them, but the disgust experienced by those who encounter them. Threatened by their own unconscious wishes, men and women have had to protect themselves by punishing those who dared to satisfy the desires they could not themselves acknowledge.[4] As a leading figure on the Left during the 1960s, Marcuse gave voice to what was perceived by rebellious students as a struggle against an antiquated sexual morality. He linked that struggle to the revolutionary attack on the prevailing social order. Concerned that the lifting of restrictions on sexual pleasure and perversions might occur without a concomitant radical social transformation, he warned against the reactionary consequences of "repressive desublimation."[5]

As Western societies have increasingly redirected their energies from the tasks of capital accumulation toward consumption, the hold of the values upon which the primacy of the procreative rested has attenuated. Though taking a form Marcuse abhorred, the search for sexual pleasure is no longer deemed antithetical to the survival of civilization and orderly social life. Renunciation, restraint, and inhibition, so crucial to the periods of human history characterized by scarcity and to the era of early capitalist development, are now perceived as old-fashioned virtues. Indeed, their replacement is virtually required by a society in which consumption is considered a condition of, rather than an antagonist to, higher levels of production. Desires and behaviors that men and women in the past felt constrained to hide or deny have become increasingly matters of public acknowledgment, tolerated when not openly encouraged.

The success of the contraceptive movement dramatically illustrates this shift. While efforts to control conception have a long history, it is a history marked by condemnation on the part of those who spoke in the name of Judeo-Christian culture. As scientific and technical advances in the nineteenth century enhanced the possibility of effective birth control, those who sought to promote the use of contraceptive devices, often under the banner of neo-Malthusian doctrines, were typically subject to assault by the state. Jail sentences imposed under statutes designed to prohibit obscenity were not unusual. Though resistance to the popular dissemination of birth control information remained fierce, pressure for change eventually prevailed.

If the success of the contraceptive movement is explained in part by the transformation of sexual values, the struggle to achieve social acceptance for birth control advanced that transformation. Leaders of the early sex reform movement like Havelock Ellis and Magnus Hirschfeld appreciated the relationship between the battle to win social acceptance for contraception and that for acceptance of other forms of nonprocreative sex. For most others, however, the weight of tradition precluded the possibility of extending to homosexuality the implications of accepting heterosexual pleasure as an end in itself. Vern Bullough, a historian of sexuality, certainly overstates the case when he argues that "once the public came to accept nonprocreative sex, then homosexuality, a form of nonprocreative sex, also had to be examined."[6]

While the first six decades of the twentieth century had witnessed many of the changes necessary for the transformation of social attitudes toward homosexuality, these changes were not in themselves sufficient for such a radical break to occur. The abhorrence of homosexual practices, so deeply rooted in the Western cultural tradition, had taken on a force of its own and could not collapse merely because conditions were ripe. Indeed, the history of the contraceptive movement provides ample evidence of the extent to which the emergence of social forces willing to struggle for change was required for the subversion of dominant sexual values. That history reveals, in addition, that for such a shift to occur, the internal cohesion of the interests opposing change must have been subject to erosion. In the case of homosexuality, the appropriate confluence of forces did not emerge until the 1960s. Thus the relative ease with which the early radical critics of society's antihomosexual posture were consigned to oblivion.

The modern homophile movement in the United States did not surface until after World War II. In its early phases, it was marked by a defensive posture and was chiefly concerned with the dangers that beset the homosexual in his or her effort to live anonymously in a society still committed to the repressive use of vice squads and the law. Only gradually did those with the audacity to identify themselves as homosexuals begin to challenge the primacy of heterosexual standards. By the late 1960s the tentative thrusts of the early leaders of the movement had become a full-blown attack, with homosexuality presented as an "alternative life style" worthy of social acceptance on a par with heterosexuality. Mere tolerance was no longer the goal; the demand was for social legitimation.

The struggle for Gay Liberation was influenced profoundly by the civil rights and feminist movements of the mid- and late 1960s. Like Blacks, homosexuals began to see themselves as an oppressed minority injured not only by the arrangement of social institutions, but also by deeply entrenched ideological standards that, in ways both subtle and blatant, denied them dignity. Like racism, antihomosexuality required both a fully developed sociocultural critique and a political assault. And homosexuals, like women, began to challenge the dominant standards of sexuality. Sexism was thus perceived as the ideological reflection of the power of male heterosexuals incapable of acknowledging the erotic desires of women or of homosexuals. Like so many other client populations, homosexuals turned on those formerly perceived as protectors, their sense of self-confidence enhanced by an awareness that they were part of an upsurge of protest directed at every social institution in America. Thus American psychiatry emerged as a primary target of their radical disenchantment.

For much of the first half of this century many homosexuals who were willing to express themselves publicly welcomed the psychiatric effort to wrest control of the social definition of their lives from moral and religious authorities. Better sick than criminal, better the focus of therapeutic concern than the target of the brutal law. By the late 1960s, however, homosexual activists had discarded whatever lingering gratitude remained toward their former protectors and in a mood of militancy rose up to challenge what they considered the unwarranted, burdensome, and humiliating domination of psychiatry. Armed with the techniques of social protest, they subjected American psychiatry to a striking series of jolts.

While the homosexual revolt against heterosexual domination mirrored the process of social upheaval on the part of marginal, disenfranchised groups, the assault upon psychiatry must be viewed as echoing the contemporary attack on what had been, until the 1960s, the unassailable status of science and technology, medicine in particular. Ivan Illich, perhaps more than any other single figure, has sounded the battle cry for this antimodernist movement. He has drawn a portrait of a civilization impoverished by its own inventions, its own scientific and technological advances. It is a portrait of the progressive alienation of the power of ordinary men and women to elites who rule in the name of superior and inaccessible knowledge.[7] Though his polemical assaults have been directed against all the professions that mask their acts of usurpation with a benign ideology of service, medicine is paradigmatic and has drawn his sharpest fire.[8] He presents the medicalization of ever wider domains of social life as inimical to the ends of health and human welfare. A new class of physicians has not only orchestrated this process, but attained with each advance of medicine a more dangerous power to dominate. Illich is not alone. Both the reception given his work and the wave of antagonistic commentaries directed at medicine suggest that he is representative of a significant and growing movement. From within medicine and without, from the Right as well as the Left, the criticism is to be heard.

The attack on medicine as a social institution was prefigured by a more narrowly framed reaction against psychiatry. In seeking to provide explanations for aberrant behavior, psychiatry has been charged with having assumed from the faltering religious tradition the function of serving as a guarantor of social order, substituting the concept of illness for that of sin. At the same time, having sought to base its formulations upon the deterministic models of the natural sciences, it has been held responsible for the subversion of the most crucial assumptions of the Western tradition. By seeking the sources of social deviance in factors beyond the will of the individual, it has denied the relative importance of human agency, and thus has made the attribution of individual responsibility for violations of socially sanctioned standards of behavior increasingly difficult to justify. As psychiatrists have sought to assume responsibility for the control of a range of behaviors previously considered immoral—criminality, violence, alcohol and drug use, juvenile delinquency, sexual deviance—they have been charged with attempting to arrogate to themselves unlimited authority, laying the foundations for a therapeutic state.[9]

What were once the lonely denunciations of Thomas Szasz, the vitriolic critic of his own psychiatric colleagues, now inform the thinking of psychiatrists, sociologists, lawyers, and philosophers.[10] These "antipsychiatrists," Szasz's epigones as well as those who have deepened his thesis, have emerged as a powerful cultural force. They can no longer be dismissed by the representatives of the psychiatric orthodoxy. The establishment has been forced to assume a defensive posture. Lamenting this turn of events, psychiatrist Robert Stoller has written, "We are in a new era in which diagnosis has such social and political implications that one is constantly on the front lines fighting on issues our forebears were spared."[11]

Faced with both external challenge and internal theoretical confusion, some of those concerned with the institutional viability of American psychiatry have begun to engage in efforts to limit its domain, pressing for a withdrawal from contested regions. Recognizing the difficulty of defending an overextended professional commitment, they have asserted that prudence dictates the importance of restricting the scope of psychiatry's concerns. They have stressed the need to reverse the tendency toward extending the concept of mental illness to the universe of social problems and have sought to narrow the range of behavioral aberrations upon which the language of psychopathology is imposed.

Those who viewed the development of psychiatry as an enormous advance over the prescientific understanding of human behavior have reacted to the move toward retrenchment with dismay. Psychiatrists like Karl Menninger had proclaimed the humanizing mission of their profession; they had anticipated an era of rational social control founded upon the progressive extension of the newly acquired knowledge. Appalled by the brutality of policies derived from the moral tradition and its retributionist principles, they had held out the prospect of a therapeutic response to aberrance designed to restore the deviant to normality. They promised a degree of efficacy unattainable by reliance on the more primitive instruments of social control. But even when they were less sanguine about their capacity to cure, psychiatrists believed that the control they exercised in custodial institutions represented an advance over what prevailed in punitive settings.

With a therapeutic vision so dominant a feature of psychiatric thinking, a divergence between the interests of psychiatry and those to whom it sought to minister was almost inconceivable. Indeed, psychiatrists often saw themselves as the protectors of deviants who had suffered at the hands of society and the more traditional forces of social control. Protected from understanding the potentially negative consequences of their own power by a benign ideology, they rarely anticipated an outraged response on the part of those to whom they proffered their concern. Only when psychiatry's vision of itself as a humanizing force is appreciated can the pain, sorrow, and anger of those who are reproached, not only by antipsychiatrists but by those they have claimed as their patients, be fully comprehended. While it is of course possible to argue that such cries

represent nothing more than the distress of those whose power
and authority have been challenged, such an interpretation
fails to capture the tragic dimension of the situation of psychiatrists whose commitment to therapeutic concern has been subjected to assault and ridicule.

Under attack from many quarters and torn by internal disputes regarding its appropriate mission, psychiatry was especially vulnerable to the challenge of an increasingly militant
Gay Liberation movement. Though symbolically powerful,
psychiatry was in fact a target that could be attacked with
relative impunity. Thus it was with stunning ease that the
Gay Liberation movement was able to force the American Psychiatric Association to reconsider the inclusion of homosexuality in its official nomenclature of disorders, the *Diagnostic and
Statistical Manual.*

To many observers the ensuing rancorous debate among psychiatrists over the status of homosexuality reflected an almost
inexplicable concern with definitions and classifications. Bemused by the American affair, one Spanish psychiatrist remarked on the irony of his colleagues in the United States—
products of a "supertechnical education"—becoming involved
in a debate comparable only to those that had engaged the
medieval nominalists.[12] To many in the United States, the focus
on the American Psychiatric Association's official listing of disorders seemed a legalistic distraction from the more serious
issue of psychiatric theory and practice, a semantic quibble
with little substantive merit.

To dismiss the significance of the debate over whether homosexuality ought to be included in the APA's nosological classification, however, is to miss the enormous importance it carried
for American society, psychiatry, and the homosexual community. By investing the dispute with great meaning, the participants had themselves transformed it from a verbal duel into
a crucial, albeit symbolic, conflict. The gay community understood quite well the social consequences of being labeled and
defined by others, no matter how benign the posture of those
making the classification. A central feature of its struggle for

legitimation therefore entailed a challenge to psychiatry's authority and power to classify homosexuality as a disorder.

With deep cultural divisions having emerged in the United States about the role of sexuality, official psychiatry had been pressed to adopt a reformist posture. In deciding to delete homosexuality from the nomenclature, the APA chose to ally itself with the movement against the still dominant antihomosexual values of American society. In so doing, it not only placed itself in opposition to the systematic pattern of formal and informal exclusions that precluded the full integration of homosexuals into American social life, but deprived secular society, increasingly dependent upon "health" as a moral category, of the ideological justification for many of its discriminatory practices.

Because concepts of disease and health take form within cultural contexts in ways that often remain hidden from view, the process of change through which certain deviations become labeled as normal or abnormal remains difficult to discern, becoming clear only when historical or social conditions permit the piercing of the veil of "the natural." The decision on the part of the American Psychiatric Association to remove homosexuality from its list of disorders was startling to many observers precisely because it diverged so dramatically from the more hidden and gradual pattern. Between 1970 and 1973, in a period of only three years, what had been an article of orthodoxy in psychopathology was reversed. Because the change occurred so rapidly, the factors that are always at play were placed in stark relief, allowing us to observe some features that are often obscure.

The struggle over the status of homosexuality also provides an extraordinary opportunity to examine the complex relationship between psychiatry and contemporary society. It has become a matter of conventional wisdom to note that psychiatry is affected by the cultural milieu within which it is embedded, tending to reflect the dominant values of the time. But psychiatry as a social institution is not so limited. It is not simply an agency of social control, autonomous only to the extent that it can develop its own explanatory schemes and modes of therapeutic intervention. Psychiatry may, under special circumstances, act upon society, using its cultural influences to challenge social values and practices. The APA's decision on homosexuality provides an instance of such an effort. Society's response reveals the limits of that reformist capacity.

Chapter 1

FROM ABOMINATION TO DISEASE

THE MORAL TRADITION AND
THE ABOMINATION OF HOMOSEXUALITY

Homosexuality, despite periods of greater tolerance, has been considered an abomination in the West for much of the past two thousand years. The very nature of anatomical design seemed to reveal a Divine plan for the morally acceptable use of the sexual organs. With life short, and human strength virtually the only source of power available for the domestication of nature, the sexual desire felt by men for women seemed a miraculous force whose intended end was procreation. Nonprocreative sexuality represented not only a violation of God's nature, but a dangerous diversion of energy from the task of human survival. It is not surprising, then, that homosexuality was the target of repression. Even when the political authorities lacked the will or the power to persecute those who engaged in homosexual practices, the religious authorities condemned them with the moral fury usually reserved for religious heretics. Indeed, in time the act of buggery and religious heresy became synonomous.

Though the twentieth century has witnessed the emergence of increasingly powerful assaults on the moral-religious tradition, the legacy of antihomosexual bias has retained a remarkable vitality derived from the strength of its deep cultural foundations. As recently as 1953 the Archbishop of Canterbury could declare: "Let it be understood that homosexual indulgence is a shameful vice and a grievous sin from which deliverance is to be sought by every means."[1]

The Biblical sources for the denunciation of homosexuality are found in both Leviticus and Deuteronomy. They make clear the gravity of the sin. "If a man also lie with mankind, as he lieth with a woman, both of them have committed an abomination: they shall surely be put to death; their blood shall be upon them."[2] The story of Sodom and Gomorrah, destroyed by God's wrath because of their unredeemable evil, provided terrible evidence of the consequences that could befall those communities in which homosexuality was practiced and tolerated. Though recent exegetical studies suggest that this interpretation of the Biblical story did not become dominant until the second century B.C., it was nevertheless available to the early Christians as a justification for their harsh rejection of homosexual practices.

The specter of Sodom thus haunted the pronouncements of the Emperor Justinian issued in A.D. 538.

Since certain men, seized by diabolical incitement practice among themselves the most disgraceful lusts, and act contrary to nature: we enjoin them to take to heart the fear of God and the judgment to come, and to abstain from such like diabolical and unlawful lusts, so that they may not be visited by the just wrath of God on account of these impious acts, with the result that cities perish with all their inhabitants.[3]

Famines, earthquakes, and pestilence were the punishments to be visited upon cities that failed to extirpate homosexual practices. Those who engaged in the "defilement of males" revealed the depths of their sinfulness; they were guilty of "sacrilegious" and "impious" acts. While holding out the possibility of repentance, Justinian sternly declared that repeated indulgence in homosexual activity would be met with remorseless severity.

Biblical sources were supplemented in the Middle Ages by

Thomas Aquinas's elaboration of the argument against unnatural sexual practices.[4] Starting from the premise that the end of "venereal acts" was procreation, St. Thomas concluded that the use of the sexual organs for any other purpose was "lustful and sinful." Like the other *peccata contra naturam* (sins against nature) homosexual acts had pleasure as their sole purpose. They therefore offended against reason. It was Aquinas's argument that provided the basis for pronouncements by later moral theologians concerning nonprocreative sexuality. With his writings, the core of the Western Christian tradition on homosexuality was fully formed.[5]

As ecclesiastical authority began to wane with the rise of the modern state, the religious abhorrence of homosexual practices was carried over into the secular law. The imprint was unmistakable in the language used to frame both the statutory prohibition of such behavior and the legal commentaries as well. In sixteenth-century England, Henry VIII removed cases of sodomy from the jurisdiction of the ecclesiastical courts and declared the "detestable and abominable vice of buggery" a felony for which the death penalty was to be imposed.[6] Commenting on the criminal law covering buggery and sodomy, Sir Edward Coke wrote a century later that, "Buggery is a detestable and abominable sin, amongst Christians not to be named, committed by carnal knowledge against the ordinance of the Creator, and order of nature. . . ."[7] Blackstone echoed these views, terming homosexuality a crime "the very mention of which is a disgrace to human nature."[8]

The criminal prosecution of homosexuals ended in the nineteenth century in those European countries that retained the *Code Napoléon* following the Napoleonic conquests. In England, however, the death penalty remained a matter of statute until 1861, when, with the passage of the Offenses Against the Person Act, the punishment was reduced to a maximum of ten years' imprisonment for the "abominable crime of buggery."[9]

It was against this background of moral opprobrium that the scientific study of homosexuality began in the nineteenth century. Part of a much broader, but still nascent, movement seeking to challenge the dominance of the moral-religious perspective on the problems posed by discordant behavior, it was inspired by the vision of a thoroughly deterministic science of human action. It rejected the "pre-modern" stress on will and the concomitant moral categories of right and wrong. Instead it sought the causes of deviance in forces beyond the control of the individual. Reflecting the rising influence of medicine, it employed the categories of "health" and "pathology," which were assumed to be morally neutral. Yet, though the new medical-scientific perspective lifted the burden of personal culpability from those who engaged in homosexual practices, the authors of this theory, with only a few notable exceptions, continued to reflect the community's antipathy toward such behavior. Rather than challenge the historical rejection of homosexuality, the new perspective seemed to buttress it. In place of a Divinely determined standard for sexuality, it put one thought to exist in nature.

EARLY SCIENTIFIC THEORIES

OF HOMOSEXUALITY

In the early decades of the nineteenth century, what medical discussion of homosexuality did take place clearly bore the mark of the more powerful religious tradition. Though it was acknowledged that in some instances such behavior could be the result of insanity, in most instances it was considered freely willed and therefore a vice. Sir Alexander Morison wrote in his "Outlines on Lectures on Mental Disease," prepared in 1825, that

Monomania with Unnatural Propensity is a variety of partial insanity, the principal feature of which is an irresistible propensity to the crime against nature. This offense is so generally abhorred, that in treatises upon law it is termed 'peccatum illud horribile inter Christianas non nominandum'. . . . Being of so detestable a character it is a consolation to know that it is sometimes the consequence of insanity: it is, however, a melancholy truth that the offense has been committed in Christian countries by persons in full possession of their reason and capable of controlling their actions.[10]

Only in the last half of the century did homosexuality become the subject of concerted scientific investigation. Those who sought to explain the "propensity to the crime against nature" were divided between those who saw it as an acquired characteristic and those who viewed it as inborn. Despite its greater compatibility with the tradition of assigning culpability to the individual homosexual, however, the acquired school did not dominate scientific inquiry during this period, but rather had to share its influence with that which focused on the importance of heredity.

Carl Westphal, a professor of psychiatry in Berlin, is credited with placing the study of homosexuality on a clinical, scientific footing[11] by publishing a case history of a female homosexual in 1869. Terming her condition "contrary sexual feeling," he concluded that her abnormality was congenital rather than acquired. In the next years he went on to study more than two hundred such cases, developing a classification of the variety of behaviors associated with homosexuality. In France, Jean Martin Charcot, the director of the Salpêtrière, also concluded that homosexuality was inherited after he failed to effect a cure through hypnosis. For his fellow countryman Paul Moreau, homosexuality was the outgrowth of both an inherited "constitutional weakness" and environmental forces. Given an inborn predisposition to perversion, a "hereditary taint," factors ranging from poverty and climate to masturbation could precipitate the manifestation of homosexuality. In a state midway between reason and madness, those afflicted were in constant danger of becoming insane and thus required the protection of the asylum. Most important of the late nineteenth-century students of sexual deviance was Richard von

Krafft-Ebing, whose monumental *Psychopathia Sexualis* had an enormous impact on informed opinion about homosexuality. Considering any form of nonprocreative sexuality a perversion with potentially disastrous personal and social consequences, he attempted, like others in this period, to explain the existence of homosexuality in terms of both environmental and inherited factors. Each of his case studies sought to document a history of family pathology—insanity, epilepsy, hysteria, convulsions, alcoholism, and physical disorders—in those who developed, as a result of their life experiences, some form of sexual pathology.

The tendency to view homosexuality as inherited was linked by many investigators to a more general interest in the extent to which various forms of degeneracy represented an atavistic reappearance of primitive tendencies. Some believed that not only did homosexuals deviate from civilized sexual standards, but they were likely to engage in uncontrolled primitive and animal-like behavior as well. These views were most notably expressed by Cesar Lombroso, the late nineteenth-century Italian criminologist, who argued that homosexuals were at a lower stage of human development than heterosexuals. Though the human race had evolved over eons, leaving behind its own primitive behavior, each child was required to recapitulate the process in the course of its own development. Those with defective heredity failed to complete that process and remained at a less civilized point in the evolutionary course. Since, in Lombroso's view, homosexuals could not be held responsible for their own failure, no justification existed for their punishment. Social defense, however, required that they be restricted to asylums because of the danger they posed.

Not only did many of those who assumed that homosexuality represented a profound deviation from the normal pattern of human sexuality turn to hereditary factors in order to explain its roots; so too did those who had begun to challenge the dominant view. Karl Ulrichs, one of the most prolific nineteenth-century defenders of homosexuals, had asserted, beginning in the 1860s, that homosexuality was a hereditary anomaly: While the genitals of homosexuals developed along expected lines, their brains did not, and so it was possible for a female soul to be lodged in a male's body. These views anticipated those of Havelock Ellis, whose work *Sexual Inversion* sought to demonstrate that homosexuality was inborn, *and therefore* natural. Finally, Magnus Hirschfeld, the great advocate of homosexual rights in Germany, held that homosexuality was not pathological but rather the result of inborn characteristics determined by glandular secretions.

Thus scientific formulations were relied upon by those with the most fundamentally divergent standpoints. Newly discovered facts did little to frame the understanding of homosexuality; rather, it was the perspective on homosexuality that determined the meaning of those facts.

PSYCHOANALYSIS AND HOMOSEXUALITY: FREUD

For Freud, as for most of those who undertook the scientific study of sexuality in the last years of the nineteenth century and the first years of the twentieth century, there was no question but that heterosexuality represented the normal end of psychosexual development. Despite the complex and uncertain process of maturation, "one of the tasks implicit in object choice is that it should find its way to the opposite sex."[12] Here Freud saw no conflict between the demands of convention and nature's course.

In his first effort to account for what he termed sexual inversion, Freud set himself in sharp opposition to those scientists who claimed that homosexuality was an indication of degeneracy. In his *Three Essays on the Theory of Sexuality* he asserted that such a diagnosis could be justified only if homosexuals typically exhibited a number of serious deviations from normal behavior and if their capacity for survival and "efficient functioning" was severely impaired. Since Freud believed that homosexuality was found in men and women who exhibited no other deviations, whose efficiency was unimpaired, and who were "indeed distinguished by specially high intellectual development and ethical culture," it made little sense to him to employ the classification "degenerate" for inverts.[13]

This perspective distinguished him from many of his earliest followers as well as from later psychoanalytic clinicians who would see in homosexuality a profound disturbance affecting every aspect of social functioning. He rejected the suggestion on the part of some of his collaborators, including Ernest Jones, that homosexuals be barred from membership in psychoanalytic societies. "In effect we cannot exclude such persons without other sufficient reasons, as we cannot agree with their legal prosecution. We feel that a decision in such cases should depend upon a thorough examination of the other qualities of the candidate."[14] To a similar suggestion by the Berlin psychoanalytic society he responded that while barring homosexuals from psychoanalytic work might serve as something of a "guideline," it was necessary to avoid a rigid posture since there were many types of homosexuality as well as quite diverse psychological mechanisms that could account for its existence.[15]

Unlike those who saw homosexuality as a thing apart from normal sexuality, Freud characterized it as a natural feature of human psychosexual existence, a component of the libidinal drives of all men and women. All children experienced a homosexual phase in their psychosexual development, passing through it on the route to heterosexuality. Even in those who advanced successfully beyond the earlier phase of development, however, homosexual tendencies remained. "The homosexual tendencies are not . . . done away with or brought to a stop."[16] They were rather "deflected" from their original target and served other ends. For Freud the social instincts such as friendship, camaraderie, and "the general love for mankind" all derived their strength, their erotic component, from the unconscious homosexual impulses of those who had achieved the capacity for heterosexual relations.

The capacity for both homosexual and heterosexual love was linked by Freud to what he believed was an instinctual, constitutional bisexuality. Activity, passivity, the desire to introduce a part of one's body into that of another or to have a part of another's body introduced into oneself, and finally, masculinity and femininity, were all reflections of bisexuality.[17] At times the active, masculine drives dominated, at others the feminine, passive drives did. In no case was a person utterly without both sets of drives. Just as with homosexual impulses, the repressed was not obliterated. Even in adults who had traversed the course to heterosexuality, masculine and feminine impulses coexisted.[18]

Given the bisexual endowments of human beings, how did Freud account for the existence of exclusive homosexuality in the adult male?* Rather than propose an elaborated theory, Freud set forth a number of explanations for the perversion of the normal course of psychosexual development. The classical mechanisms discovered during his psychoanalytic work stressed a number of possibilities, any one of which might determine a homosexual outcome. Regardless of the specific factors involved, however, all of them started from the assumption that exclusive homosexuality represented an arrest of the developmental process, an instinctual fixation at a stage short of normal heterosexuality.

Among Freud's first formulations on the etiology of homosexuality was one that focused on the male child's attachment to his own genitals as a source of pleasure. Like all boys, those who are destined to become homosexual find in the penis a

---

* Since it is not my purpose to present a full account of the various psychoanalytic theories of homosexuality, but rather to note the ways in which the issue was approached, I have decided for purposes of brevity to restrict this discussion almost exclusively to male homosexuality, leaving aside the question of the etiology of lesbianism. It should be noted that in part because of the greater clinical exposure on the part of psychoanalysts to homosexual men, women have received less attention in the literature. This tendency has, of course, also been explained in terms of the minimization of female sexuality. Nevertheless, the issue was not ignored, as is made clear by Freud's lengthy case history "The Psychogenesis of a Case of Homosexuality in a Woman" (1920) in *Sexuality and the Psychology of Love*. See also Fenichel, *Psychoanalytic Theory*, pp. 338–44.

source of enormous pleasure. But, Freud believed, there existed in future homosexuals an "excessive" inborn interest in their own genitals during the autoerotic phase of psychosexual development. "Indeed it is the high esteem felt by the homosexual for the male organ which decides his fate."[19] Like other boys, those with such a fixation initially select women, their mothers and sometimes their sisters, as objects of sexual desire. But that attraction ends when they discover that the female has no penis. Since these boys cannot give up the male organ they may turn to men for sexual pleasure. For Freud those who became homosexual for this reason had failed to traverse the course between autoeroticism and the more mature stage of object love. "They . . . remained at a point of fixation between the two."[20]

Later, Freud asserted that homosexuality was linked to the profound frustration experienced during the oedipal phase by those boys who had developed especially intense attachments to their mothers.[21] Denied the sexual gratification for which they yearned, these boys regressed to an earlier stage of development, and identified with the woman they could not have. They then sought as sexual partners young men who resembled themselves and loved them in the way they would have had their mothers love them.

In those cases where an intense attachment to the mother was combined with a fixation upon the erotic pleasures of the anus, the dynamics were somewhat different. In these instances, a desire to receive sexual gratification from the mother was transformed into a wish to enjoy sex in the way she did. "With this as a point of departure, the father becomes the object of love, and the individual strives to submit to him as the mother does, in a passive-receptive manner."[22]

While Freud saw the child's attachment to the mother as pivotal in most cases, he was careful to note instances in which the father and other male figures played a central role in the etiology of homosexuality. In some cases the absence of the mother could determine the homosexual outcome. Deprived of the presence of a woman, the young boy might develop a deep attachment to his father or another older male and as a result seek in his later sexual partners someone reminiscent of the primary object of his love. Alternatively, fear of the anger aroused in his father by the son's oedipal strivings could account for homosexuality. Terrified at the prospect of his father's retaliatory rage, the young boy could be forced to withdraw from his intense attachment to his mother. Having chosen to "retire in favor" of the more powerful male in this instance, such a boy would then leave the field of women entirely. Thereafter only a homosexual attachment to men could provide sexual gratification without anxiety about castration.[23] Finally, a later speculation of Freud's suggested yet another formulation involving a powerful male in the etiology of homosexuality. Here an older male sibling was crucial. In such cases, jealousy derived from intense competition for the mother's attention generated murderous impulses in the younger boy. Partially because of training, but more importantly because the boy recognized his own relative weakness, he was forced to repress those wishes. Transformed in the process, they would then express themselves as homosexual love for the formerly hated brother.[24]

Running throughout Freud's efforts to identify the roots of homosexuality was a complex series of combinations of inherited, "constitutional" factors and environmental or "accidental" influences. He strove to find a middle ground in the debate between those who asserted that either biology or conditioning forces were exclusively responsible for a homosexual outcome. Although acknowledging in both his case histories and his theoretical work the presence of accidental determinants in many instances of homosexuality, he could not accept an exclusive reliance upon environment. The fact that not everyone subjected to similar influences became homosexual suggested an important role for biological forces.[25] Confronted by an extraordinary richness of detail in his case studies, Freud remarked that he had uncovered a "continual mingling and blending" of what in theory "we should try to separate into a pair of opposites—namely inherited and acquired factors."[26]

As a theoretician Freud was committed to the proposition that all psychic phenomena were determined by antecedent forces beyond the conscious control of individuals. It was this determinism as well as his own more generous attitude toward the basic instinctual drives of human beings that made him so unalterably opposed to the rigid, condemnatory stance of his society toward homosexuals. That same determinism made his work anathema to those whose world-view demanded that individuals be held to account for their willful violations of civilized sexual standards. But despite his determinism, Freud acknowledged difficulty in assigning importance and predictive force to the various innate and environmental factors he had isolated in the analysis of homosexuals. These etiological elements were only known "qualitatively and not in their relative strength." Thus the anomalous situation had emerged in which "it is always possible by analysis to recognize causation with certainty, whereas a prediction of it by synthesis is impossible."[27] Unable to predict homosexuality, psychoanalysis could nevertheless unequivocally assert that in those cases where it had developed could there have been no other outcome.

Always critical of those whom he termed "therapeutic enthusiasts," Freud was especially pessimistic about the prospects for the psychoanalytic cure of homosexuality: "One must remember that normal sexuality also depends upon a restriction in the choice of object; in general to undertake to convert a fully developed homosexual into a heterosexual is not much more promising than to do the reverse, only that for good practical reasons the latter is never attempted."[28] At the basis of this profound limitation on his own technique was his belief that the cure of homosexuals involved the conversion of one "variety of genital organization of sexuality into the other" rather than the resolution of a neurotic conflict.[29] Unlike the neuroses, which were a source of pain and discomfort, homosexuality was a source of pleasure: "Perversions are the negative of neuroses." To treat a homosexual successfully would necessitate convincing him that if he gave up his current source of erotic pleasure he could again "find the pleasure he had renounced." Aware of how difficult it was for neurotics to change, Freud was unable to strike a positive therapeutic stance here. Only where the homosexual fixation was relatively weak, or where there remained "considerable rudiments and vestiges of a heterosexual choice of object" was the prognosis more favorable.[30]

Freud's therapeutic pessimism as well as his acknowledgment that many homosexuals, though arrested in their development, could derive pleasure from both love and work provides the context in which his compassionate and now famous "Letter to an American Mother" of 1935 must be read.

Dear Mrs. . . .

I gather from your letter that your son is a homosexual. I am most impressed by the fact that you do not mention this term yourself in your information about him. May I question you, why you avoid it? Homosexuality is assuredly no advantage, but it is nothing to be ashamed of, no vice, no degradation, it cannot be classified as an illness; we consider it to be a variation of the sexual function produced by a certain arrest of sexual development. Many highly respectable individuals of ancient and modern times have been homosexuals, several of the greatest men among them (Plato, Michelangelo, Leonardo da Vinci, etc.). It is a great injustice to persecute homosexuality as a crime, and cruelty too. If you do not believe me, read the books of Havelock Ellis.

By asking me if I can help, you mean, I suppose, if I can abolish homosexuality and make normal heterosexuality take its place. The answer is, in a general way, we cannot promise to achieve it. In a certain number of cases we succeed in developing the blighted germs of heterosexual tendencies which are present in every homosexual, in the majority of cases it is no more possible. It is a question of the quality and the age of the individual. The result of treatment cannot be predicted.

What analysis can do for your son runs in a different line. If he is unhappy, neurotic, torn by conflicts, inhibited in his social life, analysis may bring him harmony, peace of mind, full efficiency whether he remains a homosexual or gets changed. . . .

Sincerely yours with kind wishes,
Freud[31]

PSYCHOANALYSIS AND HOMOSEXUALITY:

RADO, BIEBER, AND SOCARIDES

Though some analysts were more sanguine, Freud's pessimism regarding the possibility of the therapeutic reversal of homosexuality dominated psychoanalytic thinking for almost forty years. Here, at any rate, the psychoanalytic movement did not differ dramatically from the congenital school, which held that homosexuality was an irreversible anomaly. A marked shift took place in the 1940s, influenced in large measure by the work of Sandor Rado and his adaptational school of psychoanalysis. Rejecting the core Freudian concept of bisexuality, Rado and his followers were able to rethink the roots of homosexuality, and adopt a more optimistic therapeutic posture.

In Rado's view Freud had made a fundamental error in assuming that the ambiguous sexuality of the zygote implied the presence of male and female attributes in the psyche. This, he declared, was an "arbitrary leap from the embryological to the psychological."[32] Unduly influenced by the ancient myth of the unity of male and female, Freud had failed to understand that

the sexes are an outcome of evolutionary differentiation of contrasting yet complementary reproductive systems. Aside from the so-called hermaphrodite . . . every individual is either male or female. The view that each individual is both male and female (either more male or less female or the other way around) . . . has no scientific foundation.[33]

Taking reproductive anatomy as a starting point, Rado went on to assert that the male-female pairing was the natural and healthy pattern of sexual adaptation. But while biology dictated the appropriate nature of sexuality, humans did not inherit biological directives regarding the use of their sexual organs.[34] Rather it was the remarkable inventions of culture that supplied the requisite instructions. In the West the institution of marriage performed this crucial role of socialization. Thus did nature and convention cooperate in the preservation of the species.

What then could account for homosexuality? Since there was no innate homosexual drive, the rejection of the "standard pattern" could only be explained in terms of some overwhelming environmental force, some profound fear or resentment. Not the triumph of a homosexual instinct, but the dethroning of heterosexual nature was at work. Homosexuality represented a "reparative" attempt on the part of human beings to achieve sexual pleasure when the normal heterosexual outlet proved too threatening. While fear and resentment could thwart the natural expression of heterosexual desire, they could not destroy it. Only "schizophrenic disorganization" could achieve that end.[35] As proof of this vitality, Rado pointed to what he believed was the otherwise inexplicable nature of the choices made by homosexuals—their selection of partners who despite their biological endowments took on the features, at least subjectively, of the opposite sex. "If male desires male, why does he seek out a male partner who pretends to be a female?"[36]

Having explained homosexuality as a phobic response to members of the opposite sex rather than a component of human instinctual life, and having assumed the ever-present existence of a strong heterosexual drive, Rado and his followers were able to assume a more positive therapeutic stance. This new optimism, conveyed primarily through the work of those at Columbia University's Psychoanalytic Clinic for Training and Research, began to affect the theoretical and clinical work of a number of psychoanalysts who were to become prominent during the 1960s, when the status of homosexuals became an issue of great social concern.

One of the most ambitious psychoanalytic studies of male homosexuality in the period following Rado's theoretical revision was undertaken by the New York Society of Medical Psychoanalysts in the 1950s. Unlike the more conventional

reports of individual analysts detailing the insights derived
from a small number of cases, the Society's study presented
in a systematic manner data on a large number of psychoanalytic patients. The project involved 77 psychiatrists who contributed information on 106 homosexual and 100 heterosexual
patients, the latter serving as controls. In order to standardize
the vast amounts of data being collected, all participating analysts were requested to complete a questionnaire of 450 items
covering a full range of familial, social, diagnostic, and therapeutic issues. The results of that study were published in 1962
under the primary authorship of Irving Bieber and entitled
Homosexuality.[37]

Placing the findings of the Society in the broad psychoanalytic tradition, Bieber made it clear that the pathological status
of homosexuality was not itself the subject of investigation.
In contrast to other theoretical orientations, which he dismissed
as inadequate, he noted that "all psychoanalytic theories *assume*
that homosexuality is psychopathologic."[38] The goal of the
project was to develop a systematic analysis of the etiological
factors responsible for the pathology, a more coherent picture
of its course, and a more accurate understanding of the prognosis for psychoanalytic cure.

Acknowledging the debt owed to Rado, Bieber explicitly
rejected the Freudian assumption of constitutional bisexuality
and an innate homosexual drive. Exclusive heterosexuality was
the "biologic norm."[39] Bieber therefore could reverse the classical psychoanalytic belief in the presence of a latent homosexual
drive in all heterosexuals and assert that "every homosexual
is a latent heterosexual."[40]

Having rejected the possibility that constitutional factors
could account for the development of homosexuality, Bieber
turned to an analysis of the families of the homosexual patients
in the Society's sample. "Our findings point to the homosexual
adaptation as an outcome of exposure to highly pathologic
parent-child relationships and early life situations."[41] Seventy
items in the questionnaire probed the relationship between
mothers and sons. In 69 percent of the cases, an intimate

mother-son dyad characterized by restrictive and binding maternal behavior was found. Such a relationship existed in only 32 percent of the heterosexual comparison cases.[42] The close-binding, intimate mothers were believed to have thwarted the normal development of their sons by responding to their heterosexual drives with hostility, often expressing "demasculinizing and feminizing attitudes"; interfering with the father-son relationship by fostering competitiveness, often favoring their sons over their husbands; inhibiting the development of normal peer relationships with other boys; and damaging the capacity for independent action, subverting every sign of autonomy.[43] Even in those instances where the mothers of the homosexual patients were not close-binding and intimate, they were more likely to have established pathological relationships with their sons than was the case with the heterosexual patients.[44]

The picture with regard to paternal relationships was equally bleak.[45] "Profound interpersonal disturbance is unremitting" in homosexual father-son relationships. Though relationships between the controls and their fathers were often not "normal," they were generally "far more wholesome." As a group the fathers of homosexuals were depicted as detached, hostile, minimizing, and openly rejecting. By failing to meet their sons' needs for affection, these fathers created a pathologic need that could be satisfied only by other males through a homosexual adaptation. These fathers were also incapable of providing the model for masculine identification crucial to a young boy's healthy psychosexual development. Finally, by failing to assume a strong presence, such fathers could not intervene in the pathological relationships between the close-binding mothers and their sons.

Following from this analysis Bieber developed a picture of the family, the "triangular system," out of which homosexuality would most likely emerge. While acknowledging that a multiplicity of combinations of paternal and maternal behavior was associated with a homosexual outcome, Bieber asserted that the "classical pattern" was one in which a close-binding, intimate mother, who was domineering and minimizing toward her husband, was paired with a detached, hostile father.[46] In such a family "the homosexual son emerged as the interactional focal point upon whom the most profound parental psychopathology was concentrated."[47]

During the oedipal phase of development, according to Bieber, when normal heterosexual drives begin to surface, the "victim" of this pathogenic family is subjected to an intolerable conflict. Sexually overstimulated by his mother, who nevertheless attempts to thwart any signs of masculinity, he is rejected by his father, who accentuates his feelings of competitiveness instead of neutralizing them. Rather than a source of positive identification, the father becomes a grave threat, a potential source of physical injury. The female genitalia become identified with danger. The heterosexual drive itself becomes identified with potential harm. It is forced "underground" and becomes latent.[48]

Because of the pathological basis of the homosexual adaptation, the possibility of establishing a stable and intimate homosexual relationship is precluded, according to Bieber. Fear of intimacy combined with a fear of retaliation on the part of other excluded males make homosexual couples relatively volatile. The hostility and competitiveness of such relationships bring to even the most apparently satisfactory among them a quality of ambivalence leading ultimately to impermanence or transience. Hence the ceaseless, compulsive, and often anonymous pattern of homosexual cruising. Despite finding many inherently destructive elements in the homosexual relationship, Bieber was able to note in it some redeeming features. These features, however, had value only within the pitiful limits of homosexual life.

There is some attempt to establish and preserve human contact and to develop and maintain meaningful relationships. It is *one* kind of adaptation in the face of crippling circumstances of growth and development; it is an attempt to participate in social living as much as is tolerable within the limits of anxiety.[49]

Undertaken when the prevailing mood among psychoanalysts about the prospects for reversing homosexuality was still quite pessimistic, the Society's investigation suggested to Bieber that Freud was wrong and that there was reason to be optimistic. "Although this change may be more easily accomplished by some rather than others, in our judgment a heterosexual shift is a possibility for all homosexuals who are strongly motivated to change."[50] As a result of that conclusion, Bieber and his colleagues urged other analysts to direct their efforts toward helping their patients achieve heterosexuality rather than adjust to homosexuality. It is remarkable, given these assertions, that the data provided by *Homosexuality* tend to suggest more modest results. Of the seventy-two patients who were exclusively homosexual at the outset of treatment, 57 percent remained unchanged at the end of the study while 19 percent had become bisexual and only 19 percent exclusively heterosexual. Only by combining the data for those who began treatment as homosexuals and those who began as bisexuals was it possible to state that 27 percent had shifted from homosexuality to exclusive heterosexuality.[51]

Those who had successfully made a shift to heterosexuality had exhibited a willingness to embark on the long, difficult, and often frustrating course of analytic therapy. Only two of twenty-eight patients (7 percent) with fewer than 150 hours of treatment had become heterosexual, while nine of the forty patients (23 percent) who had undergone between 150 and 349 hours of analysis had made the shift. Finally, eighteen of the thirty-eight patients (47 percent) with 350 or more hours of treatment had made a successful transition.[52]

Among the indicators of a positive prognosis were relative youth (being under thirty-five years of age), strong motivation, a father who was not detached, some prior effort at heterosexual experience, and erotic heterosexual activity in the manifest content of dreams. In short, analytic therapy seemed to be most successful where the homosexual adaptation was not deeply and thoroughly entrenched and where the destructive role of the father was not as pronounced as in the "triangular systems" from which homosexuals most typically emerged. Little is to be found in *Homosexuality* regarding the substance of the therapeutic process, but in a later essay Bieber indicated that in "reconstructive treatment" emphasis had to be placed on exposing the "irrational fears of heterosexuality," while helping the homosexual to resolve those fears.[53] With the irrational foundations of the homosexual adaptation eliminated, the latent heterosexuality could surface, allowing for a fulfilling sexual existence in accordance with the dictates of the biologic norm.

Like Irving Bieber, Charles Socarides was to become, in the late 1960s and early 1970s, a leading and forceful proponent of the view that homosexuality represented a profound psychopathology. Like Bieber he was to take Rado's critique of Freud as a point of departure for his own psychoanalytic discussion of homosexuality. "Heterosexual object choice is determined by two and a half billion years of human evolution, a product of sexual differentiation."[54] Unlike Bieber, however, who speculated that an inborn olfactory sense may act as a steering mechanism guiding men and women to members of the opposite sex, Socarides argued that both homosexual and heterosexual adaptations are "learned behaviors."

While rejecting a biological directive, Socarides did not deny that "anatomically outlined" factors played a crucial role in determining sexuality. In repeated and sometimes opaque formulations he attempted to prove that human culture had evolved in such a way as to foster the male-female pairing in order to perpetuate the survival of the species.

Heterosexual object choice is outlined from birth by anatomy and then reinforced by cultural and environmental indoctrination. It is supported by universal human concepts of mating and the traditions of the family unit, together with the complementariness and contrast between the two sexes. Everything from birth to death is designed to perpetuate the male-female combination. This pattern is not only culturally ingrained, but anatomically outlined. The term "anatomically outlined" does not mean that it is instinctual to choose a person of the opposite sex. The human being is a biologically emergent entity derived from evolution, favoring survival.[55]

Though the rules governing sexual behavior were thus a product of culture, they were not arbitrary. To upset them, to suppose that the demands of heterosexuality could be put aside, was to court disaster.

Like others influenced by Rado, Socarides argued that homosexuality could be explained only in terms of "massive childhood fears" that disrupted what human evolution had decreed to be the normal course of development.[56] His major contribution to the psychoanalytic theory of homosexuality has been to suggest that the disturbance responsible for those fears occurred much earlier in life than had been suggested in other formulations. Rather than oedipal, it was preoedipal in origin.[57] The failure to traverse successfully the stage of development before three years of age, when the child is believed to establish an identity separate from that of its mother (the separation-individuation phase), has dire consequences. In the case of the male child, remaining pathologically bound to the mother precludes the emergence of an appropriate gender identity. As a consequence all "true," or "obligatory" homosexuals are characterized by a feminine identification. Any effort to establish a relationship with a woman other than the mother produces profound separation anxiety. At the same time such an effort produces a terrifying dread of potential engulfment and loss of the self.[58]

By pushing the etiology of homosexuality back to the preoedipal phase of development, Socarides established the theoretical justification for characterizing homosexuality as more profoundly pathological than it was generally considered to be when oedipal conflicts were stressed. According to Socarides, almost half of those who engage in homosexual practices have a concomitant schizophrenia, paranoia, or latent or pseudoneurotic schizophrenia, or are "in the throes of 'a manic-depressive reaction.' " The remainder, when simply neurotic, are characterized as obsessional, "occasionally of the phobic type."[59] So extreme is this nosological description that many psychoanalysts who accept the classification of homosexuality as a pathological condition find it hard to accept Socarides' characterization of the general population of homosexuals.[60]

For such profoundly disturbed individuals sexuality, in all its forms, becomes in Socarides' view an elaborate and intricately developed defense designed to maintain some equilibrium. The desperate and compulsive search for sexual partners assumed to be part of gay life is interpreted as a grasping for a sense of an ever-illusive masculinity, protecting the homosexual from his fear of merger with his "preoedipal mother." "They hope to achieve a 'shot' of masculinity in the homosexual act. Like the addict [the homosexual] must have his 'fix.' "[61] The pathological nature of the homosexual solution, however, "dooms" it from the start.

Homosexuality is based on the fear of the mother, the aggressive attack against the father, and is filled with aggression, destruction and self-deceit. It is a masquerade of life in which certain psychic energies are neutralized and held in a somewhat quiescent state. However, the unconscious manifestations of hate, destructiveness, incest and fear are always threatening to break through.[62]

Under such circumstances, the effort to find pleasure, love, and stability in a homosexual relationship can only be chimerical. Like Bieber, Socarides finds in the homosexual couple little more than a pathological pairing destined to be the source of unending pain and disappointment. Heterosexual relationships provide "cooperation, solace, stimulation, enrichment, healthy challenge and fulfillment"; homosexual "masquerades" are characterized only by "destruction, mutual defeat, exploitation of the partner and the self, oral-sadistic incorporation, aggressive onslaughts, attempts to alleviate anxiety and a pseudo solution to the aggressive and libidinal urges which dominate and torment the individual."[63] The apparent capacity of some homosexuals to function successfully in their nonsexual social roles merely masks the underlying pathology that makes such adjustments fragile. Disruption of such superficial stability is an ever-present possibility.

In spite of his bleak descriptions of homosexual pathology, Socarides has presented an optimistic picture of the prospects for psychoanalytic cure, reporting that over 50 percent of the strongly motivated obligatory homosexuals he has seen in treatment four to five times a week have become heterosexual. Even among those who consciously disavow the desire for change there exists a profound unconscious desire to "alter what an early environment has so cruelly forced upon them."[64] Critical of psychoanalysts and other psychotherapists who would help homosexuals adapt to their pathology, Socarides has reserved his most vituperative remarks for behavioral therapists who have sought to enhance the sexual experiences of those whom he considers profoundly disturbed. Writing of sex therapist William Masters, he has argued that by providing homosexual couples with instruction in the techniques of sexual gratification, Masters has ignored the lessons of biology and culture and has "raised the status of the anus to the level of the vagina." Instead of aiding such homosexuals sex therapists are "in effect 'burying' them."[65]

Among the tasks Socarides has described as crucial to the psychoanalytic therapy of homosexuals are the following: uncovering of the unconscious desire to achieve masculinity through identification with the male sexual partner, understanding of the preoedipal fears of incorporation and engulfment by the mother as well as of the fears of personal dissolution that attend any effort to separate from her, analysis of the oedipal fears of incest and aggression, discovery of the role of the penis as a substitute for the mother's breast, the surfacing of the yearning for the father's love and protection, and recognition of the presence of repeatedly suppressed heterosexual interests and desires.[66] Once the crippling fear and revulsion against women are eliminated, it becomes possible for the former homosexual "to function in the most meaningful relationship in life: the male-female sexual union and the affective state of love, tenderness, and joy with a partner of the opposite sex."[67]

PSYCHIATRY AND THE "DISEASE" OF HOMOSEXUALITY

Although the theories elaborated by Bieber and Socarides gained considerable prominence in the 1960s and early 1970s, other psychoanalytic formulations retained adherents during this period, and were a guide to both theoretical developments and therapeutic intervention.[68] Such diversity was not simply the result of the creative efforts of clinicians to explain the presence of the homosexual symptom in the very different patients with whom they worked; it represented profoundly divergent theoretical orientations. Freudians and neo-Freudians, those inspired by the libido theory and those who followed Rado, proponents of the preoedipal and oedipal etiological formulations all agreed, however, on one point. Homosexuality was a pathological condition. When the dominance of psychoanalytic theory in American psychiatry began to wane in the 1960s, other schools of thought incorporated, without much difficulty, the view that homosexuality was an abnormality. For behaviorists, for example, homosexuality was simply transformed from a perversion of the normal pattern of psychosexual development into the "maladaptive consequence" of "inappropriate learning."

The virtual unanimity regarding the pathological status of homosexuality was underscored in a striking context by Karl Menninger in his 1963 introduction to the American edition of the British Wolfenden Report. That report, which had gained international attention by calling for the decriminalization of homosexual activity between consenting adults, had rejected the classification of homosexuality as a disease.[69] Applauding its criminal law recommendation, Menninger ignored the latter point, writing:

> From the standpoint of the psychiatrist . . . homosexuality . . . constitutes evidence of immature sexuality and either arrested psychological development or regression. Whatever it be called by the public, there is no question in the minds of psychiatrists regarding the abnormality of such behavior.[70]

Although the psychiatric consensus on homosexuality was still undisturbed in 1963, it had already come under serious political challenge from homosexual activists and their ideological allies.

The situation had been very different in 1952 when the American Psychiatric Association issued its first official listing of mental disorders. At that time voices of dissent were beginning to surface but had little political force. The *Diagnostic and Statistical Manual, Mental Disorders (DSM-I)* had evolved from the efforts of a working group brought together under the aegis of the United States Public Health Service to design a nosological scheme adequate to the needs of modern psychiatry. The listing of psychiatric disorders contained in the American Medical Association's *Standard Classified Nomenclature of Disease* had proved inadequate. Designed primarily for the classification of chronic mental patients, it lacked the scope required by clinicians engaged in psychiatric practice. More important, it was considered outmoded by the increasing numbers of psychodynamically oriented psychiatrists emerging from training centers dominated by psychoanalytic theory. *DSM-I* thus represented a major effort on the part of American psychiatry to establish the boundaries of its work.

In the new nomenclature homosexuality and the other sexual deviations were included among the sociopathic personality disturbances.[71] These disorders were characterized by the absence of subjectively experienced distress or anxiety despite the presence of profound pathology. Thus it was possible to include homosexuality in the nosology despite the apparent lack of discomfort or dis-ease on the part of some homosexuals.

It was the pattern of behavior that established the pathology. Explicitly acknowledging the centrality of dominant social values in defining such conditions, *DSM-I* asserted that individuals so diagnosed were "ill primarily in terms of society and of conformity with the prevailing cultural milieu."

This first classificatory scheme remained unchanged until 1968 when a revised nomenclature was issued. In the revised *Diagnostic and Statistical Manual of Psychiatric Disorders (DSM-II)* homosexuality was removed from the category of sociopathic personality disturbances and listed together with the other sexual deviations—fetishism, pedophilia, transvestitism, exhibitionism, voyeurism, sadism and masochism—among the "other non-psychotic mental disorders."[72] Despite the existence of a very well developed homophile movement at the time *DSM-II* was issued, homosexual activists appear to have been unconcerned with its publication. Two years later the classification of homosexuality in the *Manual* was to become the central focus of the Gay Liberation movement's attack on psychiatry.

In 1973, as the result of three years of challenge on the part of gay activists and their allies within the American Psychiatric Association, homosexuality was deleted from the nomenclature. That decision marked the culmination of two decades of struggle that had shattered the fundamental moral and professional consensus on homosexuality.

Chapter 2

DISSENTING VIEWS:

CHALLENGES TO THE

PSYCHIATRIC ORTHODOXY

Early in the twentieth century, under the leadership of sex reformers like Havelock Ellis and Magnus Hirschfeld, a perspective emerged within which homosexuality was viewed as a normal variant of human sexuality. As the psychiatric interpretation of homosexuality achieved cultural dominance, it eclipsed that viewpoint. With the pathological status of homosexuality a matter of broad professional and lay consensus, research tended to focus upon the question of etiology, with contending psychodynamic hypotheses vying for recognition. The second issue of interest to investigators concerned with homosexuality was the extent to which therapeutic intervention could be expected to restore normal heterosexual functioning. In both instances it was clinical populations that provided the data. Since it was assumed that all homosexuals suffered from a pathological condition there was no question about the methodological soundness of relying upon patients for a more general understanding of the disorder.

It is therefore not surprising that criticism of the pathological perspective was first voiced by researchers who did not share the dominant clinical orientation. They either came from disciplines with radically different methodological assumptions from those that dominated psychiatry or were psychiatrists who had rejected the dominant paradigm of their own profession. These critics were thus able to make a matter of question what was a given for those who saw homosexuality as a disease to be explained and if possible cured.

The challenge to the psychiatric orthodoxy began soon after the end of World War II. At first researchers pursuing quite independent lines of investigation began to uncover data that was incompatible with conventional assumptions. The existence of these findings served to provoke further challenges and, within a relatively brief period, the tradition of Hirschfeld and Ellis was given new life. In part the postwar challenge to psychiatry can be explained in terms of the impact of the relativist standpoint of cultural anthropology. More important, however, was the new wave of homosexual activism. Between the homophile movement and the critical line of research there developed a complex, reciprocal relationship. The existence of the movement had a subtle but nonetheless crucial impact upon the social context within which such research was undertaken. The findings of the research were, in turn, vitally important to the early leaders of the homophile movement, encouraging them in their early, tentative efforts at organizational and ideological development. Finally, it was the struggle for homosexual rights that ultimately transformed this research from an interesting methodological critique of psychiatric theory and practice into a weapon in the assault on the power of psychiatry.

ALFRED KINSEY

The psychiatric perspective on homosexuality was still unchallenged when in 1948 Alfred Kinsey published his empirical study of the sexual behavior of American males.[1] Unlike the reports of those who depended upon small numbers, derived largely from their clinical practices, his findings were based upon an extraordinary number of interviews with men drawn from a cross-section of the American white male population. Designed to study the patterns of sexual behavior, Kinsey's work was almost crudely empiricist, lacking any systematic, theoretical point of reference. He believed it was possible to let the data speak for itself. Assuming that the differences he found were a matter of degree rather than of kind, he rejected the conventional dichotomy between the normal and the abnormal.[2] Thus freed from the cultural perspective that framed clinical research, he was able to challenge psychiatric conceptions of normal sexuality.

The results of his study were startling to the American public, revealing a deep gulf between cultural standards and actual sexual practices. Among the most serious challenges posed by his research involved his findings on homosexual behavior. To those who had comfortably assumed that homosexual activity was a marginal, pathological phenomenon, Kinsey's study represented a disturbing revelation. He, too, was surprised by his discoveries. "We ourselves were totally unprepared to find such incidence data when this research was originally undertaken."[3] Thirty-seven percent of the male population had had physical contact to the point of orgasm with other men, at some time between adolescence and old age.[4] Equally striking was the fact that this behavior was distributed along a continuum. The male population interviewed ranged from those who had engaged in no homosexual behavior to those who had been exclusively homosexual. (Kinsey rated his respondents from 0 to 6, with 0 representing exclusive heterosexual behavior and 6 representing exclusive homosexual behavior.)[5] Ten percent of his sample reported that they had been more or less exclusively homosexual for at least three years between the ages of eleven and fifty-five.

The torrent of criticism, statistical and moral, that greeted these results indicates the depth of resistance to the idea that

the incidence of sexual deviance was so high. But for homosexuals, who were just beginning their efforts at organization and
the struggle for social acceptance and legal rights, the findings
were emboldening. No longer was there a need to behave so
fearfully; there were millions of men who shared their experiences. Indeed, homosexual activists have asserted that the Kinsey study was one important element in the creation of a social
climate conducive to the emergence of an open homophile
movement in America.[6]

Kinsey was quick to use his data to challenge the prevailing
psychiatric orthodoxy. It was inconceivable to him, given the
frequencies he had uncovered, that the homosexual reaction
could be an indication of psychopathology.[7] This was especially
the case in the light of his finding that so many men engaged
in both homosexual and heterosexual behavior during the
course of their adult lives. The histories collected from his
respondents lent further support to his contention that orthodox assumptions about the link between homosexuality and
more general psychopathic trends were unfounded.[8] For Kinsey
the statistically normal could not be psychologically abnormal.
Furthermore, he considered untenable the assertion that
heterosexuality represented a biological directive. On the contrary, he believed that the "capacity of an individual to respond
erotically to any sort of stimulus . . . is basic to the species."[9]
Our "mammalian heritage" made possible both heterosexual
and homosexual responses.

Having rejected both conventional and dominant clinical assumptions regarding patterns of sexual behavior, Kinsey was
able to dismiss discussions of a "homosexual personality" as
unwarranted.[10] In fact both his methodological standpoint,
which stressed the quantification of behavior, and his empirical
findings led him to deny the existence of *the homosexual*.[11]

In attempting to account for the patterns of sexual behavior
chosen by his respondents, Kinsey was especially critical of
the psychodynamically inspired search for pathological family
backgrounds.[12] He assumed, instead, that an enormous and
complex play of forces was at work. For him the pattern of

sexuality chosen by individuals represented but one example of the "mysteries of human choice."[13] Unlike psychiatrists, who read great meaning into the ways in which men and women chose to meet their sexual needs, Kinsey denied the inherent importance of such decisions. Sexual preferences were no different from those involving food and clothes. It was society's abhorrence of certain sexual practices that magnified their significance.

If neither biology nor psychodynamics could explain the dominance of heterosexuality, what then could? Kinsey believed that sexual orientation, like all other social behavior, was learned.[14] It was culture that transformed the originally indeterminant sexual drive, directing it, channeling it toward "appropriate ends." While clinical psychiatric interest focused on the etiology of homosexuality, Kinsey asked, instead, why it was that more men did not choose to express their homosexual potential. The answer was to be found in a heterosexual culture that was unyieldingly restrictive.

By adopting a cultural perspective on the nature of human sexual behavior and then assuming a relativist position, Kinsey was able to assume an ideological posture of extraordinary tolerance for the diversity he had discovered in his data on sexuality. It was this tolerance that led him to challenge the therapeutic orientation of most psychiatric clinicians. In assuming that heterosexuality represented a medical norm to which they were obliged to help homosexuals conform, psychotherapists were enforcing the cultural hegemony of heterosexuality instead of meeting the needs of their patients. For Kinsey, assisting human beings to accept their diverse sexual orientations was a goal of significantly greater merit.[15]

When a homophile movement emerged in the 1950s, it immediately acknowledged Kinsey as a friend, not only because he vociferously denounced the statutory prohibitions on homosexuality, but because his work presented precisely the evidence needed to challenge the psychiatric profession.[16] He and his colleagues at Indiana University cultivated warm relationships with homophile groups. His death in 1956 was mourned as a great loss. In later years the Institute for Sex Research, which he had founded, sponsored further work on homosexual behavior, all of which sought to undermine both lay and professional views of homosexuality as a unitary pathological phenomenon. The most ambitious of those projects resulted in the publication of *Homosexualities: A Study of Diversity Among Men and Women.* Its title suggests the impact of Kinsey's thought.

CLELAND FORD AND FRANK BEACH

Three years after the publication of Kinsey's investigation, Cleland Ford and Frank Beach's *Patterns of Sexual Behavior* appeared.[17] Though it took less explicit aim at the standard psychiatric understanding of homosexuality, it presented material that was ultimately subversive of the conventional view of normal sexual behavior. While Kinsey had based his conclusions on data drawn from a sample of American males, Ford and Beach relied upon a cross-cultural analysis and an investigation of the behavior of nonhuman primates. Though they explicitly rejected an evaluative standpoint, their relativism was itself a striking rejection of assumptions about the universality and naturalness of primarily Western standards of sexual normality.

Their data, derived from the Yale Human Relations Area Files, had provided them with information on seventy-six cultures besides our own. In forty-nine of the societies for which information was available, they found that homosexual activity of some variety not only was considered normal but was socially sanctioned for some members of the community. In most instances the form such activity took was similar to that of the *berdache,* who assumed "female" characteristics. In some societies some male children were actually reared to assume that role. In others, homosexual activity constituted a significant element of the pubertal initiation rights and in fact was considered quite normal before marriage. Thus their cross-cultural comparison suggested that in some societies homosexual behavior was considered appropriate for all men at one stage of life, while for a relatively small number, fulfilling special social functions, exclusive homosexuality was not only accepted but valued. They found no society where homosexuality represented the dominant form of sexual activity for adults. In the remaining societies of their sample, homosexual behavior was considered unacceptable, with explicit social pressures applied against it. But even in these there were indications of some homosexual activity, albeit hidden and rare.[18]

In an effort to determine the extent to which the human capacity for homosexual response represented an inheritance from our evolutionary past, Ford and Beach next examined the available literature on animal sexual behavior, especially that of primates.[19] Though the data was not abundant, they did find reports of sexual activity between monkeys of the same sex. Other researchers had claimed that such behavior might, in fact, represent an effort on the part of one male to achieve dominance over another. Ford and Beach acknowledged these claims, but cited evidence that in some cases homosexual activity was "accompanied by signs of erotic arousal and perhaps even of satisfaction." Finally, they rejected the claim that such behavior was substitutive, engaged in only when female partners were unavailable. Adult male monkeys had been observed in concurrent homosexual and heterosexual activity. On the basis of this material, Ford and Beach were willing to conclude that in virtually all animal species there existed an inherent biological tendency for "inversion of sexual behavior."[20] Thus the homosexual responsiveness found in humans represented an aspect of our "fundamental mammalian heritage."[21]

Having dismissed the basic premise of those who argued that homosexuality was pathological because it violated a fundamental biological directive, Ford and Beach still had to explain the predominance of heterosexuality among humans. For them, as for Kinsey, the force of cultural experience determined this outcome.

Men and women who are totally lacking in any conscious homosexual leanings are as much a product of cultural conditioning as are exclusive homosexuals who find heterosexual relations distasteful and unsatisfactory. Both extremes represent movement away from the original indeterminate condition which includes the capacity for both forms of sexual expression.[22]

For those who believed that homosexuality represented a profound disturbance in the biologically rooted course of normal psychosexual development, such a radically cultural perspective on human sexuality was unacceptable. Others who considered homosexuality a pathological condition, however, could incorporate Ford and Beach's findings; nothing they suggested denied the possibility that in our culture a homosexual orientation was most typically the outcome of a severe disturbance in the normal experience of the child. Despite the conflicting uses to which these data were put by psychiatrists, politically sensitive homosexuals in the 1950s believed that Ford and Beach had provided yet another piece of evidence undercutting claims to value-neutrality on the part of psychiatry.[23] If both heterosexuality and homosexuality were culturally determined phenomena, it was possible to contradict the authority of psychiatrists without assuming the mantle of medical expertise or usurping the appropriate role of science. If indeed both the forms of sexuality and the social responses it provoked were radically variable and founded upon social values, then the terrain of conflict could be shifted from that of science to that of human preferences. No longer was it meaningful to ask scientists to respond to the question: "Is homosexuality a disease?" To psychiatrists who believed that their profession had played a meliorative role in rescuing homosexuality from the consequence of the moral perspective, the homophile movement's insistence that the discussion be returned to a cultural level represented a bitter irony. As homosexuals gained greater self-confidence because of the emergent homophile movement, they would accept the challenge of the new period and would argue forcefully that homosexuality could be justified as a sexual orientation fully compatible with a moral standpoint. In that context psychiatry would be seen not as a beneficent force, but as a regressive social institution.

EVELYN HOOKER

While the work of Kinsey and of Ford and Beach provided evidence subversive of the view that homosexuality constituted a pathological and marginal orientation, it did not address directly the issues of greatest importance to clinicians. It was Evelyn Hooker who undertook that task and pioneered in a form of research that would in later years provide the richest source of material for those who challenged the assumption that homosexuality was a pathological condition.

A psychologist by training, Hooker was drawn into her research by a former student who was a homosexual. He introduced her to his circle of friends, a group of apparently well-adjusted men who failed to conform to the image of the tortured and disturbed homosexual. As she gained their confidence, she was exposed to ever greater numbers, discovering a richness and diversity of "worlds" hidden from the ordinary observer and clinician. At last they pressed her to carry out a scientific study of homosexuals like themselves. Because more orthodox research, focused on clinical populations, had served to buttress society's negative attitudes toward homosexuality, new research was a matter of some urgency.[24] Hooker was convinced by their arguments that a full picture of homosexuality could not be derived from the investigations of clinicians who saw only homosexuals seeking psychological help, or from those who studied homosexuals in prisons, mental hospitals, or the disciplinary barracks of the armed services.[25] With a grant from the National Institute of Mental Health, she began her work in 1954.

Hooker's research population of nonpatient homosexuals was drawn from names provided by the Mattachine Society and One Inc., two homosexual rights groups then functioning in California. Acknowledging that these men were not a random sample, she justified her procedure by arguing that since homosexuality was largely a covert phenomenon, it simply was not possible to study a more representative population. Thirty homosexuals thus selected were matched with thirty heterosexuals in terms of age, I.Q., and educational achievement, excluding from both groups those she considered manifestly pathological. Each was given a Rorschach test and two other projective tests. There were two questions to be answered: Would the homosexuals reveal higher levels of psychopathology than the heterosexuals, as might be expected from clinical research? Could the matched pairs of heterosexuals and homosexuals be distinguished from each other on the basis of the Rorschach, as would be anticipated by the assumption that homosexuality represents a distinct pathological clinical entity?[26]

Hooker's findings differed strikingly from those produced by clinical researchers. They were considered so important by the editor of the *Journal of Projective Techniques,* which published them, that he "pressed" her to put them into print despite her own belief that the analysis was still preliminary.[27] The two judges evaluating the Rorschach results categorized two-thirds of both homosexuals and heterosexuals as of average adjustment or better.[28] Analysis of the other projective tests produced similar conclusions. Equally significant was the fact that the judges were unable to distinguish the homosexuals from the heterosexuals in the matched pairs except as would have been anticipated on the basis of chance.[29] Hooker's conclusions stood as a challenge to orthodox psychiatric thinking about homosexuality.

That the personality structure and adjustment [of the homosexual] may . . . vary within a wide range now seems quite clear. It comes as no surprise that some homosexuals are severely disturbed. . . . But what is difficult to accept (for most clinicians) is that some homosexuals may be very ordinary individuals, indistinguishable from ordinary individuals who are heterosexual. Or—I do not know whether this would be more or less difficult to accept—that some may be quite superior individuals not only devoid of pathology (unless one insists that homosexuality is a sign of pathology) but also functioning at a superior level.[30]

While acknowledging that a homosexual orientation might indeed constitute a "social" maladjustment, Hooker asserted that it did not invariably affect the psychological well-being of the individual.[31]

Unlike research that portrayed homosexuality as constituting a unitary, clinical entity with a common set of underlying dynamic features, Hooker's data revealed enormous diversity. In terms of both their patterns of sexual behavior and their psychological profiles, homosexuals were heterogeneous, differing from each other as did heterosexuals. In response to the claim that the Rorschach was insufficiently sensitive as a diagnostic tool, she argued that it was the heretofore masked existence of such variation, instead of any technical flaw in the test, that explained its failure to distinguish between heterosexuals and homosexuals.[32]

Since so much of the orthodox literature on homosexuality stressed that it was a pathological development rooted in profoundly disturbed family constellations, Hooker was compelled to examine the prevalence of such factors in the backgrounds of her research subjects. From her own studies as well as from a close examination of the empirical findings of other investigators, she was able to conclude that the etiological conclusion of orthodox psychiatry represented a grave distortion. She did not deny the presence of family pathology in the backgrounds of some homosexuals, but found it the case only in those instances where homosexuality was linked to more generalized psychopathology. For most homosexuals, however, she as-

serted that disturbed family relations proved to be neither necessary nor sufficient as determinants of their psychosexual
development. For Hooker, as for Kinsey, the causes of homosexuality were infinitely complex, involving an array of many
variables, including "biological, cultural, psychodynamic,
structural and situational."[33]

Hooker was fully aware of the extent to which many of
the homosexuals she studied exhibited behavioral patterns that
clinicians had singled out as indicative of pathology. Both the
clinical and popular literature had focused special attention
on the apparent inability of homosexual men to sustain long-
term relationships, on their grim and relentless cruising behavior, and on their promiscuity. Hooker's own empirical work
had uncovered a pattern that contrasted dramatically with this
bleak picture. Two-thirds of her respondents had successfully
sustained long-term partnerships. This pattern, though less deviant than conventionally assumed, still diverged from what
was believed to prevail among heterosexuals. In attempting
to account for this behavior, Hooker denied the centrality of
psychodynamic factors. Instead she emphasized the pressures
on the homosexual world, pressures that could be traced to
heterosexual hostility. With fear of public exposure and humil-
iation dominating the homosexual's life, it was extraordinarily
difficult for relationships to last. What was a source of security
for the heterosexual was a source of risk for the homosexual.
Thus it was the social reaction to homosexuality that generated
the "fear of intimacy" cited by clinicians as evidence of homosexual pathology. The labeling process was itself the primary
pathogenic factor.[34]

Her account of other traits, such as an "obsessive concern
with homosexuality" and instances of "withdrawal and passivity," similarly stressed the importance of social rather than
psychodynamic factors. Relying upon Gordon Allport's discussion of the behavior of stigmatized minorities in *The Nature of
Prejudice*, she claimed that the "disturbed" behavioral patterns
of homosexuals were "ego defensive," traceable to the victimization they had experienced:

It would be strange indeed if all the traits due to victimization in minority groups were in the homosexual produced by inner dynamics of the personality, since he is also a member of an outgroup which is subject to extreme penalties involving, according to Kinsey, cruelties which have not often been matched except in religious and social persecutions.[35]

The implications were clear. What homosexuals needed most was freedom from the crippling effects of exclusion and stigmatization. The elimination of undesirable and "pathological" traits could only follow a fundamental transformation in the social context of homosexual existence. Social struggle rather than psychotherapy was the appropriate healing tool.

The appearance of Hooker's work in the mid-1950s was of critical importance for the evolution of the homophile movement. Her findings provided "facts" that could buttress the position of homosexuals who rejected the pathological view of their condition. She had met the psychiatrists on their own terms and provided their critics with clinical data with which to do battle. As important as her findings was her willingness to share them with the ordinary men and women of the homophile movement. Her collaborative relationship with the Mattachine Society went beyond using it as a source of informants. She spoke to its members, published in its *Review*, attended its meetings, and received its honors. She became not only a source of ideological support, but an active participant in the homosexual struggle.

Her work was ultimately acknowledged beyond the homosexual community. She was selected to write an entry on homosexuality for the *International Encyclopedia of the Social Sciences* and at the end of the 1960s was chosen to lead the National Institute of Mental Health Task Force on Homosexuality. Her influence is evident in the thrust of the *Final Report*. Though by no means critical of therapeutic efforts with homosexuals seeking heterosexual adjustment, the Task Force placed enormous emphasis on the extent to which the misery of homosexuals could be alleviated through an end to the discriminatory social practices of the heterosexual world.[36]

THOMAS SZASZ

Though Kinsey, Ford and Beach, and Hooker each attempted
to undercut some important feature of the psychiatric perspective on homosexuality, none directly attacked the assumptions
that made possible the classification of homosexuality as a
mental illness. The critiques they provided were empirical
rather than theoretical. In no way were the fundamental categories of psychiatry—mental health and psychopathology—
brought into question. As a result, their arguments and their
data were subject to rebuttal and alternative interpretation.
It was Thomas Szasz who attempted to shift the terms of discussion to a conceptual level, focusing his attack on both the
underlying ideological assumptions of psychiatry and the
power of the profession in contemporary society. For him the
classification of homosexuality as pathological was not a matter
of error. Rather it was paradigmatic of the mistaken effort
on the part of psychiatry to define its task in terms of the
"cure" of "mental illness." Though initially his work did not
focus explicit and sustained attention on the problem of homosexuality, his more general analyses and polemics provided a
"text"[37] for those in the homophile movement who would
attack the power of psychiatry to define the meaning of their
sexual orientation.

Beginning in the mid-1950s, Szasz produced a stream of
critical essays designed to expose the ways in which psychiatry,
masquerading as a medical discipline, had assumed the social
function previously performed by religious institutions. As a
guarantor of the prevailing social ethos, he argued, it sought
to redefine deviations from ethical, political and legal norms
by first the invention and then the expansion of the concept
of mental illness. Since psychiatry placed itself in the tradition
of scientific medicine, this defense of values took the form
of a value-neutral defense of health. In so doing it sought to

disarm those whose discordant behavior could be dismissed as the manifestation of illness. At the same time, Szasz argued, psychiatry camouflaged its own quest for power as a benevolent extension of medical authority.

I believe that we ought to object to all this on basic logical and moral grounds: if moral values are to be discussed and promoted, they ought to be considered for what they are—moral values not health values. Why? Because moral values are and must be the legitimate concern of everyone and fall under the special competence of no particular group; whereas health values (and especially their technical implications) are and must be the concern mainly of experts on health, especially physicians.[38]

For Szasz the fundamental self-serving error of psychiatry was its effort to claim that deviations from behavioral norms were illnesses in much the same way as deviations from biophysical norms were. In *The Myth of Mental Illness* he traced the beginnings of this process to Freud and Breuer's studies of hysteria. Here he saw a strategic move which attempted to confound real illness with a mere "counterfeit," an effort to extend through the use of metaphor the logic of the concept of disease.[39] Physical ailments were discovered through close examination of the patient or the refinement of diagnostic techniques. Mental illnesses were invented, declared, through the extension of the metaphor of disease.[40]

Central to the movement to expand the concept of illness beyond the biological realm, where Szasz claimed it had originated and ought to remain, was the increasingly appealing assumption that behavioral aberrations were often beyond the control of those who exhibited them. Szasz rejected the deterministic underpinnings of this effort. While not denying that antecedent events could, and often did, have important consequences for the way people behaved, or how they chose to solve their "problems of living," he stressed that such events were not "causes." Only in true illnesses could one speak of causal factors. Behavioral deviations "are made to happen by sentient, intelligent human beings and can be understood best in my opinion in the framework of games. Mental illnesses resemble certain moves or tactics in playing games."[41] Though psychiatry attempted to portray its concern with the victims of unconscious forces as a matter of humane understanding, for Szasz that very posture entailed a denial of the dignity and autonomy of the cared-for person. An ethical commitment to individualism thus precluded his acceptance of the deterministic premises of psychodynamic psychiatry. At the core of modern psychiatry Szasz saw a dangerous myth.[42]

Since "mental illnesses" were ways in which "patients" expressed their life choices, they were for Szasz like a language. They were to be understood and explored. Acknowledging that those who came to psychotherapists did not fully comprehend the languages in which they spoke, Szasz believed that the goal of the relationship was to provide a "translation."[43] In this scheme, strained as it seems at times, there was no room for the discussion of etiology, with its assumption of a medical problem to be solved. Thus, referring to hysteria, he wrote:

If hysteria is a language, looking for its "etiology" is about as sensible as looking for the etiology of English. A language has a history, a geographic distribution, a system of rules for its use—but it does not have an "etiology."[44]

With mental illness exposed as a myth and with the search for etiologies rejected as an inappropriate attempt to understand behavior in terms of the diction of medicine, what function was served by the psychiatric diagnosis? For Szasz the answer was clear: "terms like 'neurosis,' 'psychosis,' 'mental illness'—indeed the whole gamut of psychiatric diagnostic labels—function mainly as counters in a pseudomedical rhetoric of rejection."[45] Such diagnoses—labels applied to distasteful or otherwise unacceptable behavior—served to degrade the persons and classes to whom they were attached.[46] The diagnostic process was but the first step in the psychiatric effort to control discordant behavior. Instead of serving the interest of the "sick" through deepening our understanding, such diagnoses served the interest of power. "The chains removed from the insane by Pinel were reattached by the great psychiatric nosologists."[47]

Having elaborated his more general attack on the concept of mental illness and the social role of psychiatry as well as the allied mental health professions, Szasz was ready in 1965 to make his first fully developed statement on the question of homosexuality. In attempting to lay bare the basis for the diagnostic classification of homosexuality as a mental illness, he noted in his essay "Legal and Moral Aspects of Homosexuality" that the biological requirements of procreation seemed to justify the establishment of heterosexuality as the standard of clinical judgment.[48] Yet for Szasz the leap from the biological imperatives of the species to the norms that ought to govern human sexuality was unacceptable. It was an attempt to read from nature a set of social conventions, to claim that the priority given to heterosexuality was not a matter of human invention. "We delude ourselves . . . if because of its biological value we accept heterosexuality as a social value. The jump from biological value to social value is the crux of human morality."[49]

Just as the voluntaristic premises of his psychology assumed that individuals were free to choose from alternative life "games," his ethical perspective assumed that societies were free to choose among competing values in their efforts to guide or control the behavior of their members. Understanding why an individual chose homosexuality or why a given society condemned such behavior required an analysis of the values associated with sexuality rather than an investigation of the laws of nature.

Characteristic of Szasz's concern with the social functions of psychiatry was his argument that even more important than the theories about homosexuality was the action that followed from them.[50] Though he acknowledged that labeling homosexuality as a disease did not necessarily commit psychiatrists to the imposition of treatment upon those who were satisfied with their sexual orientations, the spectre of compulsory therapeutic intervention was a matter of overriding interest to him. Indeed, though Szasz was not explicit on the subject, it is clear that he saw the association of homosexuality with disease and heterosexuality with health as creating a coercive social situation that could easily be exploited. Thus he insisted that even in the private and voluntary setting of the psychoanalytic practice, it was imperative to recognize that the effort to change a person's sexual orientation was a matter not of curing, but of changing values. In that kind of relationship, the appropriate role of psychotherapists was not to impose, however subtly, their own values masked as health, but to let "patients" choose their own.[51]

The publication of Szasz's 1965 essay coincided with a sharpening of antagonism toward psychiatry on the part of the homophile movement. When his next major discussion of homosexuality appeared in 1970 as part of *The Manufacture of Madness*, that movement had undergone a significant radicalization, and any lingering respect for the psychiatric establishment had been swept aside. During this five-year period, Szasz's work had undergone some elaboration. Though the line of reasoning had not changed, it included new material—analogical force having been added to old arguments. More importantly, Szasz's tone had become increasingly shrill, making his work compatible with the militancy then current in the Gay Liberation movement.

His strategy in *The Manufacture of Madness* was to compare contemporary psychiatry with the Inquisition. Both were intolerant; both relied on torture.[52] Like the Church in its brutal effort to impose its religious values upon heretics, psychiatry, in alliance with the state, attempted to root out sexual deviation.

Szasz began his discussion of homosexuality with an account of the Judeo-Christian religious tradition, underscoring its hostility toward sexuality freed from a procreative function. But unlike those who saw the psychiatric effort to replace the Church's authority as a progressive step, Szasz viewed it as nothing more than the continuation of that repressive tradition.

Prefacing a bitter attack on Karl Menninger's discussion of homosexuality, he stated:

My contention that the psychiatric perspective on homosexuality is but a thinly disguised replica of the religious perspective which it displaced, and that efforts to treat this kind of conduct medically are but thinly disguised methods of suppressing it may be verified by examining any contemporary psychiatric account of homosexuality.[53]

Like the witches pursued by the Church, homosexuals were the unfortunate targets of the moral order's capacity to punish through stigmatization. Though the Church claimed that it wished to "save" the witch, in truth it wanted to torture her. Psychiatry claimed that it wished to "cure" the homosexual, but it too inflicted suffering.

Psychiatric preoccupation with the disease concept of homosexuality—as with the disease concept of all so-called mental illnesses . . . conceals the fact that homosexuals are a group of medically stigmatized and socially persecuted individuals. The noise generated by their persecution and their anguished cries of protest are drowned out by the rhetoric of therapy—just as the rhetoric of salvation drowned out the noise generated by the persecution of witches and their anguished cries of protest. It is a heartless hypocrisy to pretend that physicians, psychiatrists or normal laymen for that matter really care about the welfare of the mentally ill in general, or the homosexual in particular. If they did, they would stop torturing him while claiming to help him.[54]

As he had done five years earlier, Szasz next drew for his readers the specter of compulsory treatment, the analogue of forced religious conversion. Finally, and more convincingly, he described at length the case of a homosexual whose application for citizenship had been turned down by the Immigration and Naturalization Service, providing evidence of the ways in which psychiatry and the state collaborated in the mistreatment of those with "heterodox" sexual preferences.[55]

So unrelenting was Szasz's hostility to psychiatry and its claims to diagnostic competence that the decision on the part of the American Psychiatric Association to delete homosexuality from the *Diagnostic and Statistical Manual* in 1973 gave him the opportunity for yet a further denunciation. In an interview in *The Advocate,* a gay community newspaper, he warned its readers not to celebrate their long-sought-for victory over the Psychiatric Association.

Celebrating the APA's abolition of homosexuality as a psychiatric diagnosis tacitly acknowledges that they have the knowledge and the right to decide what is and what is not a mental illness. I think the homosexual community is making a big mistake by hailing the APA's new stance as a real forward step in civil liberties. It's nothing of the sort. It's just another case of cooptation.[56]

JUDD MARMOR

While Thomas Szasz could provide a language of combat for those who saw psychiatry as a repressive force, his far-reaching critique could not serve as the basis for the transformation of psychiatric thinking on homosexuality. To follow Szasz would have required a radical rupture with the deepest commitments of contemporary psychiatry. For those who saw in the notion of mental illness not a fundamental conceptual error, but rather a significant advance in the understanding of human behavior, his arguments failed to provide justification for a change in the psychiatric perspective on homosexuality. Indeed, the very association of Szasz's overarching attack on psychiatry with the questioning of the orthodox perspective on homosexuality may have generated some professional resistance to the reconsideration of the issue.

It was Judd Marmor, a prominent psychoanalytic practitioner, who was to serve the function of a critic within the dominant psychiatric paradigm. Because of both his status within American psychiatry and his commitment to psychoanalysis as a mode of therapeutic intervention, Marmor was able to provide a language and a line of reasoning that were acceptable to psychiatrists who were beginning to question the orthodoxy on homosexuality while remaining committed to the core principles of the psychodynamic perspective. His first major statement on homosexuality appeared as the Introduction to *Sexual Inversion*, a volume he edited in 1965. Balanced in its appreciation of the findings of social scientists like Evelyn Hooker and of psychoanalytic clinicians like Irving Bieber, it was nevertheless seen by contemporary homosexual critics as supportive of the dominant pathological view. Yet its theoretical perspective contained elements that would allow Marmor to become, within a few years, a leading advocate of removing homosexuality from the American Psychiatric Association's *Diagnostic and Statistical Manual of Psychiatric Disorders*.

Influenced by Rado, he rejected the Freudian assumption of an inborn human bisexuality. Sexuality was the product of learning and hence the result of sociocultural influences in the development of children.[57] It was that which accounted for the wide variations discussed by anthropologists in their comparative analyses of sexual behavior. However, since societal expectations and demands played such a crucial role in focusing the sexual drive, efforts to understand the significance of homosexuality in the contemporary West could not rely upon findings from other cultures. Indeed, since motivation was so central to the psychodynamic perspective of psychiatry, the problem of homosexuality could reasonably be approached only by attempting to explain why, given the demands and expectations of this culture, a person would choose such a sexual orientation.[58]

Marmor's discussion of the etiology of homosexuality thus focused on the extent to which psychoanalytic findings could account for behavior that was the subject of a condemnatory social reaction. His conclusions, though somewhat skeptical of the tendency to seek explanations exclusively in terms of the pathogenic family structure described by investigators like Bieber, supported the conventional assumptions of the psychodynamic perspective. For a homosexual adaptation to develop in this culture three elements had to be present. The child had to suffer from an "impaired gender identity," preventing the assumption of a typical male or female role. Early childhood experience had to precipitate fear of intimate contact with members of the opposite sex. Finally, opportunities had to present themselves for sexual release with members of the same sex.[59]

Despite this analysis Marmor, like other antagonists of the psychiatric orthodoxy, was extremely critical of the assumption that there was a "homosexual personality."[60] He too warned against efforts to develop an understanding of all homosexuals based upon the evidence presented by the relatively small number who sought psychoanalytic treatment. Though he believed that in our culture homosexuals were likely to suffer from "defects in ego-adaptive capacity," he nevertheless suggested that they could not be classified with a single diagnostic label. They ran the "entire gamut of modern [psychiatric] nosology."[61]

It was not however in its modest critical appraisal of dominant psychiatric themes that this essay was most significant, but rather in its discussion of homosexuality as an illness. There the impact of his cultural approach to psychiatry was reflected in its most interesting and significant form. In distinguishing between the psychiatrist as "scientist" and as "practical clinician," he wrote:

The scientist must approach his data nonevaluatively; homosexual behavior and heterosexual behavior are merely different areas on a broad spectrum of human sexual behavior, the sources of which must be determined and understood, and neither can be assumed to be intrinsically more or less "natural" than the other. The clinical psychiatrist, on the other hand, is, by the very nature of his work, deeply involved in concepts of health and disease; normality and abnormality.[62]

Having rejected Freud's assumption of a biologically rooted cause of psychosexual development, Marmor was forced to acknowledge that heterosexuality represented a culturally determined norm. It was not the end of a natural teleology. Homosexuality was not necessarily a sign of fixation or regression. Psychotherapists did not function to restore homosexuals to a biologically determined standard of health. Instead they were engaged in a process of adapting those who deviated from culturally determined standards to the demands and values of the times.

It was precisely such a claim that had led Szasz to his generalized attack on psychiatry. For Marmor, however, such a posture was not only inescapable, but fully compatible with the practice of psychiatry as a branch of medicine.

The twentieth century psychiatric clinician in the western world inevitably reflects the mores of his time and culture when he regards homosexuality as an undesirable modification of or deviation from optimum personality development and adaptation in our society. It is not my intention to denigrate the approach of the clinician. In his efforts to help the homosexual achieve a heterosexual adaptation whenever possible, the clinical psychiatrist—like any other kind of physician—is endeavoring to help his patient achieve an optimum homeostatic relationship with the environment in which he finds himself.[63]

With culture, however, as the point of reference, it was obvious that the psychiatric classification of homosexuality as an illness would have to change with the evolution of social values. While the adaptational view could, of course, be mobilized in defense of a conservative and conformist orientation, it could also serve to suggest that as older values lost their hegemonic status, a shift in psychiatric thinking was imperative. It was possible to argue that psychiatrists were obliged to permit cultural forces to develop without the fetters of a backward-looking nosology. Finally, if the appropriate task of psychiatry was to assist in the process of "optimal" adaptation, it was possible to argue that a system of psychiatric classifications which impeded the attainment of that goal was unacceptable. The way was thus cleared for asserting that psychiatry had an obligation to assist the homosexual struggle for social acceptance, the elimination of homosexuality from the psychiatric nosology being but the first step in that process.

In 1972, seven years after the publication of *Sexual Inversion* and in the midst of an intense gay campaign against the American Psychiatric Association, Marmor made explicit what was only implied earlier in his Introduction. In "Homosexuality—Mental Disease—or Moral Dilemma?" he asserted that the fundamental issue raised by the nosological status of homosexuality was neither medical nor semantic, but moral.[64] Since homosexuals were capable of making successful adaptations to society, there was no more justification for classifying homosexuality as a disease than for so designating heterosexuality. Stressing the importance of tolerance for diverse patterns of sexual behavior, he noted that the psychiatric classification of homosexuality as a mental illness had tended to justify "society's aggressive intervention into the lives of individuals."[65] Thus, on the basis of both a clinical-cultural judgment, and a political analysis of the labeling process, Marmor had become a leading psychiatric ally of the gay struggle to force the removal of homosexuality from the Psychiatric Association's list of disorders.

That the emergent homophile movement of the 1960s seized upon the work of these and other critics of the psychiatric orthodoxy is not surprising. With the professional consensus on homosexuality fractured, the movement could seek out those experts whose findings and views supported its ideological preferences. Specialists could be cast, with or without their consent, in the role of partisans in an urgent sociopolitical struggle. That the empirical material produced by the critics was generally derived from professional perspectives other than that of clinical psychiatry mattered little. Because it possessed the aura of science—albeit social science—it carried a force that would have been absent had it been based upon "less rigorous" modes of inquiry. For the homophile movement the critical literature provided a rational justification for the rejection of "facts" that cast doubt on the merits of its claims against convention. It allowed the formulation of an ideological posture which could, in the name of science, reject the view that homosexuality was a pathological condition. This was enormously important for the strategy of the most committed members of the movement as they confronted homosexuals who had accepted some or all of the orthodox psychiatric perspective on their sexual preference. As for the effort to change the opinions of the broader community, the existence of scientific evidence permitted the homophile movement to charge psychiatry with a betrayal of the norms of objectivity. This evidence was vital to the effort to strip psychiatry of the warrant granted by society to those who spoke as scientists.

Equally important, for the way in which the debate on the status of homosexuality crystallized at the end of the 1960s, was the response of the major proponents of the psychiatric orthodoxy to the critical material produced by those who challenged their views. The self-confidence with which those who viewed homosexuality as a pathology dismissed the findings of Kinsey and Ford and Beach as well as Hooker provides an important indication of the extent to which "facts" take on meaning only within the context of underlying conceptual schemes and do not in themselves have the capacity to compel fundamental changes in the way the world is viewed. Thus, while acknowledging the research of the critics of the psychoanalytic perspective on homosexuality, Irving Bieber[66] was nevertheless able to dismiss their findings as either irrelevant or the result of inadequate methodological competence. In commenting upon Kinsey's discoveries about the sexual behavior of males, he argued that there was no justification for assuming that the unexpectedly elevated frequency of homosexual behavior proved the absence of pathology. Pathological conditions could in fact be quite typical-normal in a statistical sense. In New York City having a cold in the winter months was hardly unusual. Bieber similarly criticized the work of Ford and Beach for confusing the mere existence of behavioral patterns with standards of normality for human beings. While the biological capacity for homosexual arousal may in fact have been present, as they had discovered, the inborn tendency was toward heterosexuality. It was that which accounted for its dominance rather than the existence of cultural pressures in the process of socialization. Finally, with reference to Evelyn Hooker, Bieber argued that the only plausible explanation for the discrepancy between her findings and his was that "the tests themselves or the current methods of interpretation and evaluation are inadequate to the task of discriminating between homosexuals and heterosexuals."[67]

As long as homosexuality was understood to be an "unrealistic adaptation" based upon a "fear of heterosexuality," as long as it was seen as a deviation from the biological norm of the species, it was possible to characterize the data of critical investigators as scientifically irrelevant. Only when the basic perspective on the nature of normal sexuality began to change did that data begin to assume importance. When that change did occur, in large part because of the political struggle on the part of homosexuals, the evidence that had been available for more than two decades took on new meaning. Together with more recent research it provided the justification for ending the psychiatric classification of homosexuality as a disorder.

Chapter 3

THE EMERGENCE OF

HOMOSEXUAL PROTEST

During the first half of the twentieth century the psychiatric effort to claim for itself the right to speak on the nature of homosexuality, to define its meaning, and to determine the appropriate societal response to its existence was opposed primarily by those who believed that aberrant sexuality constituted a moral challenge that should be dealt with by those social institutions responsible for enforcing behavioral conformity. In the United States, England, and Germany that task had fallen largely to the criminal law. That little was heard from homosexuals themselves regarding psychiatry's challenge to the traditional moral perspective was in large measure a reflection of the more general silence of homosexuals in that era. The fear and pervasive sense of isolation experienced in the years prior to the emergence of the homosexual rights movement generated in those who deviated from prescribed sexual patterns a desire to be hidden from a hostile society that was ever ready to impose harsh legal sanctions and social ruin. When homosexuals did speak out publicly it was to urge the repeal of criminal sanctions for consensual homosexual activity. Since the threat of criminal prosecution was the immediate danger, it is not surprising that homosexuals did not attack the standard psychiatric view of sexual deviation. With professional support hard to come by, it would have been surprising if those attempting to foster legal reform had diverted energy to the attack of those who argued that homosexuality was an inappropriate target of the criminal law.[1]

That some homosexuals saw the effort to define the problem of homosexuality in psychiatric terms as a welcome advance is doubtlessly true. After all, to the extent that psychiatry proposed an approach to homosexuality that offered the possibility of therapeutic change, it suggested that the terrible burden of isolation and shame might be lifted by the elimination of the despised social stigma. Under prevailing social conditions it would have been remarkable if homosexuals with sufficient income had not turned to psychiatrists for therapeutic assistance.

Some early opposition on the part of homosexuals to the classification of homosexuality as a pathological condition was voiced, however, at the very moment when the scientific study of sexuality was attempting to uncover the roots of the disorder. Investigators like Karl Ulrichs expended prodigious efforts to demonstrate that homosexuality was inborn and therefore a natural expression of the sexual drive. Like Havelock Ellis, they opposed the view that homosexuality was inherently undesirable.[2] Others, like Edward Carpenter, endeavored to portray homosexuality as an ethically defensible way of life. When the psychiatric perspective became synonymous with the view that homosexuality represented a pathological state, it was against psychiatrists that homosexuals who followed in the tradition of Ulrichs and Carpenter began to address their ire.

In 1932 the pseudonymous Parisex wrote, "Now that inverts have almost escaped the stake and the prison, the psychoanalysts threaten them with the new danger of the psychiatric torture chamber."[3] That homosexuality had been present in diverse societies and cultures, and that it had survived the cruelest persecution, suggested to him that it was a trait, a form of birth control, rather than a neurosis. Th to which neurosis was found among homosexuals could best be explained by the conditions under which they had been forced to live. Finally, Parisex challenged the claims of therapeutic transformation. "I doubt if there ever was a cure of genuine homosexuality." Prefigured here was virtually every element of the ideology of the homosexual struggle against psychiatry in the 1960s. It was to take more than three decades, however, for this antagonism, this challenge, to find expression in the voice of a mass movement rather than in the individual and episodic declarations of those who saw in homosexuality neither a sin nor a disease, but instead a variation of normal sexuality.

While some literary indications of opposition to the conditions of social oppression existed among American homosexuals in the period before World War II, that opposition did not take on meaningful organizational form until the postwar period. Though there were some homosexual groups before that period, they were short-lived and had little impact upon the course of later events.[4] In the aftermath of the war a number of organizations were founded that were to lay the groundwork for the contemporary homosexual rights movement. Among the first was the Veterans Benevolent Association in New York. Though it served primarily a social function, holding dances and picnics, it did organize discussions and lectures on topics of concern to homosexuals.[5] Other groups such as the Bachelors for Wallace and Knights of the Clock attempted to link the problem of homosexual life to broader political issues—in the case of the former, to the Progressive Party presidential campaign of the left-wing Henry Wallace, and in the case of the latter to the problems of American Blacks. The publication of Kinsey's study of the sexual behavior of American males, which suggested that the number of men who engaged in homosexual activities had been vastly underestimated, gave some encouragement to these efforts, but they remained extremely tentative. Donald Webster Cory, a leading homosexual publicist and activist during those years, summarized the situation in the following way:

> These are but meager beginnings. Each of these is amorphous. All of them disconnected, many functioning at cross purposes to the other. But let us not fail to see the enormous importance of the beginnings. For these are the beginnings of the groups, the movements, the activities and the struggles that will make possible the next step forward that will spread the friendly word of truth. . . . This will make it both necessary and possible for more such movements and stronger ones to arise and for their influence to spread far and wide. This is a new cycle and a dynamic one whose aim and goal of sex equality are not beyond human reach.[6]

By far the most important of the organizations to emerge in this period was the Mattachine Society. Founded in 1950 with a secret membership, by 1953 it had changed its structure to allow for the open, democratic election of leaders.[7] The Society saw as its primary function the full integration of homosexuals into American life. Concerned with discrimination in employment, the exclusion of homosexuals from the mainstream of social life, and the threat of criminal sanctions against those who engaged in sexual activity in private, it sought to dispel the image of the morally depraved pervert incapable of assuming conventional social roles. It cultivated an aura of respectability and propriety, seeking the support of theologians, lawyers, scientists, and psychiatrists in the struggle for the acceptance of homosexuals. Extreme caution characterized its every statement with regard not only to the causes and nature of homosexuality but to the tactics to be employed in achieving its ends. "The Society is determined to seek [its goals] through EVOLUTION not REVOLUTION."[8]

Against a backdrop of cultural values that saw homosexuality as a grave moral issue, the Mattachine Society asserted that the scientific study of sexual variation could lead to a rational reorientation of society's response to sexuality. Since passion characterized the traditional moral opprobrium with which homosexuality was regarded, the Society attempted to create a mood of cool neutrality. Because it believed that a full understanding of the origins of homosexuality had yet to be developed, it sought to encourage an open discussion of competing scientific formulations. In the face of the terrible costs of certainty, its strategy was to foster an agnostic posture. In 1955 the board of directors declared that the Society "neither condones nor condemns sex variation in any form."[9] Mattachine assumed that any scientific theory of homosexuality would subvert the prevailing pattern of social practices by revealing that homosexuals were not morally responsible for their sexual orientations.

Seeing in the potential development of a homosexual subculture a tendency antithetical to the goal of integration, the Mattachine Society sought to encourage the full participation of homosexuals in the life of American society.

Since variants desire acceptance in society, it behooves them to assume community responsibility. They should as individuals actively affiliate with community endeavors . . . instead of attempting to withdraw into an invert society of their own. For only as they make positive contributions to the general welfare can they expect acceptance and full assimilation.[10]

Rather than challenge American values, Mattachine affirmed a deep loyalty to the mores of society. Its goals were fully "compatible with recognized institutions of a moral and civilized society with respect for the sanctity of home, church and state."[11] As if to underline this commitment Mattachine expressly opposed "indecent public behavior and particularly excoriates those who would contribute to the delinquency of minors and those who attempt to use force or violence upon any other persons whatsoever."[12] Finally, while rejecting any affiliation with political movements and parties the Society explicitly declared its commitment to Americanism, avowing a strong anticommunist posture. In the context of the McCarthyite purges of suspected homosexuals, such a stance was hardly surprising from a group that sought to project an image of social conservatism.

In attempting to fashion a strategy of reform the Mattachine Society stressed the importance of education. Psychiatrists, psychologists, and other experts were to provide the homosexual with a fuller understanding of the causes of his sexual orientation, so that armed with some self-awareness he would be able to withstand charges of willful immorality. In addition the Society saw it as of vital importance to educate homosexuals regarding the appropriate forms of public behavior. Integration could not proceed if decorum was not maintained. "When will the homosexual ever realize that social reform to be effective must be preceded by personal reform?"[13] Of particular concern were aggressive public expressions of sexuality, as well as deviant mannerisms and forms of dress.

Not only were experts to teach the homosexual about himself, but they were also expected to speak to the broader society about the nature of homosexuality. Mattachine's effort to cultivate the interest and support of those who could speak with some authority on the problems of sexual "variation" was intrinsic to its strategy of changing public opinion in a reasoned and gradual manner. Homosexuals themselves could not affect the nature of social policy and the climate of opinion; they required the help of those who could speak in a disinterested fashion from the vantage point of scientific neutrality.

Education and gradualism seemed imperatives in the reformist strategy, given the extremely hostile environment within which the first tentative efforts to gain a modicum of social acceptance for homosexuals were made. So fearful was the leadership of the Society that it even cautioned against aggressive collective lobbying for changes in laws and policies affecting the status of homosexuals. "If it could be shown that a pressure group was exerting untoward influence on lawmakers and law enforcement agencies . . . it would provide them with an abundant source of hysterical propaganda with which to permit an ignorant fear-inspired campaign against sexual variants."[14] The Society could function most effectively as a provider of information regarding policy, leaving it to individuals acting as individuals to contact the appropriate political officials. Thus the Society denied itself the option of acting in a forceful way on behalf of homosexuals as a disadvantaged social group. While this peculiar individualism recognized the social roots of the homosexual's plight, it rejected the standard forms of collective social protest.

Though Mattachine was not officially restricted to male homosexuals its membership and leadership were almost exclusively male. It is thus not surprising that lesbians, too, moved to create an organization capable of meeting their needs. The Daughters of Bilitis was, like the Mattachine Society, cautious in both the formulations of its program and its strategy for change. Indeed, given its relatively smaller size and its own sense of vulnerability, it seems to have been the more conservative of the two.

Since the Mattachine Society and the Daughters of Bilitis shared an extraordinarily open ideological perspective on the nature and causes of homosexuality, they tended to lack the singlemindedness often associated with movements of social protest. As a consequence their meetings served as rather remarkable forums. That openness also characterized their official publications, the *Mattachine Review* and the *Ladder*.[15] The *Review* was by far the more important of the journals in the period before 1960, and the most free-wheeling debates were to be found in its issues. And while the early editors of the *Review* were officially agnostic on the question of the causes of·homosexuality, its status as a pathological condition, and the appropriateness of efforts to "cure" homosexuals voluntarily seeking heterosexual orientation, proponents of fiercely antagonistic views on these questions were free to express themselves in its pages.

No feature stands out more sharply in the early issues of the *Mattachine Review* than the presence of the conflicting views of psychiatrists, psychologists, and other therapists on the causes of homosexuality, its status as a mental illness, and the possibility of cure. Its first issue, in January 1955, presented a summary of Evelyn Hooker's work which suggested that since homosexuality did not constitute a distinct clinical entity, efforts to classify all homosexuals as disturbed could not stand the test of rigorous psychological analysis.[16] So vital did the editors consider Hooker's research that they took the unusual step, three years later, of publishing a rather technical paper in which she challenged the assumption that homosexuals invariably suffered from psychopathology.[17] Others who questioned psychiatric orthodoxy were given frequent opportunities to present their views. For such experts homosexuality was "fully compatible with subjective well-being and objective efficiency."[18] The discomfort homosexuals experienced was not inherent in their condition, but was a reaction to the socially restrictive conditions under which they were forced to live.

The views of those who saw a profound psychological disturbance in homosexuality were also represented in the *Review*. Often their arguments were presented as humane and rational alternatives to the assumptions that underlay the reliance upon the criminal sanction as a social response to homosexuality.[19] Since homosexuals were always fearful of police harassment and arrest, it is not surprising that Mattachine was receptive to those who argued that homosexuality was a disease rather than a crime. Invariably psychiatrists and psychologists writing from this perspective suggested that cure was not only possible but desirable. With few exceptions, however, they acknowledged that clinical experience indicated that the transformation of homosexuals into heterosexuals was difficult to attain. But sober assessment of psychotherapeutic efficacy did not alter the fact that heterosexuality was preferable to homosexuality and that acceptance of one's homosexuality was a solution representing something of a tragic compromise.

The views of the lay—primarily homosexual—contributors to the *Review* must be read against this backdrop of professional disagreement. Reflecting the tendency to grant a central role to experts in the discussion of the causes of homosexuality, many writers assumed that homosexuals themselves should not take sides. It was for scientists to resolve such complex issues. "Where medical men, psychoanalysts and social scientists fail to agree laymen can only cower in silence."[20]

While these authors believed that homosexuals did not have the professional skill required to judge among alternative etiological formulations, they did appreciate the fact that all scientific explanations of homosexuality rejected the assumption that it was a willful choice representing a decision to reject the moral values of society. Therefore homosexuals need experience neither shame nor guilt. They ought to accept themselves and inform both family and friends of their sexual preference.[21]

Alongside such agnostic expressions, the *Review* published more partisan statements. Those who were critical of psychiatric orthodoxy repeatedly cited the work of Evelyn Hooker and Alfred Kinsey. Luther Allen, a frequent contributor to the Mattachine journal, rejected as a "psychiatric cliche" the view that homosexuality constituted a crippling condition, and asked, "Why not regard homosexuality as merely a difference in the direction of the sexual instinct? Why not view the heterosexual life as the sexual superhighway, the homosexual as one of the by-roads of love?"[22] While acknowledging that homosexuality represented a social handicap, he asserted that this was so only because of the world heterosexuals had created. For Allen, as well as other opponents of the pathological view, it was necessary to challenge the idea that sexuality took on its primary human significance from its linkage to procreation. "This view degrades human sexuality to the level of the stud farm."[23] In an era when birth control was still viewed by some as posing a serious moral problem, when the sale of contraceptive devices was restricted and even prohibited, the implications of the argument that sexual pleasure had no end but itself were indeed radical. When stated in its most aggressive form this position became an argument for the social utility of homosexuality. With the birth rate rising and with population growth an increasing cause of concern, "It seems to me that homosexuality as an alternative form of love . . . is a sort of sexual and social safety valve rather than a menace."[24]

Yet while such forthright defenses of homosexuality were being presented to the homosexual community, other laymen were still asserting that to be homosexual was indeed a great tragedy. At times this perspective was reflected in the tacit acceptance of the views of the psychiatric experts whose work was being commented upon in the *Review,* at other times in the sympathetic reception of their findings. This was strikingly the case in a review of Abram Kardiner's *Sex and Morality* that uncritically accepted his assertion that homosexuality was a "price extracted" by the pressures of civilization, affecting those individuals with "developmental vulnerabilities and acquired weakness in masculinity."[25]

Those who regarded their homosexuality as a normal variation denied the centrality of procreation to the human experience, but those who believed it a crippling condition were explicit in affirming procreation's importance.

Many of us homosexuals regard our inversion as a handicap because it precludes a complete life. And no life is complete emotionally or biologically without the extension of love in the upbringing of children of one's own. And this limitation on our lives imposed upon us in our childhood could have been prevented in most cases. . . . To boast of being glad for an exclusively homosexual condition is but a defense mechanism.[26]

The extent to which this position was shared by the leaders of the homophile movement is demonstrated by the tone of the keynote address delivered by Ken Burns, chairman of the board of the Mattachine Society, at its Third Annual Convention in 1956. After asserting that homosexuals "cried out" for assistance in controlling the social and family patterns out of which homosexuality developed, he stressed the importance of prevention in the overall effort to solve the problem of homosexuality.[27]

Attitudes toward the therapeutic posture of psychiatry also reflected the sharp divisions within the homophile movement. Those who believed that psychotherapeutic intervention could effect a shift toward heterosexuality raised no objection to therapeutic work with those who voluntarily sought such a change. Deep concern was expressed, however, over the threat of coercive psychiatric intervention, the fear being fueled by the specter of court-mandated treatment for homosexuals charged with violating sodomy statutes. Others, less sanguine about the likelihood of successful therapy and aware of the doubts expressed by psychiatrists themselves, asserted that to hold out the possibility of change was both dishonest and cruel. Psychotherapy under such circumstances became yet another device for torturing the homosexual. "When psychotherapy attempts to be more than just the key to free the poetry in man then it becomes another tyranny."[28] It was not yet the moment to declare that the very attempt to treat homosexuality, regardless of therapeutic efficacy, was morally unacceptable. Finally, and indicative of the warm regard in which psychiatry was held by the homophile movement in its early years, both those who accepted and those who rejected the possibility of reversing the homosexual pattern approved of the psychotherapeutic effort to help homosexuals find greater self-acceptance.

The more general conflict over the pathological status of homosexuality, as well as over the appropriate functions of psychiatry and psychology, crystallized around the work of Albert Ellis, a psychologist who had considerable clinical experience with homosexuals. A frequent lecturer at Mattachine discussion groups and a contributor to the *Review*, Ellis argued that exclusive homosexuality could be explained only as a phobic response to the opposite sex and a compulsive fixation on members of the same sex. It was, because of its rigidity and exclusivity, neurotic.[29] Though he asserted that exclusive heterosexuality also represented a neurotic pattern of sexuality, such consistency was lost upon those concerned primarily with his pronouncements on homosexuality.

Ellis rejected the claim that homosexuality was in most cases irreversible, asserting that virtually every homosexual who wanted to achieve satisfactory heterosexual relations could do so with the aid of a competent psychotherapist.[30] At a time when considerable doubt existed within the psychiatric profession about the efficacy of therapeutic intervention with homosexuals, Ellis's therapeutic enthusiasm was striking. Because he saw homosexuality as a neurosis, and because he believed that change was possible, he rejected the proposition that for most homosexuals the function of psychotherapy was to foster a satisfactory adjustment to their sexual orientation.[31]

Ellis's articles were often greeted by critical letters which rejected his premises at their root. "We are not sick and don't ask treatment; we seek only understanding. . . . We are human like the rest." The editorial response to this smoldering controversy was to strike a characteristically neutral stance.

We hesitate to comment that either Ellis or his critics is to be regarded as wrong or right. While we welcome critical letters don't expect everyone to agree with you, just as we don't expect everyone to agree with everything we publish. Our goal is to get at the TRUTH— good or bad. . . . We shall not evade an issue simply because it may be controversial and Albert Ellis dared to face it.[32]

Since Ellis was accorded a certain privileged status as a respected antagonist in the debate on homosexuality, the growing hostility of many homosexual activists toward those who argued that homosexuality was a disease was somewhat hidden from view in the reactions to his work. That was not so in the case of Edmund Bergler. The publication in 1956 of his *Homosexuality: Disease or Way of Life?* was greeted with an outpouring of denunciatory rage that was striking given the tone of earlier discussions of psychiatric perspectives on homosexuality.

Bergler had, in aggressive and sometimes intemperate language, gone beyond the more conventional discussion of homosexuality as a psychiatric disorder, asserting that homosexuals tended to be unreliable troublemakers who were "injustice collectors," having a deep wish to suffer.[33] Among Bergler's most vitriolic comments were those reserved for Mattachine's ally, Alfred Kinsey, "a medical layman."[34] As a result of his influence, homosexuals had become so outspoken that "they are now virtually asking for minority status."[35]

The critique of Bergler began in early 1957 and continued into the next year with major articles in both the *Review* and the *Ladder*. Having learned the lessons of Evelyn Hooker, the critics charged that Bergler had drawn his conclusions from an unrepresentative sample of homosexuals.[36] His diagnoses were said to be based upon the examination of a "tribe of malcontents and vagrants," and his approach was compared to a sociological study of "mankind" based upon a population drawn from San Quentin.[37] Rejecting Bergler's characterization of homosexuals as miserable souls, one critic wrote that there were "countless homosexuals who do lead lives that are happy, stable, productive, rich in achievement, devoid of obsessive and paralyzing conflicts."[38] Since he had *defined* homosexuality as a disease, Bergler had not spoken as a scientist. Not objectivity but a "maniacal moralism" informed his work.[39] While some effort was made to distinguish him from other more responsible psychiatric investigators, there were indications that he was perceived as more representative of the profession than not. "Authorities like Bergler . . . are among a growing sect of pompous neo-Freudians who have substituted 'sick' for sin and who damn souls with it as sanctimoniously as any Calvinistic minister."[40] Finally, there was a recognition that the work of psychiatrists like Bergler could be used by those opposed to the advance of the homosexuals' cause and that the very authority upon which homosexuals had relied in their effort to win social acceptance could be used to buttress prevailing social conventions or exploited by "opposing bigots."[41]

The outrage that greeted Bergler's book signaled a shifting tone in the discussion of psychiatry within the homophile movement. The *Review*'s editorials began to take on an air of impatience when commenting on the psychiatric orthodoxy. In a 1958 anniversary issue, looking forward to the ninth year of the Society, the editors wrote:

Every year sees an evolving and more complete definition of the Mattachine philosophy. While this idea attacks ancient antisexual attitudes that are still prevalent in Western cultures, it nevertheless declares that the concept of homosexuality as a disease is unacceptable. It holds that this . . . orientation is rather one of the phenomena of nature, and one which society as yet has been unable to understand

and loath to permit those whose personalities fall into this category
to make their fullest contribution for mankind.[42]

With the rejection of the view that homosexuality was a disease, cure increasingly became anathema, "self-acceptance"
and adjustment being "vastly preferred."
    It is thus not surprising that Irving Bieber's *Homosexuality*,
which reported far greater success with psychoanalytic intervention than had previously been noted by analysts, was
greeted with derision. Indeed, his volume was scornfully referred to as a "new Bible" for those psychiatrists who saw
homosexuality as a pathology requiring clinical intervention.
Throughout the 1960s Bieber's name became synonymous with
all that was hateful in American psychiatry, he and his colleagues being labeled "talmudic propagandists."
    While the attack on Bieber followed a pattern set by the
earlier critiques of Ellis, Bergler, and psychiatry in general, it
was not until 1964 that a specific corporate representative of
the medical profession was challenged. In that year the prestigious New York Academy of Medicine issued a report on homosexuality containing all the views that had become
unacceptable to the homophile movement. The editors of the
Ladder denounced the Academy's effort as

a reminder of the sly desperate trend to enforce conformity by a
"sick" label for anything deviant. The doctors of this medical group
in prescribing heterosexuality simply because it is "normal," are practicing moral manipulation in the guise of scientific leadership.[43]

The increasing militancy in the tone of the declarations in
this period was a cause for some alarm within established homophile groups. To those who had carefully fashioned organizational profiles designed to reassure the heterosexual world,
the new thrust appeared disastrous. The Daughters of Bilitis
quite candidly acknowledged this tension by expressing, in
1962, its own commitment to a strategy more conservative
than that being pursued by others. The goal was mutual understanding between homosexuals and society rather than "the
beating of the drums."[44] Nevertheless, the Daughters of Bilitis

traversed this period without experiencing a severe challenge to its organizational integrity. Indeed, the *Ladder* was to emerge during the mid-1960s as the most important forum of homosexual opinion in the United States.

The Mattachine Society did not fare so well. In part because of the fear that some of its local groups might move in directions unacceptable to the parent organization, the local Mattachine councils were disbanded. As a result Mattachine as a national organization lost much of its strength. In place of a single Mattachine Society there emerged a number of independent local Mattachine groups each free to pursue its own course, some taking on the new militancy, others pursuing the more conservative course charted in an earlier phase of the homophile movement. The *Review* ceased to be the vital journal it had been, and was gradually eclipsed by the *Ladder*.

A MORE MILITANT MOVEMENT

The growing intolerance for traditional psychiatric formulations on the part of those active in the homophile movement created the conditions under which the movement could make a radical break with its own past. No one was of greater importance during this period of transition than Frank Kameny, president of the Mattachine Society of Washington, D.C. Not only was he able to bring coherence to the critique of psychiatry that had surfaced in the preceding years, but he was of central importance in pressing the movement into a more militant phase, one that would provide the backdrop for the explosive emergence of Gay Liberation in the late 1960s. In a stream of essays, lectures, and articles, Kameny set himself the task of articulating an ideology for the homophile movement. Deeply concerned with the implications of the continued official neutrality of the established homophile organizations, Kameny argued that the struggle for homosexual equality required an ideological position which affirmed that homosexuality was no less than a normal variant of sexual behavior. "I feel that the entire homophile movement . . . is going to stand or fall upon the question of whether or not homosexuality is a sickness, upon taking a firm stand on it."[45]

Like those before him who had been critical of the psychiatric orthodoxy, Kameny asserted that the corpus of clinical studies of homosexuality was flawed on methodological grounds.[46] Lacking statistically verifiable evidence that homosexuality constituted a pathological condition, psychiatric researchers had *defined* homosexuality as a disease. He characterized their conclusion as a "theological position" thinly disguised as objective science.

Had Kameny's contributions been limited to this critique, he would have been no more important than those who preceded him. It was his perception that the diagnosis of psychopathology served as the fundamental prop for the entire pattern of social exclusions and his insistence that homosexuals must not cede to the scientific experts the right to speak on this question that set him apart. "I for one am not prepared to play a passive role in . . . controversies over psychopathology letting others dispose of me as they see fit. I intend to play an active role in the determination of my fate."[47] The experts had forfeited their right to speak on homosexuality because they had shown themselves both incompetent and compromised. They lacked the skill to study the question of homosexuality. They lacked the capacity to withstand the distorting, value-laden assumptions of the broader society. Indeed they collaborated in the oppression of homosexuals. "We are right; those who oppose us are both factually and morally wrong. We are the true authorities on homosexuality whether we are accepted as such or not."[48]

Because he believed that the question of pathology was a matter of definition, Kameny rejected the longstanding commitment of the homophile movement to research. In a series of furious exchanges with Florence Conrad, director of research of the Daughters of Bilitis, he charged that concern with the causes of homosexuality was directly related to the postulation of a pathological state that required explanation. "Those who allege sickness have created *their* need for *their* research. Let *them* do it."[49] He acknowledged that Evelyn Hooker's work had served an important role in combating psychiatric "propaganda," but asserted that "in logic" not even her work was of fundamental significance.

Linked to Kameny's rejection of the scientific community was his dismissal of the dominant tactical posture of the homophile movement. For more than a decade, education and reason had been perceived as the most effective means for winning social acceptance and overcoming discriminatory practices. With the civil rights movement of the 1960s as a referent, Kameny stressed that militant action in the courts and on the picket line was the only effective tool available to those seeking social change. "We would be foolish not to recognize what the Negro rights movement has shown us is sadly so. Mere persuasion, information and education are not going to gain for us in actual practice the rights and equality which are ours in principle."[50]

Finally, it was Kameny more than any other spokesperson at that point who understood the political needs of a protest movement, who sensed the importance of developing a deep sense of solidarity. Unlike those who saw the homophile movement as serving the individual needs of its participants, he argued that priority had to be given to the collective cause of homosexual freedom and equality.[51] No separatist, he nevertheless understood that homosexuals had to have their own movement to which they could turn for the strength required for their struggle.

The extent to which . . . homosexuals are heartened by knowing that someone, anyone is actually standing up before the public and standing up to the "experts" and trying to counter psychiatric propaganda—as they cannot do—is almost indescribable. If there were no other reasons for our taking the position that homosexuality is not pathological than bolstering the morale of our own people we would have justification enough.[52]

While with increasing frequency Kameny and other leaders of the homophile movement had been rejecting the psychiatric perspective on homosexuality, others, ideologically more cautious and maintaining the original Mattachine position of neutrality, found the new thrust a matter of deep concern. Among the most prominent objectors was Donald Webster Cory, who had been a central figure in the days when the only organizational commitment of the movement had been to the civil rights of homosexuals. He expressed his profound disagreement with the emergent ideology in an impassioned introduction to Albert Ellis's *Homosexuality: Its Causes and Cure*. Defending Ellis against the attacks of his homophile critics, Cory wrote:

> Once the name was Edmund Bergler: today it is Albert Ellis. Public enemy No. 1 of the homosexual, the whipping boy of the homophile press, the *bête noire* of the friend of the deviant, Albert Ellis is scorned, laughed at, ridiculed, hated, feared and admired. Though he has spoken out for the rights of homosexuals he continues to be denounced with a fury that might be expected were he on a puritanical crusade. . . .[53]

Arguing that homosexuality was in fact a "disturbance," Cory expressed his deep disagreement with those who asserted that cure was impossible and undesirable. With faith in the role of science reminiscent of the early days of the Mattachine Society, he attempted to demonstrate the dangers inherent in subjecting the search for truth to the influence of "ideological prejudice."[54] More disturbing to Cory was the spectre of a rupture of the historical alliance between scientists and the homophile movement.

> I am more and more convinced that the homophile movement in the United States is fighting a righteous struggle for justice, freedom and personal dignity; that it will do great harm to its struggle if it gets into a head-on clash with men of science whose work it finds threatening: and that there is nothing inconsistent between acceptance of the work of psychotherapists who report success, nay cure, and the struggle for the right to participate in the joys of life for those who cannot, will not or do not undergo such change.[55]

But Cory's appeal was an echo of the past. The initiative had passed to those like Kameny who denied the validity of the psychiatric perspective on homosexuality, who questioned the scientific merits of the clinical approach to sexual deviation, and who challenged the very morality of the therapeutic posture.

In the first years of the homophile movement, controversy over the issue of cure had centered upon the technical question of whether it was possible for a homosexual to become heterosexual as a result of therapeutic intervention. Those who argued that such change was possible never insisted that all homosexuals should attempt to change. Those who argued that such change was impossible never assumed that such efforts were in principle wrong. A new theme was now emerging: The therapeutic posture itself was morally wrong. An increasingly affirmative stance toward homosexuality suggested to activists that those who offered assistance to *voluntary* patients who expressed profound distress over their sexual orientation, did so as the agents of society and should be attacked. In a climate increasingly affected by the rise of nationalist movements abroad, the Black struggle at home, and a new wave of feminism, "psychiatric cure" became the equivalent of white supremacy, of patriarchal domination in the case of lesbianism—a "final solution" to the problem of homosexuality.

In an essay entitled "The Heterosexual Obsession," one author told of physicians in South Africa who were bleaching Chinese to make life easier for them in that racist society, and compared such efforts to those of psychotherapists who attempted to cure homosexuals.

Adding insult to injury the members of the psychological profession pretend they are doing it for the homosexual's own good. . . . But just as the *real* purpose of the South Africans is to assert the rightness of whiteness, the psychotherapists are insisting on the rightness of the society's heterosexual bias.[56]

Although the focus of such denunciations was unmistakably upon psychotherapeutic practitioners, there were also the first hints of the argument that homosexuals who attempted to change were not only foolish and misguided but renegades, hints that the goal of homosexual emancipation required of homosexuals that they, like Blacks, accept their identities rather than seek freedom through self-denial.*

As homophile groups moved to withdraw the *bona fides* from those psychiatrists and psychologists who they felt had forfeited the claim to speak as objective scientists, they bestowed credibility upon others who came forward to side with their struggle. Characteristic of these new-found allies was a willingness to denounce the psychiatric profession for its collaboration in society's moral crusade against homosexuality. Ernest Van Den Haag, Hendrik Ruitenbeek, and George Weinberg were significant partisans in this period. They provided homosexuals with evidence and also with a vocabulary of criticism that were invaluable in the effort to tear the mantle of authority from those who claimed that science itself had discovered the psychopathology inherent in homosexuality. The role of the expert at homophile meetings shifted from that of providing homosexuals with insight into the etiology of their sexual preferences to that of providing insight into the illegitimate power of psychiatry.

Van Den Haag repeatedly urged the homophile movement to understand that the psychiatric effort to portray homosexuality as a disease was part of a broader tendency to replace moral judgments with ostensibly value-neutral, scientific ones. In a tone characteristic of Thomas Szasz's antipsychiatric critique, he told the Third National Convention of the Daughters of Bilitis in 1964, "Today people are reluctant to make moral

---

* In later years such homosexuals were to be compared to Blacks attempting to "pass." The review of Edward Sagarin's *Odd Man In*, a study of deviant subcultures in America, reflects the ire directed against those who, having rejected a homosexual identification, become defenders of the psychiatric perspective. Refusing to mention the name by which he was known in the homophile movement because of a "code of honor," the reviewer nevertheless went on to state: "Could it be that he is one of the homosexuals who has surrendered . . . to the 'sick sick sick' school? Right, but I assure you that if you knew who this man really is, then you'd wonder, really wonder, for he is as responsible for the founding of the homophile movement as any other single man. We are sorry, truly sorry that he got so lost . . . we hope he doesn't suffer too much." (*The Ladder*, February–March 1970, pp. 33–34.)

statements. We have no evil persons, only sick persons. Many use the authority of science to make wholly unscientific statements reflecting . . . our moral norms disguised as scientific statements of fact."[57] Ruitenbeek, who had edited a volume on homosexuality and was a practicing psychotherapist, denounced the tendency of psychiatrists and psychoanalysts to stress the psychological origins of homosexual behavior. For him, that focus diverted professional attention from the more crucial task of helping homosexuals, who had been subject to social exclusion, to function well in society.[58] Finally, George Weinberg cautioned homosexuals to "beware the psychoanalyst." He argued that it was virtually impossible to convince psychoanalysts that homosexuals could function well in society without giving up their sexual orientation. As a result, he warned, those who sought the help of analysts would be doing great damage to themselves. The process of psychoanalysis itself was dangerous under prevailing conditions since the attempt to change the homosexual could only result in the subversion of his or her capacity to thrive as a human being with a basic guiding "fantasy."[59]

While Kinsey, Hooker, and Ford and Beach had provided empirical material for homosexuals seeking to challenge the psychiatric orthodoxy, these new partisan experts provided more general arguments of an invaluable kind in that struggle. It is not that some of the thoughts they expressed had not been anticipated by homosexuals themselves, but rather that they framed them in such a way as to suggest that disorder existed within the therapeutic establishment. Both the empirical findings of the earlier period and the more general perspectives articulated in the mid-1960s were to become part of the ideological armamentarium of homosexuals in their intensifying battle with psychiatry.

Despite these changes, the first efforts to get homophile groups to adopt formally the antipathology perspective as a matter of policy met with resistance. Even Frank Kameny's effort to press his own Washington Mattachine Society to adopt this position provoked a series of internal conflicts. Only after a protracted debate was he successful. Then in March of 1965, with only one vote in opposition,[60] the Society declared:

> The Mattachine Society of Washington takes the position that in the absence of valid evidence to the contrary homosexuality is not a sickness, disturbance or other pathology in any sense but is merely a preference, orientation or propensity on a par with, and not different in kind from, heterosexuality.[61]

With the Washington group having broken the barrier, the refusal of homophile organizations to defend homosexuality, rather than individual homosexuals, began to give way. In New York the question of whether to follow this new course became the central issue in the 1965 electoral campaign within the Mattachine Society. Donald Webster Cory's name had been placed in nomination for president-elect. His opponent was Dick Leitsch.

Noting that the issue of illness had become "the greatest obstacle in the path of the homosexual community's fight for full citizenship in our Republic," Leitsch pledged that if elected he would press the New York Society to adopt the resolution recently voted by Washington Mattachine. He pointed to Cory's introduction to Ellis's book by way of contrast and asked the membership to make a presidential choice based upon their position as to whether homosexuality was an illness.[62] Cory lost the election, and soon after, New York Mattachine followed Washington in declaring its opposition to the view that homosexuality constituted a clinical disorder.

GAY LIBERATION:

THE RADICALIZATION OF PROTEST

The increasing militancy of the homophile movement was accompanied by a marked expansion in the constituency of homosexual activists. Early homophile groups had been small, somewhat secretive, and limited geographically to a few major urban centers, mostly on the two coasts. By the mid-1960s the number of such groups was beginning to grow, with active homophile organization evident in the Midwest as well. Membership figures began to show a significant rise, as larger numbers of homosexuals were willing to identify publicly with a homophile posture.[63] In large measure these changes reflected a dynamic process internal to the homosexual struggle itself. Yet the pace of the transformation and its very character were inseparably linked to the sociopolitical context within which they occurred. Just as early organizational efforts bore the mark of the political quiescence and anticommunist hysteria of the early 1950s, the efforts of this period were affected by the political activism of the early and mid-1960s—an activism that was virtually synonymous with the civil rights struggle.[64]

The political climate of the United States had been transformed in the first half of the 1960s by the emergence of a vast number of civil rights groups which, though linked by an overriding commitment to the assault on racism, had a multiplicity of foci. The political geography of America became increasingly dense with such organizations. Smaller cities and university campuses experienced the impact of challenges to the gravest as well as the most subtle manifestations of racism. The existence of the civil rights movement thus prepared the way for the emergence of local homophile groups ready to attack long-tolerated expressions of cultural and social bias against homosexuality, and at the same time stood as a provocative reminder to homosexuals of the need to develop organizational forms capable of giving vent to their discontent. Just as the newer civil rights groups did not supplant the older, more conservative organizations that had struggled in earlier years for Black rights, the newer homophile groups did not displace the older organizations that had emerged in the 1950s. Yet the often fierce antagonism of the more militant civil rights groups toward those who had led the earlier struggle signaled to many homosexuals the necessity of casting off older ide-

ologies, older forms of organization, and older styles of protest.

On an ideological level the civil rights struggle had also been
transformed when the earlier defensive posture was replaced
by an affirmation of blackness. In part this reflected the powerful impact of African nationalism and the anticolonial struggles;
it also represented a rediscovery of the nationalist tendency
in American Black thought. Implicitly a negation of the hegemony of white culture, the affirmative stance provided Blacks
with a sense of value independent of the judgments of the
broader society. That ideological tone not only set the stage
for a similar affirmation on the part of homosexuals, but actually provided some of the language that would be used. The
appropriation of slogans was self-conscious and indicated an
awareness of the debt owed to the civil rights movement. Thus,
in 1968 the North American Conference of Homophile Organizations (NACHO), a coalition organized in an effort to bring
some unity to the homosexual struggle, unanimously adopted
the following resolution introduced by Frank Kameny:[65]

BECAUSE many individual homosexuals, like many of the members
of many other minority groups suffer from diminished self-esteem,
doubts and uncertainties as to their personal worth, and from a pervasive false and unwarranted sense of an inferiority and undesirability
of their homosexual condition, and from a negative approach to that
condition; *and*

BECAUSE, therefore, many individual homosexuals, like many of
the members of many other minority groups, are in need of psychological sustenance to bolster and to support a positive and affirmative
attitude toward themselves and their homosexuality and to have in-
stilled into them a confident sense of the positive good and value
of themselves and of their condition; *and*

BECAUSE it would seem to be very much a function of the North
American Homophile Conference to attempt to replace a wishy-washy
negativism toward homosexuality with a firm no-nonsense positivism,
to attempt to establish in the homosexual community and its members
feelings of pride, self-esteem, self-confidence, and self-worth, in being
the homosexuals that they are and have a moral right to be (these
feelings being essential to true human dignity), and to attempt to

bring to bear a counter-vailing influence against negative attitudes toward homosexuality prevalent in the heterosexual community; *and*

BECAUSE the Negro community has approached similar problems and goals with some success by the adoption of the motto or slogan: *Black is Beautiful*

RESOLVED: that it be hereby adopted as a slogan or motto for NACHO that

GAY IS GOOD

Finally, the civil rights movement had transformed the culture of political protest by the popularization and legitimation of direct action as an instrument for the expression of discontent. An end was put to the older and exclusive reliance upon legislative lobbying and litigation. The rally, the march, the picket line, and the sit-in captured the imagination of those most directly involved in the struggle for Black rights. Hence a style of protest that involved the direct and repeated mobilization of bodies became a standard of the era, with older forms of political action and their reliance upon intermediaries and experts perceived as inherently conservative.

Despite its increasingly militant tone, the homophile movement had relied upon the older forms of protest into the mid-1960s. While it had shed the caution of the first Mattachine pronouncement on aggressive lobbying and had begun to make open appeals to homosexual voters to use their ballots as weapons in the struggle against discrimination, the first efforts at more militant protest against such practices were slow in coming. It was even more difficult to translate the ideological antagonism toward psychiatry into action. Demonstrations against those who wielded both political and economic power seemed quite appropriate. There was, however, no model to draw upon for a confrontation with psychiatric power, exercised as it was primarily through cultural influences. The essentially literary critique of psychiatric orthodoxy had attempted to meet ideology on its own grounds. Yet the growing awareness on the part of homosexual activists of the influence of psychiatric thought on the social status of those whom it defined as sick made clear the necessity of a more potent response. Here the homophile movement provided the model, charting a course of political protest against psychiatry by lending force to the ideological critique that Thomas Szasz and his followers had been elaborating for a number of years. Picket lines began to appear at lectures by those who defended the standard psychiatric position on homosexuality. In 1968 the convention of the American Medical Association in San Francisco was leafleted by homosexual activists who took the opportunity of a lecture by Charles Socarides to demand that those who opposed the pathological view of homosexuality be represented at future conventions. They demanded in addition that representatives of homophile groups be invited to participate in such discussions. Finally, they argued for a redirection of scientific research with the antihomosexual bias of the psychoanalytic perspective being replaced by a value-neutral search for "facts."[66]

A similar protest took place at Columbia University's College of Physicians and Surgeons the same year. Protesting the composition of a panel on homosexuality led by Lawrence Kolb, director of the New York State Psychiatric Institute, the demonstrators demanded "to be participants in considerations of our condition and in the disposition of our fate. It is time that talk stopped being *about* us and started being with us."[67]

The emergence of militant homophile groups on American campuses was especially significant for later developments, since it brought homosexual politics to the center of radical ferment in the United States. Proximity to students engaged in a broad array of countercultural, feminist, antiimperialist, antiracist, and anticapitalist activity was to have a major impact on the language, style, and intensity of homosexual activity in the late 1960s and early 1970s.

The smoldering rage on the part of homosexuals that had been evident in episodic demonstrations in the late 1960s exploded in June 1969 after a raid on a bar in Greenwich Village by the New York City police. The gay community fought back, and the Stonewall Bar on Christopher Street assumed the symbolic status of birthplace of a new phase in the homosexual struggle. Though there had been earlier signs that the homosexual community had entered a period of determined action, for gay activists the events surrounding these riots suggested a rupture with the past.

We consider the Stonewall Riots to mark the birth of the gay liberation movement, as they were the first time that homosexuals stood up and fought back.[68]

We are truly the children of Christopher Street.[69]

Emerging from the battles between the police and the homosexuals of Greenwich Village was the Gay Liberation Front (GLF), a radical organization that sought to make its opposition to the social order manifest through the assumption of a name evocative of the communist struggle in Vietnam against American military intervention. Soon after, Liberation Front groups were organized across the country in Berkeley, Boston, Los Angeles, and Minneapolis.[70] Even when other names were chosen by groups in other cities there was a surge of activity that sought to link the homosexual struggle to the other forms of radical protest then shaking America.

From the outset these groups attempted to deny their ties to the older homophile groups, which were charged with attempting to seek "a quiet accommodation with a fundamentally sexist society."[71] The Mattachine Society was characterized as the NAACP of the gay movement and was denounced as an obstacle to change.[72] Most important was the assertion by these groups that the era of restrictive organizational politics had ended and had been replaced by a popular mobilizational style.

Running through the manifestos and declarations of Gay Liberation groups was a Fanon-like emphasis on the importance of struggle not only for the social ends it was to achieve but for the personal "healing" it could bring. Though not necessarily couched in terms of violence, "action" and "rebellion" were seen as antidotes to the shame, self-doubt, and self-hatred that had been imposed upon homosexuals by society.

Characteristic of the ideological thrust of Gay Liberation Front militants was a conscious linking of the struggle for homosexual liberation with the struggle of the underclass against social deprivation, of Blacks against white racism, and of the Vietnamese against American imperialism. Perhaps most important was the acknowledgment of the common nature of the gay struggle against heterosexual domination and the struggle of women against male domination. In both instances the enemy was the heterosexual male, who had arrogated to himself the power to define sexuality so as to guarantee his own superordinate position in society. It was that power which had to be overturned. Each of these struggles represented but another facet of the overarching rebellion against capitalism. "Our oppression as homosexuals stems from the same source as that of other repressed groups: the restrictive competitive social roles necessitated by a capitalist economy and a ruling elite."[73] And so the liberation of homosexuals required the radical transformation not only of America's sexual mores—"a mere epiphenomenon"—but of its socioeconomic structure as well. Such a struggle required the mobilization of homosexuals into a broad anticapitalist front just as it required the 'fraternal support" of other militant groups in the struggle for homosexual freedom. "The struggle for sexual liberation is a necessary part of making the Revolution by any means necessary."[74]

While gay ideology strove to express its argument against the social order on a theoretical level, it also recognized the importance of intimate and personal revelations on the part of homosexuals. Such a fusion of the social and the personal was not, of course, limited to homosexuals during this period. The women's movement saw in such testimony, either in consciousness-raising groups or in more public "speak-outs," a source of vitality for feminist ideology. Indeed, the refusal to recognize the traditional distinctions between the private and the social characterized much of both the countercultural and New Left critiques of everyday life in America. Since the radical transformation of human relationships was seen as the goal of political struggle, it could not have been otherwise.

There was a long tradition among homosexuals of discussing

the difficulty of "coming out," of telling parents and friends of one's homosexuality. Now, with increasing frequency, homosexuals discussed publicly their very painful experiences with psychiatrists and other mental health professionals. These descriptions were often angry, portraying the ways in which therapists attempted to force their view of sexual normality upon guilt-ridden and often confused patients. Howard Brown, who had been commissioner of health in New York City, wrote: "The few insights I gained during analysis were nothing compared to its overriding message—I was inherently impaired because of my sexual orientation and that if I could not change it, I was doubly a failure. I left analysis convinced that I had no talents."[75] For Brown it took twenty years to "recover" from that experience, twenty years before he could regard himself and other homosexuals as worthwhile and capable.

One of the most sensitive and interesting of these revelations was written by Christopher Hobson. Lacking the rancor of many accounts of the same genre, Hobson's essay accused his therapists of neither venality nor psychological brutality. "My therapists—there were three over the years—were all intelligent, somewhat sensitive men."[76] Instead he tells of his growing realization that he could be happy only by coming to grips with his homosexuality instead of denying it. That was a task in which psychotherapy could play no part since its theoretical assumptions characterized his homosexuality as a condition to be explained rather than a sexual orientation to be encouraged. Indeed it was his therapists' inability and unwillingness to encourage his homosexual love which, for Hobson, indicated their basic failing. Finally, he used his own very personal encounter with psychiatry to reach out to others—calling them to the Gay Liberation movement.

All over the United States there are thousands in psychotherapy and millions more under the pervasive social influences of psychiatric dogma, who never will make this step towards self-acceptance until they are reached, not by doctors but by the winds of social protest.[77]

Unlike earlier homosexual activists who had evidenced a willingness to discuss differences of opinion with psychiatrists and others in the mental health professions, those inspired by the new militancy had little interest in such exchanges. Since discussions would impart a modicum of credibility to those with whom one spoke, they were politically unacceptable. Psychiatrists were war criminals, the enemy; they were to be defeated, not won over. It became a matter of principle for Gay Liberation to denounce discussions with psychiatrists as acts of "collaboration."

While those associated with the Gay Liberation Front were able to capture the political and ideological initiative among many homosexuals in the months following the Stonewall riots, they were not able to hold within their ranks the vast number of homosexuals who, at least in part as a result of those events, had been drawn into a public identification with the struggle for homosexual rights. What had appeared to be the strength of the Gay Liberation Front—its open identification with radical forces throughout the society—was for other militant defenders of the homosexual cause the mark of excessive ideological orthodoxy. That Front-identified militants expressed their utter contempt for the political values and tactics of less radical homosexual groups made a split within the ranks of the "Children of Christopher Street" inevitable.

When Gay Liberation Front groups disrupted the August 1970 meeting of the North American Conference of Homophile Organizations, the tension, thus far contained, broke into the open. Commenting bitterly on the disruption, the gay newspaper *The Advocate* declared:

We watch the activities of the most disruptive gay militants with fascination. We try in vain to detect some rationale in their tactics and philosophy. . . . But it becomes more and more apparent that the so-called gay militants are not so much pro-gay as they are anti-establishment, anti-capitalist, anti-society. They lash out in all directions, destroying everything in sight—gay or straight.[78]

Ideological disagreement with the Gay Liberation Front, as well as concern that the opportunity to attain civil and social rights for homosexuals within the context of the American social order not be lost, created the conditions out of which new organizational forms developed within the homosexual community. In New York for example, the Gay Activist Alliance was established in an explicit effort to provide a political base for homosexuals of all political persuasions who were willing to work together on the basis of their commitment to one issue—gay rights. While such groups were less socially radical than the Front groups, they were no less militant, no less aggressive in their affirmative stance with regard to homosexuality, and no less hostile to every indication of social and economic discrimination. To that extent they too exemplified the ardor and commitment of the era following the June 1969 riots, and looked back upon the earlier experience of homophile organizations as a prehistory.

Barbara Gittings, a lesbian activist with a finely developed sense of the history of gay politics and ideology, noted:

At first we were so grateful just to have people—anybody—pay attention to us that we listened to and accepted everything they said, no matter how bad it was. That is how different the consciousness at the time was. But I must emphasize, it was essential for us to go through this before we could arrive at what we now consider our much more sensible attitudes. You don't just spring full blown into an advanced consciousness. You do it step by step. . . . By the late 1960s we began to see that discussing the cause and the nature of homosexuality would not help us. We began to insist on our rights . . . to demand what was ours.[79]

Armed with that new "consciousness," homosexuals in the early 1970s were mobilized for mass politics, one of the most striking features of which was the series of "gay pride" demonstrations commemorating the Stonewall Riots. On the first anniversary of the police raid, thousands rallied in New York's Central Park. Never before had so many homosexuals declared in so public a fashion their rejection of the stigma associated with their sexuality. They demanded an end to the sodomy laws which made their most private acts a public crime and the enactment of legislation protecting them from discrimination. "We'll never have the freedom and civil rights we deserve as human beings unless we stop hiding in closets and the shelter of anonymity. This march is an affirmation and declaration of our new pride."[80] With evidence that such mass actions could mobilize large numbers of homosexuals into the streets, demonstrations were organized in successive years, each larger than the preceding one. Across the country, and especially on the west coast, the experience of New York was repeated. Homosexuals had at last made an entry into the politics of mass protest.[81]

In addition to these marches, and drawing inspiration from the same mood of militancy, gay groups organized pickets and demonstrations directed at every institution that buttressed the pattern of discrimination against homosexuals. The Catholic church became a target,[82] as did the mass media. Psychiatrists who gave public lectures on the disease of homosexuality could always expect to be greeted by hostile picket lines and fliers denouncing them and denying their right to speak as experts. "We interrupt this program and psychiatric propaganda to bring you a message from Gay Pride," proclaimed one leaflet. It was bigotry and not its victims that required medical attention.[83] University departments that used articles and books considered unacceptable were beset by demands for the exclusion of such material and the inclusion of works considered favorable to Gay Liberation. At the University of Pennsylvania, for example, gay activists successfully engineered the removal of David Reuben's popular *Everything You Always Wanted to Know About Sex but Were Afraid to Ask* from the reading list of a course sponsored by the Sexual Counseling Service, getting it replaced by a book that presented a more favorable picture of homosexuality.[84]

Far more significant, however, was a shift in the role of demonstrations from a form of expression to a tactic of disruption. In this regard gay activists mirrored the pattern of confrontation politics that had become the cutting edge of radical and antiwar student groups. The purpose of protest was no longer to make public a point of view, but rather to halt unac-

ceptable activities. With ideology seen as an instrument of
domination, the traditional willingness to tolerate the views
of one's opponents was discarded. Those who sought intellectual justification for this change found it in Herbert Marcuse's
essay "Repressive Tolerance."[85]

On more than one occasion television was the focus of such
actions. In 1971 the taping of an interview with David Reuben
in Chicago was interrupted by homosexuals challenging his
right to present his views.[86] Two years later gay activists held
a sit-in at the offices of the American Broadcasting Company
to demand that a Marcus Welby show be withdrawn because
it characterized homosexuals as "guilt-ridden mental cases."[87]

No longer content with the mere picketing of professional
meetings, homosexuals began to engage in disruptions, "zaps,"
designed to put a halt to discussions considered inimical to
their interests. In October of 1970 the Second Annual Behavior
Modification Conference in Los Angeles was the target of such
an action. During the showing of a film depicting aversive
conditioning techniques designed to eliminate homosexual behavior, members of the Gay Liberation Front interrupted with
cries of "barbarism," "medieval torture," and "This is disgust-
ing." Philip Feldman, whose therapeutic techniques were demonstrated in the film, attempted to justify his work by arguing
that he did not serve society's bidding but rather responded
to the needs of those who wanted to achieve a heterosexual
adjustment. He was shouted down. One demonstrator announced to the startled and furious audience:

We are going to reconstitute this session into small groups with equal
numbers of Gay Liberation Front members and members of your
profession and we are going to talk as you have probably never talked
with homosexuals before, as equals. We're going to talk about such
things as homosexuality as an alternative life style.[88]

This disruption was in fact a replay of one that had occurred
in San Francisco six months earlier, when homosexuals created
a chaotic situation after their first direct attack on the American

Psychiatric Association. That action represented the opening salvo in a battle that was to last three years, and was to bring homosexuals into direct conflict with organized psychiatry over its official classification of homosexuality as a disease.

Chapter 4

DIAGNOSTIC POLITICS:

HOMOSEXUALITY AND THE

AMERICAN PSYCHIATRIC

ASSOCIATION

THE AMERICAN PSYCHIATRIC ASSOCIATION

UNDER ATTACK: 1970–1972

Though the struggle on the part of homosexuals had, by the end of the 1960s, taken on the features of a broad social movement, it remained, like other expressions of discontent in this period, radically decentralized. Local groups inspired by the ideological tone of the movement would seize, often in an ad hoc manner, whatever opportunities presented themselves to demonstrate their demands for change. Since the targets of such protest—the media, government, economic institutions, and professional meetings where unacceptable views were being expressed—were so numerous, there tended to be almost no continuity from one effort to the next. With little overall coordination of activity, what coherence appeared to exist was the result of the observations of those aware of the patterns of protest.

Thus the American Psychiatric Association became the target of homosexual attack in 1970, when gay activists in San Francisco saw in the presence of the APA convention in their city yet one more opportunity to challenge the psychiatric profession. That decision was no different from the many others that had preceded earlier challenges to psychiatry. It was the status of the Association that gave the decision its significance. With the APA designated as a target, gay groups throughout the country could direct their wrath against a common organizational foe. Furthermore, the generalized antagonism toward psychiatry as a social institution could be transformed into a focused assault upon the psychiatric profession. Most importantly, the outrage against the view that homosexuality was a mental illness could be translated into a demand for the deletion of homosexuality from the APA's official *Diagnostic and Statistical Manual of Psychiatric Disorders.*

In the wake of the American invasion of Cambodia in May 1970, the killings at Kent State, and the subsequent convulsion of protest that swept the nation, gay groups in alliance with feminists engaged in the first systematic effort to disrupt the annual meetings of the American Psychiatric Association. "When we heard that Bieber and company were coming," said one activist, "we knew we had to be there."[1] Guerrilla theater tactics and more straightforward shouting matches characterized their presence. At a panel on transsexualism and homosexuality, Irving Bieber experienced his first face-to-face denunciation. Having become accustomed to the written attacks of those who had labeled him Public Enemy Number One, he was still unprepared for the kind of rage that greeted him. His efforts to explain his position to his challengers were met with derisive laughter. Since the norms of civility were considered mere conventions designed to mute outrage, it was not difficult for a protester to call him a "motherfucker."[2] "I've read your book, Dr. Bieber, and if that book talked about black people the way it talks about homosexuals, you'd be drawn and quartered and you'd deserve it."[3] This verbal attack with its violent tone caused Bieber considerable distress.

It was not, however, the confrontation with Bieber that provided the most dramatic encounter at the convention, but one that occurred at a panel on "issues of sexuality."[4] In a room filled with several hundred psychiatrists, homosexuals and feminists expressed their strongest outrage during the presentation of a paper by Nathaniel McConaghy, a young Australian psychiatrist, who was discussing the use of aversive conditioning techniques in the treatment of sexual deviation. Shouts of "vicious," "torture," and "Where did you take your residency, Auschwitz?" greeted the speaker. As that paper came to an end, and the chair prepared to announce the next presentation, demonstrators exploded with the demand that they be heard. "We've listened to you, now you listen to us." When urged to be patient, they retorted, "We've waited five thousand years." At that, the meeting was adjourned and pandemonium ensued. As one protester attempted to read a list of gay demands, he was denounced as a "maniac." A feminist ally was called "a paranoid fool" and "a bitch." Some psychiatrists, enraged by the intrusion and the seeming inability of the Association to protect their discussions from chaos, demanded that their air fares to San Francisco be refunded. One physician called for the police to shoot the protesters. While most of those who had assembled for the panel left the room, some did not, staying to hear their profession denounced as an instrument of oppression and torture.

It was after this disruption that Kent Robinson, a psychiatrist from Maryland, met Larry Littlejohn, one of the organizers of the protest. Robinson, who was sympathetic to the plight of homosexuals, seeing in their struggle a movement analogous to that of Blacks, women, and students, agreed with Littlejohn that the tactics employed at the meeting were necessitated by the Association's systematic refusal to let homosexuals appear on the official program. When told that homosexuals wanted to present a panel at the next APA convention, to be held in Washington, D.C., he agreed to convey that demand to the Association's leadership.

It was against the background of this chaotic challenge to the APA that Robinson approached John Ewing, chair of the Program Committee, warning him that unless the request for a panel was met, there was a grave risk that the entire 1971 meeting would be disrupted. "They're not going to break up just one section."[5] Noting the coercive terms of the request, Ewing quickly agreed, stipulating only that, in accordance with APA convention regulations, a psychiatrist chair the proposed session.

Since Robinson knew no homosexual psychiatrists, he somewhat reluctantly agreed to chair the gay panel. At the suggestion of Littlejohn, Robinson contacted Frank Kameny, the most notable homosexual activist in Washington. A decision was reached to invite the participation of gay women and men who could speak on homosexuality as a life style. And so the first panel discussion by homosexuals at an APA convention was organized. The long-sought-for goal of homosexuals speaking about themselves to psychiatrists in a forum that rejected the assumption of psychopathology had been attained. To those who had so boldly challenged the professional authority of psychiatry it was clear that only the threat of disorder or even of violence had been able to create the conditions out of which such a dialogue could occur. That lesson would not be forgotten.

Despite the agreement to allow homosexuals to conduct their own panel discussion at the 1971 convention, gay activists in Washington felt that they had to provide yet another jolt to the psychiatric profession. Accepting a limited role in the program without engaging in a more direct attack on psychiatry might have slowed the momentum necessary to force a retreat on the central issue, the classification of homosexuality as a mental disease. Too smooth a transition toward the institution- alization of protest would have deprived the movement of its most important weapon—the threat of disorder. Aware of the organizational weakness of his own Mattachine Society as well as of its relative conservatism, Frank Kameny turned to a Gay Liberation Front collective in Washington to plan the May 1971 demonstrations. Together with the collective, Kameny developed a detailed strategy for disruption, paying attention to the most intricate logistical details, including the floor plan of the hotel in which the convention was to be housed.

Hoping to avoid the chaos of its previous meeting, the APA prepared for the expected disruption by hiring a special security consultant who was to map a strategy for diffusing potentially explosive confrontations. Special considerations regarding the security of the convention were also called for, since it was known that antiwar activists were planning to converge on Washington during the first week in May to engage in massive civil disobedience. In an effort to limit the extent of possible violence, the APA's leaders decided to avoid, at all cost, any reliance upon a show of force by uniformed guards or police. A less provocative posture, one that entailed a willingness to ride out rather than to prevent demonstrations, was agreed upon.

The planned disruption occurred on May 3, when gay and antiwar activists stormed into the prestigious Convocation of Fellows. During the ensuing uproar, Kameny grabbed a microphone and denounced the right of psychiatrists to discuss the question of homosexuality. Borrowing from the language of the antiwar movement, he declared, "Psychiatry is the enemy incarnate. Psychiatry has waged a relentless war of extermination against us. You may take this as a declaration of war against you."[6] Fist-shaking psychiatrists, infuriated by the invaders, compared their tactics to that of Nazi stormtroopers.

The tone and mood of intimidation produced by this encounter pervaded the convention from that point. Using forged credentials, gay activists gained access to the exhibit area and, coming across a display marketing aversive conditioning techniques for the treatment of homosexuals, demanded its removal. Threats were made against the exhibitor, who was told that unless his booth was dismantled, it would be torn down. After frantic behind-the-scenes consultations, and in an effort to avoid violence, the convention leadership agreed to have the booth removed. Robinson, who had been acting as an intermediary between the APA and the homosexuals, was himself taken aback by the intensity of the rage and cautioned Kameny to temper the tactics of his codemonstrators. His call for moderation was dismissed. Robinson continued to perform the self-described function of "bagman" with the Association's quest for order being held at ransom.[7]

In contrast to these events, the officially sanctioned panel put together by Kameny posed a quieter challenge to orthodox psychiatric thinking on homosexuality. Its very title, "Lifestyles of Non-Patient Homosexuals," suggested a critique of both the diagnostic posture and the methodology of clinical research. In addition to Kameny, the panel included Larry Littlejohn of the Society for Individual Rights in San Francisco, Del Martin, a founder of the Daughters of Bilitis, Lilli Vincenz, a lesbian activist, and Jack Baker, the gay president-elect of the student body at the University of Minnesota. Though differing in matters of detail, they were unanimous in rejecting the clinical perspective on their lives, all expressing utter disdain for psychiatry's claim that it sought to heal and aid the homosexual. Kameny, whose vocal presence during the convention had made him an unmistakable antagonist, portrayed psychiatry's therapeutic posture as masking a pernicious desire to preserve a proprietary relationship to the homosexual: "We're rejecting you all as our owners. We possess ourselves and we speak for ourselves and we will take care of our own destinies."[8] The antipathy toward psychiatry was underscored by Del Martin, who asserted that what she had seen and heard during the course of the convention had reinforced her belief that psychiatry was the most dangerous enemy of homosexuals in contemporary society. The other panelists described the very painful lives endured by homosexuals as a result of social exclusions, legally sanctioned discrimination, and familial rejection, pointing to the role psychiatry played in nurturing these sources of despair. Equally important was the striking stance of self-affirmation contained in these presentations. Larry Littlejohn declared:

I think the homosexual lifestyle for those people who want to live it, is beautiful and I think it should be appreciated . . . for many people, hundreds of thousands of people [it] is a valid, healthy . . . lifestyle.[9]

Both the tone and the content of the open discussion that followed the panel suggest that those who opposed the homosexual presence at the convention had either avoided the session or been intimidated into silence. Only one psychiatrist ventured a criticism of the panelists, and he focused upon the extent to which they had unfairly assumed that all APA members were followers of Bieber and Socarides. The panelists responded by challenging sympathetic psychiatrists to break the monopoly enjoyed by those who characterized homosexuality as a disorder.

Toward the end of the convention Kameny and Littlejohn informed Robinson that they wanted to present their demands for the deletion of homosexuality from the APA's official nosology, *DSM II*, to members of the Association's Committee on Nomenclature. A meeting was hastily arranged with Robert Campbell of New York, who promised to convey their message to his colleagues. Though little came of that effort, it represented the first attempt on the part of gay activists to enter into direct discussions with those within the APA leadership who were responsible for the classification of psychiatric disorders. The process of transforming general outrage into a specific political demand had been set in motion.

Reliance upon disruptive tactics and rancorous denunciation was largely absent from the homosexual involvement in the 1972 APA convention held in Dallas. Kent Robinson again played a central role, this time making arrangements for a fully institutionalized gay presence at the annual meeting. Since the Psychiatric Association had accommodated itself to the inevita-

bility of homosexual pressure, those who continued to challenge the designation of homosexuality as a disorder displayed
a willingness to meet their opponents on terms less threatening
to professional decorum.

A grant from the Falk Foundation covered the travel expenses
of several gay activists as well as the cost of a booth in the
scientific exhibition area. The display, entitled "Gay, Proud
and Healthy," was designed to win the support of psychiatrists
in the struggle to end the classification of homosexuality as
a disease. A special flier produced by Frank Kameny for the
exhibit stressed both scientific and social themes: Psychiatrists
had acted unscientifically in labeling homosexuality as a disorder; the social consequences for gay women and men of being
so stigmatized had been disastrous. More significant than the
reiteration of these oft-repeated positions was the conciliatory
tone of the statement:

> We are trying to open dialogue with the psychiatric profession.
> . . . In past years it has been necessary, on occasion, to resort to
> strong measures against a resisting profession in order to achieve such
> discussion of *our* problems *with* us instead of merely about us. We
> sincerely hope that resolution, constructive discussion and dialogue
> followed by meaningful reform of psychiatry will soon proceed. . . .
> Psychiatry in the past—and continuingly—has been *the* major single
> obstacle in our society to the advancement of homosexuals and to
> the achievement of our full rights, our full happiness and our basic
> human dignity. Psychiatry *can* become our major ally.[10]

The flier concluded by calling upon psychiatrists both individually and collectively to renounce the "sickness theory," to work
for the reform of public opinion regarding homosexuals, and
to support law reform and equal opportunity legislation.
Through consultations psychiatrists could engage in a new co-
operative relationship with the homosexual community.

> Our themes are: Gay, Proud and Healthy and Gay is Good. With
> or without you we will work vigorously toward [their acceptance];
> and will fight those who oppose us. We would much prefer to work
> with you than against you. Will you join us, to our mutual benefit?[11]

The panel on homosexuality organized by Robinson brought together Frank Kameny; Barbara Gittings, a long-time lesbian activist and chair of the Task Force on Gay Liberation of the American Library Association; Robert Seidenberg, a psychoanalyst and clinical professor of psychiatry at New York's Upstate Medical Center in Syracuse; Judd Marmor; and most dramatically, Dr. Anonymous, a masked and cloaked psychiatrist who was also homosexual.

Kameny's presentation was not very different in content from the brochure he had prepared for the gay booth at the convention. More importantly, after an expected denunciation of his most prominent psychiatric antagonists, he evidenced an understanding of the extent to which the profession was divided, reaching out to those who might ally themselves with the homosexual struggle. "We do not want psychiatry as our foe, nor do we want any other foes." Barbara Gittings's talk was of a very different character. After asserting that it was not her purpose to "scold" the psychiatric profession, a task "well done and very properly done" at the 1971 convention, she went on to discuss the existence of the hidden minority of homosexual psychiatrists. Quoting extensively from the remarks of those whom she had met, she drew a portrait of psychiatrists who lived anguished lives, terrified at the prospect of professional ruin because of exposure. Like Kameny, Gittings ended with an appeal for serious and ongoing discussions, stressing, however, the importance of a new understanding between gay psychiatrists and their professional colleagues.

This year you are being offered an antidote [to the poisoned climate created by psychiatric orthodoxy]—invitations to open up dialogue with members of your own profession who are gay—to help, no longer to hurt. Gay is proud and gay is loud and gay is getting louder outside and inside the profession. What are *you* going to say in the dialogue that *we* are ready to enter into.[12]

By far the most dramatic event of the panel was the address of Dr. Anonymous. "I am a homosexual. I am a psychiatrist," he proudly announced. His attire not only seemed to protect his own identity, but perhaps more importantly was designed to stress that he spoke not only for himself but for all homosexual psychiatrists. He informed his audience that there were more than two hundred homosexual psychiatrists attending the convention. In fact there had been for some time a Gay-PA, an underground gay psychiatric association that met socially during the course of the annual meetings. Underscoring the situation Gittings had described, he stated:

As psychiatrists who are homosexual, we must know our place and what we must do to be successful. If our goal is high academic achievement, a level of earning capacity equal to our fellows, or admission to a psychoanalytic institute, we must make sure that we behave ourselves and that no one in a position of power is aware of our sexual preference and/or gender identity. Much like a black man with white skin who chooses to live as a white man, we can't be seen with our real friends, our real homosexual family, lest our secret be known and our doom sealed. . . . Those who are willing to speak out openly will do so only if they have little to lose, and if you have little to lose, you won't be listened to.

He ended with an appeal to both homosexual psychiatrists and their nonhomosexual colleagues. From the former he called for the courage to struggle for change; from the latter he called for acceptance.

The gay participants having made their plea, the two remaining psychiatrists responded by echoing the criticism of their profession, providing evidence that the gay cause had powerful and articulate allies within the APA. Robert Seidenberg contrasted the increasingly liberal attitude of religious groups toward homosexuality with the rigid and hostile attitude of psychiatry. In the most contemptuous of terms he described the "litany of atrocities" to be found in the professional literature dealing with the treatment of homosexuals. "As charitable as I can possibly be towards my own discipline and profession, I cannot . . . say that psychiatry or psychoanalysis is a friend of the homosexual."

Finally, Judd Marmor described his own effort to develop a critique of the prevailing psychiatric orthodoxy, defending

his 1965 Introduction to *Sexual Inversion* but adding an extended
comment from his as yet unpublished 1972 essay "Homosexuality—Mental Illness or Moral Dilemma?"[13] While noting that
there were an increasing number of psychiatrists who shared
his views, he pointed to the existence of intense and powerful
resistance on the part of many of his colleagues to the effort
to bring about a change in prevailing opinions. Though he
singled out for denunciation Charles Socarides, whom he accused of having written a "monstrous attack" on homosexuality for the *Journal of the American Medical Association*, as well as
the classical psychoanalytic societies, he made it clear that the
pattern of antihomosexual bias within the profession was pervasive. "The cruelty, the thoughtlessness, the lack of common
humanity, in the attitudes reflected by many conservative psychiatrists is I think a disgrace to our profession." Under such
circumstances it was impossible, in good faith, to call upon
homosexual psychiatrists to shed their anonymity. The potential costs were simply too great.

In reflecting upon the extraordinary nature of both the presentations at this panel and the role of gay activists at the convention, Frank Kameny noted with discernible pleasure that
for the first time at these meetings the only views on homosexuality heard in public forums were those that could be considered friendly. The impact of the increasing power of gay groups
had been revealed in the successful intimidation of old
enemies.[14] *The Advocate* reported the events in Dallas with similar
satisfaction, commenting that the panel might well have represented a "turning point" in the relationship between psychiatry
and the gay community.[15]

In accounting for the willingness of the APA to tolerate a
panel so blatantly critical of psychiatric practice and theory,
Barbara Gittings commented that it would have taken decades
for such an event to occur "if gay people had politely waited
to be asked." The tactical reliance upon disruption and force
in earlier years had been vindicated. What psychiatrists saw
as a gradual shedding of their own unfounded beliefs, the
product of reason, was for gay activists a confirmation of the
strategy of social protest.

CHANGING PERSPECTIVES WITHIN PSYCHIATRY

The presence at the 1972 APA meetings of psychiatrists critical of their own profession's attitude toward homosexuality was indicative of a much broader process of reevaluation that had begun to take place. Not long after the convention, the issues involved in the dispute over the classification of homosexuality were given full exposure in the *International Journal of Psychiatry*. In a lengthy discussion entitled "Homosexuality as a Mental Illness," Richard Green, director of the Gender Identity Research and Treatment Program at the University of California Medical School at Los Angeles, subjected the orthodox psychiatric perspective on homosexuality to a series of critical questions.[16] To those who spoke with certainty about etiology, psychodynamics, and psychopathology, he offered a number of provocative challenges. Less concerned with providing answers than with exposing the extent to which heterosexual biases had colored the work of psychiatrists, he suggested a range of diagnostic problems for which no firm data were yet available. For him evidence did not exist to support the claim that homosexuality was a disease or that sexual relations between partners of the opposite sex were preferable to those between partners of the same sex. Green challenged his readers to reconsider the issues pressed upon psychiatry by its homosexual critics.

At the risk of being charged with heresy I have asked the above questions in a friendly but troubled spirit. They are not challenges although they may be experienced as such by those for whom the issues have long been decided. . . . To my thinking in this issue there has been premature closure or premature order. I believe it is again time for inquiry and questioning of accepted, comfortable givens.[17]

Green's essay was followed by six formally invited responses, at least four of which were calculated to sharpen awareness of the profound disagreements that had begun to characterize psychiatric opinion on homosexuality. Rather than expressions of doubt and uncertainty, they were unmistakably partisan declarations. Judd Marmor[18] and Martin Hoffman[19] expressed clear and unambiguous support for the position that the classification of homosexuality as a mental illness represented nothing more than the cloaking of moral judgments in the language of science. Charles Socarides[20] and Lawrence Hatterer[21] defended the traditional psychiatric perspective. Especially for Socarides, there was no reason to reopen the issue of the pathologic status of homosexuality. Indeed, he perceived Green's agnostic stance as a rejection of the findings of science—a rejection cloaked in the guise of a scientific posture.

The theoretical ferment reflected in this exchange was mirrored in discussions within the American Psychiatric Association's task forces as well as in some of its local branches. As early as November 1971 the Task Force on Social Issues had recommended that the *Diagnostic and Statistical Manual's* classification of *all* homosexual behavior as pathological be reconsidered. Though limited to a suggestion that homosexual behavior in certain settings, such as prisons, might not necessarily be an indication of pathology, the recommendation did reveal a growing uneasiness with the certainty that had characterized the psychiatric nosology.[22] Upon receiving this recommendation Henry Brill, chair of the Committee on Nomenclature, wrote that there was strong sentiment within his committee to recognize "that homosexual behavior was not necessarily a sign of psychiatric disorder: and that the diagnostic manual should reflect that understanding."[23]

The most significant indication of the growing unwillingness to embrace automatically the standard pathological view occurred in the New York County District Branch of the American Psychiatric Association. Soon after the San Francisco disruption in May 1970, Charles Socarides approached the leadership of the New York District Branch with a request to establish a task force on sexual deviation. In accordance with well-established procedure, the request was granted, and

Socarides was appointed chair with the power to select its members. The Task Force report was completed in March 1972 and presented for discussion to the council of the New York body the following month. After a rancorous discussion between Socarides and the council, the report, which bore the psychoanalytic imprint of its authors, was rejected.[24] In justifying its decision the council stressed that though the clinical conclusions of the Task Force about the pathological status of homosexuals were acceptable, the overemphasis upon psychoanalytic theory was not.[25] Enraged by the decision, Socarides attacked the council's action as an act of "collusion" between the leadership of the New York District Branch and the national leadership of the APA. Suspecting that the latter was moving toward the "normalization" of homosexuality, Socarides charged that the officers of the New York Branch did not dare to take contrary action. For him this represented yet one more instance of the corruption of psychiatric science, with politics assuming preeminence over truth.[26] Robert Osnos, who had been appointed by the council to discuss the report with Socarides' group, dismissed these allegations, suggesting instead that the New York Branch had been reluctant to embrace the Task Force report because of its controversial nature. Interested in avoiding conflict, the leadership chose to sidestep the dispute over homosexuality.[27] Despite their sharply divergent evaluations of the motives of those involved, Socarides stressing venality and Osnos timidity, both provided unmistakable evidence of the extraordinary degree to which political factors and a fractious spirit had begun to affect psychiatric decision-making on the issue of homosexuality.

The erosion of certainty about homosexuality among American psychiatrists had its analogue among other mental health professionals. In October 1970, the Executive Committee of the National Association for Mental Health adopted a declaration against the criminalization of homosexual behavior between consenting adults in which it took a noncommittal stance in the conflict over whether such behavior could best be understood as the result of an underlying psychopathology or as an "accidental natural variant of mammalian sexual development."[28] Less than a year later the San Francisco affiliate of that association went further by adopting, with the prodding of two lesbian activists, a resolution asserting that "homosexuality can no longer be equated only with sickness, but may properly be considered as a preference, orientation, or propensity for certain kinds of life styles."[29] Clearly under pressure from the same quarters, the Golden Gate Chapter of the National Association of Social Workers adopted a similarly worded resolution in 1972.[30]

With psychiatrists as well as workers in the allied mental health professions beginning to doubt the merits of classifying homosexuality as a disease, and with the gay movement increasingly sophisticated in the use of tactics designed to create disorder, the stage was set by the end of 1972 for a full-scale effort to demand the amendment of the *Diagnostic and Statistical Manual of Psychiatric Disorders (DSM-II)*. What was now required was an appropriate triggering event that would set in motion the intellectual, professional, social, and political forces that had been generated during the prior years of protest. That event occurred in October 1972, with a disruptive demonstration at a meeting of behavior therapists in New York City.

THE POLITICS OF DIAGNOSTIC CHANGE

On October 8, 1972, the New York Gay Activist Alliance organized a "zap" of the Association for the Advancement of Behavior Therapy to protest the work of its members who, though rejecting the *language* of psychopathology in relation to homosexuality, were perceived by homosexuals as engaging in a brutal assault on the dignity of those whose sexual preferences deviated from the heterosexual norm. In a flier entitled "Torture Anyone?" circulated to mobilize supporters, the Alliance called for "an end to the use of aversion techniques to change the natural sexual orientation of human beings." Raising the specter of a totalitarian assault on human diversity, it demanded an end to "experiments in social engineering." More than one hundred demonstrators protested on the steets outside the New York Hilton Hotel while a smaller number gained access to a room crowded with conference participants anticipating a disruption. During a discussion in which one therapist was discussing his techniques, Ronald Gold of the Alliance led gay demonstrators in challenging those present to acknowledge the antihomosexual bias implicit in their therapeutic stance.[31]

It was at this session that Robert Spitzer of the New York State Psychiatric Institute, a member of the APA's Committee on Nomenclature, came into contact for the first time with homosexuals demanding a revision of psychiatry's attitude toward homosexuality.[32] Impressed by both their passion and their arguments, he agreed to arrange for a formal presentation of their views before a full meeting of his committee and to sponsor a panel at the APA's 1973 convention on the question of whether homosexuality ought to be included in the Association's official listing of psychiatric disorders. While such promises had been made before, these were to set in motion a series of events with far greater momentum.

Within the Gay Activist Alliance, Gold's success in eliciting from Spitzer a promised meeting with the Nomenclature Committee was met with considerable discontent. For many, such a formal discussion would represent a tacit recognition of the authority of the APA, and would be an act of collaboration with the enemy.[33] Yet for Gold and Bruce Voeller, president-elect of the Alliance, the opportunity to go beyond disruptive tactics in the gay struggle for social acceptance presented an opportunity that should not be lost. To avoid the impression of an officially sanctioned overture to psychiatry, gay activists insisted that the first meeting at which Spitzer's offer was discussed be termed a "gathering of individuals." Despite their initial caution, and the risk of a serious split within the Alliance, those present quickly agreed to accept the invitation to speak before the Nomenclature Committee. Charles Silverstein of the Institute for Human Identity, a homosexual and bisexual counseling center, was chosen to prepare a statement outlining the gay critique of the psychiatric orthodoxy. That a divisive controversy within the Alliance did not follow this decision can be attributed to the existence of widespread support for Bruce Voeller, who had just been elected by an overwhelming majority. A less popular leader might well have lacked the capacity to open formal discussions with the APA.

In an effort to create a receptive climate for his presentation at the Nomenclature meeting, Silverstein enlisted a number of sympathetic psychiatrists and psychologists to address the committee with statements supporting the deletion of homosexuality from the *Diagnostic and Statistical Manual.* Seymour Halleck, a psychiatrist widely acknowledged as a critic of the abuse of psychiatric authority, wrote that scientific evidence was lacking to support the view that homosexuality was a developmental disorder and stated that homosexual behavior could best be considered a "common behavior[al] variant." Noting the social consequence of being labeled with a psychiatric diagnosis, he concluded that "deletion of the diagnosis of homosexuality is not only a humanistic step, it is dictated by the best scientific information available."[34]

Wardell Pomeroy, a collaborator with Kinsey in his study of male sexual behavior, cited sections of the 1948 work that had been sharply critical of psychiatric orthodoxy. Stressing the extent to which reliance upon data drawn from clinical populations had created a distorted perspective, he called upon the Nomenclature Committee to acknowledge homosexuality as a normal variant, suggesting with only thinly disguised contempt that psychiatry would have done well to accept the conclusions he and Kinsey had put forth twenty-five years earlier. "I have high hopes that even psychiatry can profit by its mistakes and can proudly enter the last quarter of the twentieth century."[35]

Finally, Alan Bell of the Institute for Sex Research at Indiana University, and an investigator in the Kinsey tradition, cited both his own work and that of Evelyn Hooker in arguing that homosexuality fell "within the normal range of psychological functioning." For him, well-adjusted homosexuals and hetero-sexuals had more in common psychologically than disturbed and well-adjusted persons of either sexual orientation.[36]

Silverstein made his presentation to the Nomenclature Com-mittee on February 8, 1973. In a lengthy written statement he surveyed the current research findings of psychologists, psy-chiatrists, and social scientists, presenting an impressive array of citations which indicated that the classification of homosex-uality was inconsistent with a scientific perspective. Starting with the early work of Evelyn Hooker, Alfred Kinsey, and Ford and Beach, the document included material from more recent studies by investigators using both psychometric tests of psychological well-being and structured psychiatric inter-views designed to probe the extent of psychopathology. In addition, he referred to the work of Judd Marmor, Richard Green, and Martin Hoffman,[37] indicating that even among prominent psychiatrists and psychoanalysts serious doubt ex-isted about the validity of classifying homosexuality as a dis-ease. Finally, he cited a letter by Freud, which had not yet been published, to prove that even the founder of psychoanaly-sis was distressed by the conclusion of some of his early follow-ers that homosexuals were so disturbed as to be inappropriate candidates for membership in psychoanalytic societies.[38]

Having exposed the "scientific errors" involved in listing homosexuality as a psychiatric disorder, Silverstein's statement went on to document the manner in which this diagnostic label had served to buttress society's discriminatory practices against gay women and men. It cited federal court cases involv-ing the Defense Department's refusal to grant security clear-ance to avowed homosexuals because they suffered from a mental illness; a demand on the part of the New York Taxi Commission that a homosexual receive a psychiatric evaluation twice a year in order to assure his "fitness" to drive; the refusal of a university to grant a charter to a Gay Liberation group because the presence of such an organization on campus would not be "beneficial to the normal development of our students"; and the denial of a license to a homosexual to practice law. The statement held psychiatry culpable for the suffering of gay men and women deprived of their social rights because of the label of pathology. Lastly, the Nomenclature Committee was pressed to consider the psychological havoc that resulted from the labeling of the homosexual preference as pathological.

> We are told, from the time that we first recognize our homosexual feelings, that our love for other human beings is sick, childish and subject to "cure." We are told that we are emotional cripples forever condemned to an emotional status below that of the "whole" people who run the world. The result of this in many cases is to contribute to a self-image that often lowers the sights we set for ourselves in life, and many of us asked ourselves, "How could anybody love me?" or "How can I love somebody who must be just as sick as I am?"[39]

Thus, with a mixture of academic discipline and passion, the case was developed for a change in psychiatric nomenclature. To accommodate the sense of urgency felt by the homosexual community, an appeal was made for immediate action, despite the existence of plans to publish a revised edition of the *Manual* in 1978. Such a step would place psychiatry in the position of "bringing to pass a more enlightened medical and social climate."

Charles Silverstein's oral presentation at the February 8 meeting covered much of the same ground as his written statement, stressing the absence of any empirical basis for classifying homosexuality as a disorder. In contrast to the rich scientific literature, psychoanalytic theory was depicted as "subjective," "unsubstantiated," a series of "adult 'fairy' tales." Pointing both to the work of social scientists, and to the actions taken by mental health groups that had already rejected the pathological view, he concluded:

> I suppose what we're saying is that you must choose between the undocumented theories that have unjustly harmed a great number of people and continue to harm them and . . . controlled scientific

studies. . . . It is no sin to have made an error in the past, but surely you will mock the principles of scientific research upon which the diagnostic system is based if you turn your backs on the only objective evidence we have.[40]

Nothing impressed the members of the Committee on Nomenclature more than the sober and professional manner in which the homosexual case was presented to them. After several years of impassioned denunciations and disruptions, here, at last, was a statement that could be assimilated, analyzed, and discussed in a scientific context. Since none of the committee members was an expert on homosexuality, there was considerable interest in the data that had been presented, much of which was new to those who would have to evaluate the issues raised by the call for a revised nomenclature.[41] That the Silverstein presentation and the discussion that followed it produced such a reaction was remarkable, given the absence on the committee of any psychiatrist who had publicly expressed uncertainty about the diagnostic status of homosexuality.

For the homosexual activists who had succeeded in obtaining a formal hearing for their case and who had raised issues of sufficent seriousness to warrant a thoroughgoing review, the significance of the February 8 meeting cannot be overestimated.[42] Concerned, however, that subsequent discussions of the issues would be concealed from public view under conditions that would favor conservative professional tendencies and an unfavorable decision, they concluded that the press should be informed of the meeting. Only with such exposure could they sustain the kind of pressure that years of experience had demonstrated was vital to the process of change.[43] On February 9, under the headline "Psychiatrists Review Stand on Homosexuals," the *New York Times* reported the events of the preceding day. It quoted Henry Brill, chair of the committee, who indicated ready acknowledgment by his colleagues that the psychiatric labeling of homosexuality had led to unwarranted discriminatory public policies and attitudes. While the majority had also rejected the view that homosexual relations were invariably an indication of mental disorder, Brill noted that some members saw homosexuality as a "central feature of a psychiatric problem." With the reevaluation of the status of homosexuality a matter of public record, Brill reported that he hoped to present a statement on the appropriate direction of change within four months, in time for the May 1973 APA convention.[44]

With every indication that the Nomenclature Committee would attempt to resolve the dispute on homosexuality rather quickly, opponents of a change in *DSM-II* mobilized to forestall an undesirable outcome. An Ad Hoc Committee Against the Deletion of Homosexuality from *DSM-II* was organized under the leadership of Irving Bieber and Charles Socarides to focus the forces of resistance. Concerned with the absence on the Nomenclature Committee of psychiatrists who could be considered allies, the Ad Hoc Committee anticipated an unfavorable vote. On April 9, Bieber wrote to Walter Barton, medical director of the APA, urging him to appoint a special committee, "balanced in its composition," to review any decision by the Nomenclature Committee to delete homosexuality from *DSM-II*.[45]

Psychoanalytic societies were the most outspoken in their expression of opposition to change. In March the Council of the Association for Psychoanalytic Medicine passed a resolution opposing a change in *DSM-II*. Noting that exclusive homosexuality was a form of "disordered psychosexual development" resulting from early childhood experiences, and that it was treatable through psychotherapeutic intervention, the council asserted that such behavior could not be considered normal.[46] Little more than one week later Harry Gershman, dean of the Institute for Psychoanalysis of the Karen Horney Institute, and a member of the Socarides-Bieber committee, reported to the APA that its board of trustees had unanimously passed a resolution identical to that approved by the Council of the Association for Psychoanalytic Medicine opposing the removal of homosexuality from *DSM-II*.[47] Finally, in more cautious and less committed terms, the Executive Council of the

American Psychoanalytic Association voted at its Sixtieth Annual Meeting early in May to urge a delay in any action to remove homosexuality from the *Diagnostic Manual*, suggesting the need for "more time for useful study and consideration."[48] It is clear that the question of the diagnostic status of homosexuality aroused deep concern for these groups not only because of its potential impact on psychiatric thinking and practice with regard to sexuality, but because of what this change would portend for the status of psychoanalytic theory in the organization of a nosology of mental disorders.

While general public and professional attention was focused on the prospect of a nomenclature shift by the American Psychiatric Association, pressure for change was mounting in local psychiatric societies as well. Most important was the activity within the Northern New England District Branch of the APA, which included Massachusetts and New Hampshire. Toward the end of 1972 Lawrence Hartmann, chair of the Branch's Social Issues Committee, decided to have his group take up the issue of homosexuality. Concerned about both the scientific and civil rights aspects of the problem, he thought it an appropriate moment for the Branch to go on record as favoring the deletion of homosexuality from *DSM-II* as well as supporting an aggressive campaign to combat discrimination against gay men and women. These actions might have the further result of prodding the APA's leadership into what he believed was long overdue action. To inform the deliberations of his committee, Hartmann called upon Richard Pillard, a gay psychiatrist who had been publicly identified with gay causes ever since he had helped found the first homophile counseling center in the East. After making an oral presentation to the Social Issues Committee, Pillard was asked by Hartmann to prepare a formal resolution for its consideration. By the end of December 1972 his work was done.

Acknowledging that data were lacking on many questions having to do with homosexuality, the resolution nevertheless called for the deletion of homosexuality from *DSM-II* and its replacement with a broader category of "sexual dysfunction." Because many homosexuals were capable of functioning normally, they could be diagnosed as ill only if "homosexuality itself is arbitrarily considered an illness." By contrast, the new diagnostic category "sexual dysfunction" would include frigidity, impotence, and homosexuality in those instances when "in the opinion of the physician this is a problem area for the patient." After linking the prevailing pattern of social discrimination to the psychiatric classification of homosexuality as a disorder, the resolution went on to call for an end to such practices, as well as for the repeal of all sodomy legislation affecting consenting adults. Finally, in order to help young people becoming aware of their own homosexual desires, the resolution asked for an end to the exclusively heterosexual orientation of sex education programs.[49]

With the exception of the last provision, the resolution was enacted by the Social Issues Committee. In March 1973 the Northern New England District Branch endorsed this action, making it the first APA affiliate to take a stand for the deletion of homosexuality from *DSM-II*.[50] Soon afterward it was endorsed by the APA's Area Council I, which included all of New England in addition to Ontario and Quebec.

For the homosexuals who had been engaged in the politics of confrontation with the American Psychiatric Association for more than two years and who had, less than six months earlier, begun a process of negotiation with Robert Spitzer and the Nomenclature Committee, passage of the complete resolution by the New England District Branch and Area Council I was the first indication that their effort might well end in success.[51]

Within the Nomenclature Committee itself, discussions following the presentation of the gay case in February were affected by pressures to act quickly despite the fact that no member considered himself expert on the theoretical or clinical dimensions of homosexuality. Though Henry Brill had titular authority over the committee, Robert Spitzer, who was committed to an expeditious resolution of the controversy, zealously assumed a central role in directing its considerations, suggesting appropriate clinical and research literature to his colleagues for study. The intensity of his involvement, however, was not linked initially to any strong allegiance to a substantive position. Certainly he was not at first a supporter of the effort to delete homosexuality from the nomenclature. Indeed, when paired with Paul Wilson, a psychiatrist from Washington, D.C., to draft a discussion paper for the committee, Spitzer could not accept Wilson's version because of its support for declassification.[52] What is remarkable is that because of his sense of mission he was, despite his unformed views, able to dominate both the pace and the direction of the committee's work. In fact it was Spitzer's own conceptual struggle with the issue of homosexuality that framed the committee's considerations.

By the time of the May 1973 APA convention in Honolulu, Spitzer's views had moved quite far. The justification for including homosexuality per se among the psychiatric disorders had become increasingly inconsistent with his understanding of the appropriate focus of a nosological system.[53] His attention had been drawn to critical analyses of standard psychoanalytic works like Bieber's and to empirical studies indicating that homosexuals were quite capable of satisfactory adjustments to the demands of everyday life.[54] Contact with gay activists had made it clear that many homosexuals were fully satisfied with their sexual orientations. It began to seem to him that the inclusion of homosexuality in *DSM-II* constituted an unjustifiable extension of the concept "psychiatric disorder." Furthermore, as the issues unfolded, Spitzer was forced to reconsider the foundations of the psychiatric nosology itself. In rethinking the basis for the classification of aberrant behavior, he concluded that an important distinction existed between what was suboptimal and what could appropriately be considered a psychiatric disorder. Wrestling with the implications of this conceptualization, he began to recognize how great a distance he had traveled from his own psychiatric and psychoanalytic training.

At the same time as he was shifting his own position, Spitzer was engaged in planning a panel discussion for the 1973 psychiatric meetings in fulfillment of his second pledge to gay activists in October 1972. Indicative of the seriousness with which he took this mission was the professional stature of the participants he sought to engage. In contrast to prior attempts in which homosexuals and their psychiatric allies were brought together to speak out against the profession, the panel brought together by Spitzer would incorporate the major proponents of the antagonistic views then dividing American psychiatry. Representing the orthodoxy, now so clearly under attack, were Irving Bieber and Charles Socarides.[55] Arrayed against them were psychiatrists Judd Marmor, Richard Green, Robert Stoller, and gay activist Ronald Gold. Marmor, a vice-president of the APA, and for years clearly identified as a critic of the standard psychiatric position, concluded his expected assault by challenging his colleagues to relinquish their unwarranted and unscientific defense of the supremacy of heterosexuality. "It is our task as psychiatrists to be healers of the distressed, not watchdogs of our social mores."[56] To Stoller, not only was the listing of homosexuality as a diagnostic category untenable, but the entire system of psychiatric classification was flawed and in need of radical revision.[57] Finally, Ronald Gold made an impassioned appeal to psychiatrists to withdraw from their clinical stance. "Stop it," he declared. "You're making me sick."[58]

Nothing more clearly indicates the extent to which this controversy had gripped the membership of the APA than the size of the audience that turned out for the session—almost one thousand conference participants were present. From the air of self-confidence that characterized the remarks of those who only three years ago had represented a distinctly unpopular view, and from the response evoked by their comments, it seemed to attentive observers that the long-sought-for goal of homosexual activists would soon be attained. Commenting on the events of the APA convention, *Newsweek* noted, "The indications seem to be that the [Nomenclature] Committee will decide to drop homosexuality from its list of mental aberrations."[59]

Yet despite the apparent certainty of ultimate success, gay activists remained concerned about Robert Spitzer's failure to arrive at an unambiguous position on the deletion of homosexuality by the date of the convention, fearing that he might delay the process of change. Ronald Gold decided that a meeting between Spitzer and homosexual psychiatrists at the convention might provide the necessary pressure.[60] Without warning those who were attending a Gay-PA social function, Gold appeared with Spitzer, who at an earlier date had said that he had never met a homosexual psychiatrist. The initial response to Spitzer's presence was outrage. Dismayed by Gold's action, many of the gay psychiatrists complained that he had thoughtlessly exposed them to an outsider, one whom they feared could easily ruin their careers. Gold prevailed over those who had demanded that Spitzer leave by arguing that they now had a unique opportunity to convey their sense of urgency about the diagnostic change. In this emotionally charged situation, Spitzer heard homosexual psychiatrists declaring to Gold that "their lives had been changed by what they had heard at the panel discussion."[61] The occasion not only succeeded in substantiating Spitzer's belief that being homosexual had little to do with one's capacity to function at a high level, but perhaps more importantly provided an emotional jolt that moved him to prepare, within a month, a proposal for the deletion of homosexuality from the nomenclature.

His first draft, entitled "Homosexuality as an Irregular Form of Sexual Development and Sexual Orientation Disturbance as a Psychiatric Disorder" was circulated in June. It reflected an effort to steer a middle course between those like Marmor who saw homosexuality as a normal variant of sexuality and those like Bieber and Socarides who characterized it as a psychopathology. Spitzer's strategy entailed the development of a restricted definition of psychiatric disorders that excluded homosexuality while avoiding the implication that it was no different from heterosexuality—in his view the preferred form of human sexuality.

From a review of the available empirical literature he concluded that a significant proportion of homosexuals were satisfied with their sexual orientation, showed no signs of manifest psychopathology (other than homosexuality, if that were considered pathological, per se), and functioned in a socially effective fashion; some, however, were distressed by their sexual orientation and sought the assistance of psychiatrists to help them achieve either a heterosexual life style or a better adjustment to their homosexuality. He turned next to the more problematical question of the appropriate scope of a manual of psychiatric disorders. For Spitzer the answer was now obvious. Only clearly defined mental disorders ought to be included and "not all of the forms of human psychological development which are judged by the profession or some members of the profession as less than optimal." His restricted definition of mental disorders, articulated *after he had decided that homosexuality had been inappropriately classified,* entailed two elements: For a behavior to be termed a psychiatric disorder it had to be regularly accompanied by subjective distress and/or "some generalized impairment in social effectiveness or functioning." With the exception of homosexuality and some of the other sexual deviations, Spitzer argued, all other entries in *DSM-II* conformed to this definition of disorder.

The inclusion of homosexuality in the nomenclature would have required the expansion of the concept of psychiatric disorder to include all "suboptimal" conditions. From such a theoretical perspective, Spitzer warned, the classification of disorders would become a listing of a vast array of odd behaviors. As if to suggest the absurdity to which psychiatry would be forced by such an all-embracing concept of mental disorder, he listed the following potential candidates for inclusion in a broad nosological classification: celibacy (failure to achieve optimal sexual functioning), religious fanaticism (dogmatic and rigid adherence to religious doctrine), racism (irrational hatred of certain groups), vegetarianism (unnatural avoidance of carnivorous behavior), and male chauvinism (irrational belief in the inferiority of women).

Spitzer was careful to underline that he was not asserting that either these behaviors or homosexuality were "normal." Fully aware of the possibility that gay activists would claim the deletion of homosexuality from *DSM-II* as indicating that psychiatry had recognized it as being as desirable, as "normal," as heterosexuality, he flatly asserted, "They will be wrong." Only homosexuals troubled by their sexual orientation—those who sought either adjustment or change—ought to be the subject of psychiatric classification. Only they exhibited the distress that was so central a feature of the newly defined "disorder." Thus Spitzer recommended that a new classification, "sexual orientation disturbance," be substituted for "homosexuality" in *DSM-II*.

This category is for individuals whose sexual interests are directed primarily toward people of the same sex and who are either bothered by, in conflict with or wish to change their sexual orientation. This diagnostic category is distinguished from homosexuality, which by itself does not constitute a psychiatric disorder. Homosexuality per se is a form of irregular sexual development and like other forms of irregular sexual development, which are not by themselves psychiatric disorders, is not listed in this nomenclature of mental disorders.[62]

For Spitzer there were a number of significant advantages in this reformulation. Psychiatry would no longer be in the position of claiming that homosexuals who insisted on their own well-being and who were clearly able to function socially were nevertheless sick. Furthermore, removing the label of mental illness from homosexuals would eliminate a major justification for the denial of their civil rights. Finally, such a definition would protect the professional standing of clinicians who sought, through therapeutic intervention, to assist homosexuals seeking a heterosexual adjustment.

The position paper as well as the proposed new diagnostic category thus attempted to provide a common ground for those who had been locked in combat for the past three years. To homosexual activists it granted the removal of homosexuality from the *Diagnostic Manual*, allowing them to claim a stunning victory. To psychoanalytically oriented psychiatrists, it stated that their own view of homosexuality as suboptimal was not being challenged, but rather was not central to the restricted concept of psychiatric disorder. To those seeking an end to the pattern of disruptions that had beset psychiatric meetings, the new classification provided a formula that could remove the APA from the center of controversy. Finally, for psychiatrists concerned with the extent to which the psychiatric nosology had become a tool in the hands of government officials attempting to deprive homosexuals of their rights, the proposed shift promised to put an end to such unwanted collaboration. That all of this could take the form of a theoretical refinement rather than a political accommodation made the proposal more attractive to those willing to yield the polar positions defined in the course of conflict.

At the same time as the classification change was being considered, a formal statement on the civil rights of homosexuals, drafted by Robert Spitzer and Ronald Gold, was before the Nomenclature Committee. This more patently political declaration sought to put the APA on record as opposing the discriminatory practices that had been justified for so long on the grounds that homosexuals were mentally ill. That this kind of declaration could have emerged from the committee charged with overseeing the consideration of nosological issues can be explained only in terms of the appreciation, shared by those involved in this process, of the enormous social importance of making a clean and comprehensive break with the antihomosexual past.

Unanimous support existed for the civil rights resolution within the Nomenclature Committee.[63] This was not the case with regard to the deletion of homosexuality. When both proposals were delivered to Walter Barton, medical director of the APA, Henry Brill noted in a covering letter that his committee was "completely divided," with some opposing action, others being undecided, and only "one or two" favoring quick approval. Not surprisingly, he caustically characterized Spitzer as being "quite sympathetic" to the viewpoint of the "Gay

Liberation Group." Brill's emphasis upon the degree of dissension may have reflected his own indecision and his discomfort with Robert Spitzer's aggressive assumption of leadership on this issue. In describing his own position, he stated, "From the social point of view there appears to be a very good case in favor of dropping homosexuality from the *Manual,* but from the medical and psychiatric point of view the issues are by no means so clear-cut."

Because of both his own ambivalence and his tendency toward caution, Brill suggested to the medical director that a formal survey of a stratified sample of APA members be undertaken to elicit responses to Spitzer's nomenclature proposal. Such a survey would alert the leadership of the Association to the possibility of either strong negative or strong positive reactions to the proposed deletion of homosexuality from *DSM-II,* thus avoiding the potentially disruptive consequences of a decision unacceptable to the majority of America's psychiatrists. While not a suggestion for a binding formal referendum of the kind that would ultimately be held on this question in 1974, Brill's request for a survey indicated not only the extremely delicate nature of the issues involved, both social and scientific, but the remarkable extent to which he and his colleagues understood that political factors were at play in this dispute. The decision by the APA's leadership not to undertake such a survey indicated its own concern about the potential divisive impact of the further politicization of the nomenclature discussion. The Association had little difficulty in justifying its rejection of Brill's procedural proposal. To do otherwise would have implied a willingness to subject scientific questions to the democratic process. Russell Monroe, chair of the Council on Research and Development, termed Brill's suggestion "ridiculous," asserting, "You don't devise a nomenclature through a vote."[64]

It was to Monroe's council, comprised of five senior psychiatrists who were responsible for providing the APA with advice on matters of policy and with information on current issues in psychiatric research, that Spitzer's proposal was first sent for consideration.. Though officially coming from the Committee on Nomenclature, in fact it had never been formally approved by its members and thus represented Spitzer's own effort to resolve what many APA leaders considered a "hot potato."[65]

Just prior to the regular October meeting of the Council on Research and Development, its members received a letter from Ronald Gold, now of the National Gay Task Force (NGTF), spelling out the concerns of the gay community on this issue.[66] Written with extraordinary attentiveness to the sensibilities and professional prerogatives of those who would be making the crucial decision, it sought in almost deferential terms to avoid the impression that pressure was being brought to bear upon them. While supportive of the proposed deletion of homosexuality, the letter expressed concern about both the new diagnostic category of "sexual orientation disturbance" and the tone of the Spitzer position paper. Gold argued that a serious error had been made in restricting the new diagnostic category to homosexuals. Heterosexuals too could be in conflict over their sexual orientations and need assistance in making a homosexual adjustment. Most importantly, the new classification would provide a warrant for "indiscriminate attempts" by psychiatrists to change the orientation of homosexuals "suffering from the internalized effects of anti-homosexual bigotry." The Spitzer paper was criticized not only because it did not embrace the view that homosexuality was a normal variant of human sexuality, but also because of its emphasis on the extent to which homosexuality was "suboptimal." Referring to Spitzer's comparisons of homosexuality, religious fanaticism, and racism as "egregious," Gold asserted that the paper's discussion of "valuable" and "optimal" behavior was unscientific, revealing an attitude that ought to be irrelevant to psychiatry and the diagnosis of disorders. However, because he feared that a thorough review of the issues raised in his letter would delay a decision to delete homosexuality from *DSM-II*, Gold offered the expedient of simply sidestepping the question of a new diagnostic category while moving ahead with the more important task of deletion. Though ostensibly reasonable, such a move in effect would have undermined the very delicate balance upon which Spitzer had constructed his proposed change, which sought to gain the support of the broadest possible psychiatric constituency.

Despite this tactical effort to diffuse the atmosphere of pressure that had forced this issue on the APA, it would have required a state of self-imposed amnesia for the members of the Council on Research and Development to consider the question of the diagnostic status of homosexuality without taking into account the sociopolitical struggle that had placed this item on their agenda. For some members that pressure had created an unacceptable situation in which patient populations could determine the pace at which matters of serious consequence for psychiatry would be considered. An unwarranted intrusion of extraprofessional forces was perceived by many as posing a threat to the integrity of the APA. In addition, some felt that Robert Spitzer and his supporters on the Nomenclature Committee had been so eager to bring the discussion of homosexuality to a predetermined resolution that they had repeatedly violated accepted procedures for the consideration of such matters. The captives of extraprofessional interests, they had attempted to short-circuit the institutional framework designed to guarantee the scientific evaluation of issues. Yet it was precisely the same sense of urgency that suggested to other council members the need to move swiftly. With homosexuals rightly claiming that inclusion in the *Manual* had become a source of great suffering, it was necessary to handle their demand in an ad hoc fashion rather than to wait for the formal reconstruction of *DSM-II*.[67]

After considering both Spitzer's proposal and other opinions on the nomenclature change, the council voted unanimously to approve the deletion of homosexuality from *DSM-II*. While the members generally had agreed with the reasoning offered in favor of deletion, the principal explanation for their unanimity was the council's desire to act according to the well-established procedural norm of accepting the findings of the task

forces established under its aegis. Since such task forces typically were appointed on the basis of expertise, to override their
conclusions would have represented a violation of the principles of scientific authority. In this instance, however, the invo-
cation of that standard served to mask a very complex
relationship between the premises of psychiatric diagnosis and
more overtly social considerations. The proposal that had been
brought before the council was not the considered conclusion
of the full Nomenclature Committee, but rather the work of
one of its members. Though the absence of any outcry from
its members suggested a willingness to let Spitzer have his
way, Brill himself had alerted Monroe to how divided the
group was. More importantly, the task force had not been
appointed on the basis of expertise on the question of homosexuality; indeed none of its members including Spitzer considered
himself expert on the question. That some reading and discussion had been undertaken could hardly have materially affected
this situation. Significant in this regard was the council's reluctance to raise serious questions about the conceptual basis of
Spitzer's conclusions, for within a year even he was to recognize
its inadequacy.

The council's unanimous endorsement of Spitzer's effort provided the first indication of the tactical wisdom in his decision
to answer the question of whether homosexuality was a psychiatric disorder with a definitional device. The new restrictive
definition of psychiatric disorder had proved itself capable of
providing a common ground for those with quite disparate
views on the nature of homosexuality. Thus it was possible
for Louis Jolyon West, a strong advocate on the council of
the Spitzer proposal, to believe nevertheless that "homosexuality usually represents a maturational disturbance of
personality."[68]

Despite the apparent capacity of Spitzer's formulation to
win the support of powerful figures in the APA's leadership,
many gay activists remained extremely reluctant to embrace
his effort. More enthusiastic about the declaration of Area
Council I, they attempted to mobilize psychiatrists to support

it in the Assembly of District Branches.[69] Before it could be voted on, however, the leaders of the Area Council withdrew it from consideration for tactical reasons, leaving only the Spitzer proposal on the agenda of the Assembly for full formal consideration in November.

Because the Assembly tends to reflect a clinical rather than an academic perspective in psychiatry, many observers anticipated resistance to the deletion of homosexuality from the nomenclature. Though there were some who strongly opposed the declassification of homosexuality, the overwhelming majority voiced approval. More significantly, the Assembly expressed concern about the wording of the new diagnostic category because of its reference to homosexuality as an "irregular" form of sexual behavior.[70] Siding with a criticism voiced early in June by Judd Marmor, they called upon the Council on Research and Development to reword the resolution, eliminating such pejorative phrasing.[71]

Having passed the Assembly, the proposal next appeared before the Reference Committee, comprised of the chairs of the various APA councils and the president-elect of the Association. At its November 15 meeting it endorsed the diagnostic category of "sexual orientation disturbance," thus paving the way for the board of trustees to act at its mid-December meeting.[72]

With every indication that the board of trustees would supply the final approval necessary for the change in nomenclature at the December 15 meeting, homosexual activists began to prepare for the celebration of victory. Concerned that the APA would attempt to mute the significance of the deletion of homosexuality from *DSM-II*, gay activists exerted intense pressure upon Alfred Freedman, the liberal president of the Psychiatric Association, to create an appropriate setting for the announcement of the board's expected decision. In an atmosphere charged with both anticipation and unflagging militancy, there were demands for a "gay presence" at the board's meeting. Threats of mobilizing a major picket of APA headquarters were made. When warned that too obvious an effort to highlight the significance of political pressure in the process might have disastrous consequences, leaders of the homosexual cause decided to settle for a press conference at which representatives of both the gay movement and psychiatrists would explain the significance of the decision to remove homosexuality from the nomenclature and of the accompanying civil rights declaration.[73]

On December 10 the APA publicly announced plans to hold a press conference, at which Robert Spitzer, Alfred Freedman, and others would be present. The National Gay Task Force planned to participate with a full contingent of the activists who had been long involved in pressing the APA to make the desired change. Among those to be present were Howard Brown, former commissioner of health in New York and chair of the National Gay Task Force; Bruce Voeller, its executive director; Barbara Gittings, the long-time lesbian activist; and Frank Kameny. In a memorandum to the gay participants, Ronald Gold urged them to stress the symbolic importance of the anticipated board decision. He asked them to underline their intention to use it in the attack on sodomy laws, immigration restrictions, custody cases, and the use of antihomosexual textbooks. Finally, he asked them to note their dissatisfaction with the new diagnostic category of "sexual orientation disturbance." While accepting a truce with the profession as a whole, he called upon the gay participants to indicate that individual "homophobes" would remain the subject of continued "exposure."[74]

Though they had had only the most limited formal input at the earliest stages of discussion, three leading opponents of the change in the status of homosexuality were invited to state their case before the board of trustees when it met to make a final decision on December 15. With the outcome all but a foregone conclusion, the presentations of Irving Bieber, Charles Socarides, and Robert McDevitt were received respectfully, but coolly. Bieber reiterated his familiar claims regarding the etiology of homosexuality, stressing the dire consequences of a diagnostic shift for the "pre-homosexual child."[75] Socarides, appealing to the authority of scientific expertise, charged that those with the greatest experience on the question of homosexuality had been systematically denied the opportunity to have their views heard during the months preceding the board meeting.[76] He went on to draw a sharp distinction between the legitimate struggle for civil rights on the part of homosexuals and the scientific issue of the nomenclature, in a futile attempt to drive a wedge between those who supported the social aspirations of the gay community and those who rejected the psychopathological view of homosexuality. Finally, McDevitt argued that since clinical evidence made clear that homosexuality was a pathological state, the desire to alter the nomenclature could be explained only on "political and philosophical grounds."[77] Far from helping homosexuals, the declassification of homosexuality would represent a "cold and unfeeling response" to those in need, creating "more despair than hope" for such individuals.

Having satisfied the formal requirements of providing a fair hearing, the board met in executive session to render its verdict. Among the fifteen trustees who were present (three were absent), a clear majority accepted the distinction drawn by Spitzer between sexual behavior that was not normal and that which ought to be termed a psychiatric disorder.[78] Some who felt privately that homosexuality was indeed a disorder, even in Spitzer's more limited sense, nevertheless acknowledged that the evidence required to substantiate their position was lacking.[79] Opposition to the proposed deletion tended to focus on the degree to which, under the pressure of homosexual activists and concern for civil rights, the Association had attempted to move too summarily, and with inappropriate haste.[80]

On the first formal vote, the classification of "sexual orientation disturbance," as amended to meet the objections raised by Assembly members won the support of nine members with four casting negative ballots and two abstaining. On a motion of Ewald Busse, it was suggested that the phrase "homosexuality . . . by itself does not constitute a psychiatric disorder" be altered to read "homosexuality . . . by itself does not *necessarily* constitute a psychiatric disorder."[81] When that motion passed, it was possible for those who wanted to avoid the impression that the psychiatric status of homosexuality was no longer a matter of debate to vote for the new diagnostic category. On a final poll, with a vote of thirteen to zero and two abstentions, the board approved the deletion of homosexuality and its replacement with the classification "sexual orientation disturbance."

This category is for individuals whose sexual interests are directed primarily towards people of the same sex and who are either disturbed by, in conflict with, or wish to change their sexual orientation. This diagnostic category is distinguished from homosexuality, which by itself does not necessarily constitute a psychiatric disorder.[82]

In addition, the trustees, with only one abstention, approved Spitzer's far-reaching civil rights proposal, placing the American Psychiatric Association on record as opposing both the use of the criminal sanction against private consensual homosexual activity and the deeply embedded pattern of social discrimination against gay men and women. While advocates of the nomenclature change had repeatedly argued that the two issues were conceptually distinct, it is clear that much of the force of the civil rights resolution was derived from the prior nosological decision.

Whereas homosexuality in and of itself implies no impairment in judgment, stability, reliability, or vocational capabilities, therefore, be it resolved, that the American Psychiatric Association deplores all public and private discrimination against homosexuals in such areas as employment, housing, public accommodation, and licensing, and declares that no burden of proof of such judgment, capacity, or reliability shall be placed upon homosexuals greater than that imposed on any other persons. Further, the APA supports and urges the enactment of civil rights legislation at local, state, and federal levels that would insure homosexual citizens the same protections now guaranteed to others. Further, the APA supports and urges the repeal of all legislation making criminal offenses of sexual acts performed by consenting adults in private.[83]

And so, eleven months after their first presentation before the Nomenclature Committee, homosexual activists had succeeded in achieving their long-sought goal. If continued distrust prevented the perception of psychiatry as a true ally in their struggle, at least it had been neutralized. What Frank Kameny had been referring to for years as *the* major ideological prop of society's antihomosexual bias had been shattered.

In the press release that followed the December 15 decision, Alfred Freedman, the APA's president, underscored the limited scientific meaning of the vote to delete homosexuality from *DSM-II* while emphasizing its enormous social significance. Closely following Spitzer's line of reasoning about the classification of psychiatric disorders, he asserted that the board had declared neither that homosexuality was "normal" nor that it was as desirable as heterosexuality. With regard to the civil rights statement, he declared that the APA wished to add its voice to the struggle to root out the irrational social practices that so cruelly victimized homosexuals. He expressed the hope that the trustees' action on both resolutions would "help to build a more accommodative climate of opinion for the homosexual minority in our country, a climate which will enable homosexuals to render the maximal contribution to society of which they are capable."[84]

Across the country newspapers headlined the American Psychiatric Association's decision. Washington's two major dailies, the *Post* and the *Star,* reported "Doctors Rule Homosexuals Not Abnormal"[85] and "Victory for Homosexuals."[86] The *New York Times* noted in a front-page story: "Psychiatrists in a Shift. Declare Homosexuality No Mental Illness."[87] The gay press exultantly announced the decision in *The Advocate,* declaring, "Gays Leave Psychiatric Sick List,"[88] and "Sick No More."[89]

PSYCHIATRY DIVIDED: VOTING ON

THE STATUS OF HOMOSEXUALITY

While discussions within the APA's committees and councils had been conducted in an atmosphere of striking consensus, the board's decision provoked a response by many psychiatrists that revealed how profoundly divided American psychiatry was on the issue of homosexuality. The public reaction to the deletion of the older diagnostic category was largely, though certainly not exclusively, expressed in language compatible with the standards of professional decorum. But just beneath the surface, always fueling the intensity of the debate and sometimes breaking through in startling expletives, was a deep bitterness. Denunciations and vilifications, most often muttered in private discussions, characterized the politicized dispute among psychiatrists over their association's new position.

Those who supported the board quite naturally praised its sobriety and wisdom in breaking with the past. They perceived in the attempt to narrow the definition of mental illness a serious effort to respond to psychiatry's conceptual confusion, reflected in the apparent success of antipsychiatrists like Thomas Szasz in gaining a sympathetic hearing. Finally, they welcomed the openness with which their leadership had responded to the legitimate concerns of the homosexual community. The tone of these congratulatory reactions was, not surprisingly, subdued; after all, they represented affirmations of official policy. That was not the case with those who had lost out in the debate.

Stung by the significance of the ideological rebuff they had suffered, those who continued to view homosexuality as pathological perceived themselves as having been expelled from the center of psychiatric authority. The liberal, socially oriented leadership of their association had usurped the mantle of science; the APA's councils had fallen victim to a Babylonian captivity. In letters to the Washington headquarters of the Association and to _Psychiatric News_, the APA's official publication, they expressed dismay and outrage.

On a conceptual level, opponents of the board's decision found it utterly astounding that "subjective distress" could provide a standard by which to determine the presence or absence of psychopathology. Indeed, it was the absence of such discomfort that often revealed the depths of pathology. Furthermore, Spitzer's emphasis on the importance of social functioning implied that a number of patently pathological conditions, expecially the sexual perversions, had been improperly classified as disorders. Instead of providing a sound basis for a psychiatric nosology, the board had made a shambles of the nomenclature.

On a clinical level, concern was greatest over the implications of the Association's decision for the psychotherapeutic effort to assist adolescents experiencing conflict over their sexual identities. The removal of homosexuality from the list of psychiatric disorders would signal to these confused young men and women that it mattered little whether they chose a homosexual or heterosexual orientation. One psychiatrist wrote to *Psychiatric News:* "The Board of Trustees has made a terrible, almost unforgivable decision which will adversely affect the lives of young homosexuals who are desperately seeking direction and cure. That . . . decision will give young homosexuals an easy way out and make the job of practitioners like myself much more difficult."[90]

In attempting to explain the decisions of the board and the other APA bodies, dissenting psychiatrists frequently asserted that those who had supported the deletion of homosexuality from *DSM-II* acknowledged privately that such sexual behavior represented a pathological condition, but refused to say so publicly. The Spitzer formulation, which allowed for a distinction between the suboptimal and the disordered, was characterized as providing a clever subterfuge for those whose clinical insights conflicted with their socially inspired desires to justify declassification.

The most sympathetic view among this group was that declassification reflected a willingness to bend the psychiatric nosology to serve laudable social goals. More contemptuously it was viewed as a craven capitulation to the power of the mob.[91] For the opponents of the board's December 15 vote the central issue was the desertion of psychiatry's scientific posture. It was that which drew the most venomous comments. "I think the Board of Trustees did not have the strength and guts to resist superficial social pressure from homosexuals who, having a collective Oedipal complex, wish to destroy the American Psychiatric Association. It is a bad day for psychiatry."[92] The dissenters were haunted by the specter of a politicized psychiatry that would be defenseless against an endless wave of protests. "It now seems that if groups of people march and raise enough hell they can change anything in time. . . . Will schizophrenia be next?"[93]

For these critics of the APA decision, it was psychiatry as a scientific discipline, as a subspecialty of the medical profession, that would be the ultimate victim of this self-inflicted wound. Having forsaken the canons of science, psychiatry had revealed itself to be a subdivision of theology, its board having behaved "like a church council deciding on matters of dogma."[94] Harold Voth, a psychiatrist at the Menninger Foundation who was to become a major figure in the effort to overturn the decision on deletion, charged that the board of trustees had not only done society a grave harm, but in the process "disgraced itself."[95] Perhaps the gravest prediction of the costs to psychiatry came from Abram Kardiner, a senior figure who had pioneered in the effort to merge the insights of psychoanalysis and anthropology. Viewing homosexuality as a symptom of social disintegration, he wrote to the editors of *Psychiatric News*:

> Those who reinforce the disintegrative elements in our society will get no thanks from future generations. The family becomes the ultimate victim of homosexuality, a result which any society can tolerate only within certain limits.
> If the American Psychiatric Association endorses one of the symptoms of social distress as a normal phenomenon it demonstrates to the public its ignorance of social dynamics, of the relation of personal maladaptation to social disharmony, and thereby acquires a responsibility for aggravating the already existing chaos.[96]

Given the existence of such a sharp outcry against the December 15 vote, it is not surprising that the Ad Hoc Committee Against the Deletion of Homosexuality from *DSM-II*[97] attempted to mobilize the forces of dissent in an effort to reverse the decision. Seizing upon by-law provisions designed to provide for a measure of democratic professional control over the APA's corporate life, the committee circulated a petition demanding a referendum of the Association's membership. Since little more than two weeks remained before such requests had to be filed, Socarides' group was forced to move quickly. On December 16 a text was drafted and brought to the annual meeting of the American Psychoanalytic Association in New York City, where it met with an enthusiastic response. More than two hundred signatures were gathered with ease. Armed with these names, the committee sought and gained approval for a referendum to be held in conjunction with the upcoming general election of the Association's officers.

That a decision presented as being based upon the scientific examination of the standards that should apply to the classification of psychiatric disorders would be subject to ratification in a democratic vote of America's psychiatrists astonished many observers. It suggested that psychiatry's claim that it constituted a clinical science like other branches of medicine was at best a self-deception. It is thus rather remarkable that the same psychiatrists who had charged the APA's board with an unscientific and unseemly capitulation to political pressure now invoked the referendum procedure. When the APA's constitution had been amended to permit such votes, it was to guarantee psychiatrists a voice in the "extra-scientific" policy of the Association. Certainly there had never been an expectation that diagnostic matters would be opened to a vote.

In defending the decision to employ a referendum on this issue, Socarides argued that it was "a wonderfully democratic, vital tool."[98] Irving Bieber attempted to justify the Ad Hoc Committee's strategy by stating that though he was unalterably opposed to democratic decision-making in matters of science, it was the board of trustees that had violated the standards of scientific inquiry by voting on the classification of homosexuality. Since that narrowly constituted group had demonstrated a disregard for scientific authority in both its procedures and its decision to remove homosexuality from *DSM-II*, it seemed only appropriate to subject the December 15 statement to a "complete vote."[99] This vote would at least reflect the collective scientific wisdom of the profession in contrast to the more political orientation of the Association's leadership. Those within the APA's decision-making bodies who had been intimately involved in the discussions of the status of homosexuality saw in the referendum a dangerous assault on the principles that ought to govern the resolution of scientific disputes. While recognizing the importance of eliciting the opinions of America's psychiatrists on the issue, Robert Spitzer nevertheless expressed "severe discomfort" over the recourse to a referendum on this "presumably scientific" matter.[100] John Spiegel, the APA's president-elect at the time, charged that a vote of the Association's membership would make a "popularity contest" out of what had been a soberly considered question.[101]

So concerned was the APA's leadership about the implications of this referendum, the ridicule to which it might subject psychiatry, and the precedent it could set, that the Reference Committee felt called upon to discuss the possibilities of remedial action. While quickly concluding that democratic votes were appropriate for organizational policy questions and not for matters of science, it found that distinguishing between the two was not quite so simple. As a result that committee asked the executive committee of the board of trustees to establish a task force to study the problem. The board responded swiftly, endorsing the creation of a group that would "investigate the whole issue of referenda and what is or is not proper use of the procedure."[102]

Despite these objections the decision was made to permit the referendum; to do otherwise would have been politically untenable considering the intensity of the opposition aroused by the deletion of homosexuality, and the existence of an apparently unrestricted right to demand such a vote. The leadership of the APA calculated that it would be worth the risk of reversal, profound embarrassment, and violation of scientific principle to avoid provoking a full-scale revolt by a grass-roots movement that would merge the forces of those ideologically opposed to the substance of the decision on homosexuality and those who would consider rejection of the petition a high-handed infringement of their democratic professional rights. Following their decision to meet the challenge of the Ad Hoc Committee, the officers of the Association undertook a campaign to gain support. On February 6, 1974, a statement calling for rejection of the Socarides committee effort, endorsed by President Alfred Freedman, President-elect John Spiegel, Speaker of the Assembly Warren Williams, Chair of the Council on Research and Development Russell Monroe, and Robert Spitzer, appeared in *Psychiatric News*. After explaining the basis for the board of trustees' decision, the authors confronted the argument that the December 15 vote had confounded a legitimate political concern with a scientific question.

The revision in the nomenclature does not sacrifice scientific principles in order to further the struggle for the civil rights of homosexuals. Quite the contrary: it has been the unscientific inclusion of homosexuality per se in a list of mental disorders which has been the main ideological justification for the denial of the civil rights of individuals whose only crime it is that their sexual orientation is to members of the same sex.[103]

Having dismissed the principal charge of their opponents regarding the scientific integrity of the board's action, the authors attempted to underscore the very limited nature of the change that had occurred. It represented a "scientifically sound . . . compromise" between two polar positions: one that viewed homosexuality as a normal variant of sexuality and one that saw it as a mental disorder.

For gay activists the possibility of a reversal after such a hard-won victory was alarming. They sought therefore to map an aggressive strategy that would enhance the political strength of their allies within the Psychiatric Association. Kent Robinson, who as a result of his role as an intermediary between the APA and the gay community in earlier years had proven himself so useful a friend, was asked to seek Judd Marmor's support for a statement to be mailed to all APA members urging them to vote for the nomenclature change. Marmor, then engaged in a campaign for the presidency of the APA, agreed to sign such a letter, but suggested that its strength would be enhanced if it were cosigned by the two other candidates for office as well as by the current officers. Robinson then contacted Louis Jolyon West and Herbert Modlin, Marmor's competitors in the presidential election. They, as well as the Association's two vice presidents, Harold Visotsky and M. Mitchel-Bateman all agreed, in principle, to support the effort. Drafted jointly by Robert Spitzer and Ronald Gold, of the National Gay Task Force,[104] the statement was then submitted by Gold to each of the potential signers for final approval.

The most striking features of the statement were its avoidance of the substance of the conflict over homosexuality and its attempt to win allegiance based on the need for organizational and professional integrity.

The undersigned recognize the complexity of the many issues involved in this decision and the diversity of views within our Association. Nonetheless, we feel that it would be a serious and potentially embarrassing step for our profession to vote down a decision which was taken after serious and extended consideration by the bodies within our organization designated to consider such matters. We therefore urge you to vote to retain the nomenclature change.[105]

The National Gay Task Force orchestrated the process of obtaining signed copies of the letter,[106] purchased the necessary address labels from the American Psychiatric Association, and underwrote the full cost of the mailing. In order to raise the required funds ($2,500), the NGTF sent an urgent request to its supporters:

It is essential that this referendum be defeated, and the best guess is that the vote will be close. We are convinced that this mailing could be the deciding factor in that vote. Now is the time for gay people to show that they care about their own lives. Now is the time for anyone who cares about civil rights and human dignity to show that they care.[107]

Though the NGTF played a central role in this effort, a decision was made not to indicate on the letter that it was written, at least in part, by the Gay Task Force, nor to reveal that its distribution was funded by contributions the Task Force had raised. Indeed, the letter gave every indication of having been conceived and mailed by those who signed it. What remains in doubt is the extent to which the signers collectively either encouraged or acquiesced in that decision. Though each publicly denied any role in the dissimulation, at least one signer had warned privately that to acknowledge the organizational role of the gay community would have been the "kiss of death."[108]

There is no question, however, about the extent to which the officers of the APA were aware of both the letter's origins and the mechanics of its distribution. They, as well as the National Gay Task Force, understood the letter as performing a vital role in the effort to turn back the challenge.[109]

Since a public solicitation of financial support had been made, though presumably to those sympathetic to the gay cause, it is not surprising that information regarding the role of the NGTF surfaced quickly. At the end of February, Charles Socarides wrote to Walter Barton, medical director of the APA, that the *Chicago Daily News* had reported the purchase by the Gay Task Force of the Association's computerized mailing labels. He asked for an explanation.[110] Barton, clearly side-stepping the issue of the very special nature of the transaction being questioned, responded simply that any candidate for office was free to purchase those labels for electioneering purposes.[111]

The first major attack on the relationship between the NGTF and the signers of the statement came from Harold Voth, a member of the Socarides committee. In a bitter letter to Alfred Freedman, president of the APA, he wrote:

I was absolutely shocked when I learned that a Gay Lib group originated, financed and distributed the enclosed letter. The letter is written in such a way as to suggest that the signatories initiated it. . . . Nowhere is there the slightest hint that they responded to the lobbying of the Gay Lib group or groups. I think it is imperative that you write a letter to the entire membership explaining how this letter came about, who financed it. . . . Furthermore, I think the Ethics Committee of the Association should make a thorough investigation of the entire matter. I believe each of the signatories should be required to state in writing how and by whom he was contacted and what he was told in the way of an inducement to sign the letter. In my opinion this letter represents an act of fraud.[112]

Several days later, on March 21, 1974, the Ad Hoc Committee filed a formal request demanding that a "proper body" be established to investigate the issues raised in the Voth letter.

Though the leadership of the APA felt that the charges directed against the signers of the statement were exaggerated, and denied that any real ethical issues were involved, they were sufficiently concerned to call for a discussion of the entire matter at the April 1974 executive committee meeting of the board of trustees. The existence of this dispute did not, however, delay the referendum, which was conducted as scheduled.

Accompanying their mailed ballots, APA members received copies of the board's new classification "Sexual Orientation Disturbance," a brief statement supporting the December fifteenth action, and one opposing it. The supporting statement reiterated the arguments published in the February sixth issue of *Psychiatric News*, underscoring the scientific merits of the decision as well as the negative social consequences that had flowed from the unscientific inclusion of homosexuality in the list of psychiatric disorders. The opposing statement stressed the extent to which homosexuality was a disorder resulting from the conflicts of early childhood, which reflected a disturbance in the normal relationship between anatomy and psychosexual identity. The attempt to remove homosexuality from *DSM-II* was portrayed as a step backward in the evolution of the psychiatric understanding of human behavior. Finally, the opponents of the board's action stressed the degree to which it had sacrificed the "standards of excellence in diagnosis," serving neither the "goal of individual liberty nor the best interests of society."[113]

Just over ten thousand psychiatrists participated in the vote. The results were a clear, though not overwhelming, expression of support for the nomenclature change.

Results of the Referendum on Homosexuality

	Number	Percent
Favoring the board's decision	5,854	58
Opposing the board's decision	3,810	37
Abstaining	367	3
Invalid votes	9	*
Not voting on this issue	51	*
Total casting ballots	10,091	

* less than 1%
Source: American Psychiatric Association

Since no systematic analysis is available of the backgrounds of those who voted, or of those who did not take part in the election, it is not possible to determine with any degree of certainty how professional backgrounds and status affected the outcome. What does require some explanation, however, is the fact that though each of the central decision-making bodies of the APA had supported the nomenclature change unanimously (the board with two abstentions), almost 40 percent of those who voted in the referendum expressed their opposition.

Those who opposed the removal of homosexuality from *DSM-II* argued that it was the civil rights issue rather than the logic of Spitzer's position that was uppermost in the minds of those who had voted in favor of the diagnostic shift. Since the stigma of mental disorder had become a source of pain, an iatrogenic disability, and a justification for discrimination, politically liberal psychiatrists had allowed their social values to interfere with their scientific judgment. Further, it was asserted that those supporting the board tended to be younger psychiatrists with less clinical experience in dealing with homosexuals, a situation that permitted extrascientific values to assume a distorting and preeminent role. Finally, they noted that the board and its allies had successfully convinced a majority of the voters that the status of psychiatry as a profession would suffer if the effort to return to the older diagnostic label were to prevail.

The supporters of Socarides' initiative characterized themselves as adhering to sound scientific principles. Removed from the center of psychiatric politics in Washington, they had been less subject to the social pressure of gay activists. Concerned with clinical issues rather than with the status of psychiatry as a political institution, they were able to avoid the seduction of compromises that were unrelated to the scientific validity of insights derived from psychodynamic practice and research. Above all, those who continued to view homosexuality as a psychiatric disorder saw in the 37 percent vote against deletion a stunning refutation of the board's claim that its decision represented a scientific consensus. Rather it represented the precipitous and unwarranted imposition of the board's own, quite unjustified, understanding of homosexuality.

Generally, those who supported the removal of homosexuality from *DSM-II* provided explanations for the breakdown of the vote that were the mirror image of those put forth by their opponents. They viewed support for the board as representing a recognition of both the merits of the case for change, as elaborated by Robert Spitzer, and the appropriateness of assenting to a decision arrived at as a result of the full scientific airing of the complex issues by the Association's duly appointed committees and councils.

They explained the substantial opposition to their position as reflecting a conservative tendency among American psychiatrists, which was an expression of the intimate link between psychiatric values and the social outlook of the general population. It was assumed that those who supported Socarides tended to come from socially conservative backgrounds, "the hinterlands." In contrast to the leadership of the APA, which was liberal and sophisticated because of its exposure to cosmopolitan values and current empirical research, those who continued to see homosexuality as a psychiatric disorder were depicted as occupying entrenched positions, inaccessible to the evolving understanding of the nature of psychiatric disorders. Warren Williams, the speaker of the Association's Assembly of District Branches, remarked: "In the APA membership at large, many psychiatrists finished their education years ago. They are locked up in an office and don't change very much on any issue. The tendency is to vote conservatively."[114] Heinz Lehman, a member of the Committee on Nomenclature, underscored this point when he noted that had he not been exposed to the intense discussions of that body, and especially the presentation of the gay leaders, he too might have voted with the 37 percent. Speaking of those who adhered to the conservative view, he said, "They didn't have new information. Key information."[115]

Narrow professional self-interest was also cited as a partial explanation for the conservative vote. Since psychiatrists had assumed a socially sanctioned role in both the discussion of the meaning of homsexuality and the treatment of homosexuals, they were loath to cede that authority. Not only did declassification represent a narrowing of their professional domain, but it posed a specific challenge to the financial interest of those with large homosexual case loads.

Finally, it was argued that the politics of the APA were such in the early 1970s that any major departure by the leadership from a conservative course would be certain to arouse significant opposition. Liberal psychiatrists committed to social activism had recently mounted a successful challenge to the Association's old guard, and those who were threatened by the orientation of the new leadership could be counted upon to react almost viscerally in opposition. For them, the decision on homosexuality was not an issue that could be considered on its merits, but represented a consolidation of the power of liberal, younger psychiatrists who were redirecting the energies of American psychiatry.

What stands out so sharply in both sets of interpretations is the positive value placed upon "science" and the negative conception of "politics." The former was presented as providing a standard of judgment free of debasing social values. The latter was characterized as posing a potentially catastrophic threat to the integrity of psychiatry as a branch of scientific medicine. Those who opposed the nomenclature change believed that the psychiatrists who voted to reverse the board's decision had rallied to the banner of science and objectivity while those who voted to affirm the December 15 action were guilty of attempting to impose their own social values under the guise of science. On the other hand, those who supported the change portrayed their own affirmative votes as indicating their commitment to the scientific tradition of psychiatry, and they excoriated those who supported the Socarides position for their value-laden attachment to an unscientific perspective on homosexuality.

This was a struggle in which neither side could acknowledge the merits of its opponents' case. Instead of resolving the issue of the appropriate classification of homosexuality, the referendum had revealed the deep fissure within psychiatry. Perhaps more serious than the split over homosexuality, however, was the confusion over the principles that ought to govern the structure of its own diagnostic nomenclature.

With the referendum having demonstrated a profound division within the Psychiatric Association, it is not surprising that the Socarides committee and its allies attempted once more to prevent what it considered premature closure of the debate on homosexuality. The strategy adopted was to force exposure of the relationship between the National Gay Task Force and the signers of the letter supporting the board of trustees, in hopes of demonstrating that the outcome of the vote had been affected by an act of fraud. At least one effort was made to compel the APA's newspaper *Psychiatric News* to reveal the nature of the "collusion."[116] The matter was given broad publicity when Mike Royko, the syndicated columnist, wrote an exposé that appeared in the *Chicago Daily News* on May 17, 1974.[117]

It is clear that the opponents of declassification cooperated with Royko in the preparation of this article with the intention of generating the pressure for action that they believed internal APA maneuvers could not possibly achieve.

Finally, on June 22, 1974, three months after Socarides' group had requested an investigation, the executive committee of the APA's board appointed the Ad Hoc Committee to Investigate the Conduct of the Referendum. Fritz Redlich was selected as its chair. Showing deep irritation over the entire issue and the way in which the Association had been exposed to public ridicule, the board asked the committee to examine not only the conditions under which the referendum was held, but also the appropriateness of Charles Socarides having turned to the press to charge his colleagues with unethical behavior.

Two weeks later *Psychiatric News* published a statement from those who had signed the document that had become so central an element in the conflict over the referendum. It denied all charges of culpability. The text of the disputed letter had been prepared by Robert Spitzer. The National Gay Task Force had assumed administrative responsibility for obtaining the necessary signatures. While acknowledging that they knew that the National Gay Task Force had underwritten the cost of the mailing, they denied any foreknowledge of the decision not to reveal the role of the Gay Task Force to the APA's membership. "We think it would have been more correct for them to have done so. However, we do not see this failure as dishonest. The statement that was mailed was ours, the signatures ours, and the membership had a right to know our views."[118]

When the Redlich committee met at the end of September 1974, it heard testimony from those who had made the original charges of fraud as well as from Bruce Voeller of the National Gay Task Force. None of the signers of the letter was present, nor were they called upon, in any formal way, to defend themselves.

In its final report the committee declared that neither the disputed letter's signers nor Socarides had acted unethically, though it had been "unwise" to circulate the document in

question without a clear indication of the Gay Task Force spon-
sorship and funding.[119] The committee recommended that unambiguous guidelines be promulgated to avoid any similar
occurrences in the future. Refusing to speculate on the extent
to which the outcome of the vote would have been materially
affected by a revelation of the NGTF's role, the committee
nevertheless rejected Socarides' claim that such information
would have resulted in a reversal of the outcome of the ballot.[120]
Most important, Redlich's committee denounced not only the
use of a referendum to decide on the status of homosexuality,
but the procedures of the board of trustees itself in handling
scientific questions.

The Ad Hoc Committee is opposed to the use of referenda to decide
on scientific issues. This is the principal reason why the committee
does not recommend another referendum. It also does not recommend
to declare the referendum invalid. This would cause further confusion
without any benefit to anyone. Referenda on facts of science makes
no sense. . . . Scientific matters should be discussed by a broad and
informed panel of experts. The Board of Trustees may or may not
choose to accept the statement of experts; but neither they nor the
membership in its entirety should be put into the position of deciding
scientific questions by vote.[121]

Here, in the face of a wrenching political dispute, the ideology
of science was invoked in its purest form as the only acceptable
standard for resolving conflicts in which psychiatrists held such
disparate views.

Socarides' group responded to the report with derision.[122]
Redlich's committee had failed in its responsibility to call before it those charged with misconduct. It had acknowledged
the accuracy of the assertion that the undisclosed role of the
National Gay Task Force raised serious questions about the
referendum, while proposing only future guidelines. Lastly,
it had endorsed an antidemocratic principle to defend the ideological authority of the dominant forces in the APA leadership.
Since their perspective on homosexuality was incompatible
with that of the leaders of the Association, Socarides and his
supporters invoked the principle of democracy in their struggle

to win for themselves the warrant to speak in the name of science.

At its December 1974 meeting the board of trustees accepted Redlich's findings on the conduct of those accused of unethical behavior. It also approved the recommendations on the principle of public disclosure for all material designed to influence the membership of the Association. The trustees sidestepped, however, the difficult question of the appropriate role of referenda in "scientific" and "nonscientific" disputes.[123] Having experienced the consequences of their action on homosexuality, they sought to avoid a potentially disruptive debate on this fundamental question touching on the scientific status of psychiatry.

Chapter 5

THE AFTERMATH OF DIAGNOSTIC

CHANGE: PSYCHIATRY AND

THE SOCIAL STATUS

OF HOMOSEXUALITY

THE STRUGGLE FOR HOMOSEXUAL RIGHTS

The struggle waged by gay groups against the American Psychiatric Association between 1970 and 1973 was just one element in the far broader assault on the social status accorded to homosexuals in America. The seriousness with which the battle against psychiatry was waged and the concern with which the ideology of pathology was viewed indicated how great a transformation the homophile movement itself had undergone since its beginnings. No longer content with mere tolerance, gay activist groups sought social acceptance, and the legitimation of homosexuality as an alternative sexual orientation.

The same persistence that had forced upon the APA a rethinking of homosexuality compelled religious and professional
groups throughout the United States to confront their own
antihomosexual biases. Churches were urged to make whatever
doctrinal changes were necessary to accommodate homosexuals
as congregants, and to ordain to the ministry those previously
condemned as sinful. Professional societies were urged to defend the prerogatives of their members regardless of sexual
orientation.

In a social climate charged with radical discontent, and with
reformist movements challenging the social and cultural status
quo, it was possible for gay activists to forge a broad-based
alliance with liberal political figures, religious organizations,
and civic leaders in order to press local, state, and federal governments to adopt new social policies toward homosexuals.
Demands were made for the deletion of the hated sodomy
statutes which, though rarely enforced, often served as the
basis for blackmailing homosexuals. Pressure was mounted for
the enactment of civil rights legislation that would extend to
"sexual minorities" the same protections recently extended to
racial and ethnic minorities as a result of the agitations of
the 1960s. Religious groups as diverse as the Society of Friends,
the Lutheran Church in America, the National Council of
Churches, and the National Federation of Priests' Councils
joined in these efforts.[1] The struggle against the criminalization
of homosexual behavior won the support of the American Bar
Association,[2] the American Medical Association,[3] and the
American Psychological Association.[4]

As a result of this pressure, by 1976 fifteen states had deleted
sodomy statutes from their criminal laws. Equally important,
local governments across the nation began to enact civil rights
codes designed to protect homosexuals; between 1972 and
1976 thirty-three cities had done so as a result of either legislation or executive order. These included the major metropolitan
centers of New York, San Francisco, Washington, Detroit, Boston, Cleveland, and Los Angeles, as well as a number of smaller
university-dominated communities such as Ann Arbor, Berke-

ley, Palo Alto, Amherst, and Ithaca.[5] In 1975 the United States Civil Service Commission ruled that homosexuality, in itself, could not constitute a basis for excluding women and men from federal employment.[6]

Significant as these advances were, they were extremely limited in scope; typically they extended the rights of homosexuals only to public employment. Nevertheless, the struggle to win even these guarantees had encountered bitter opposition from those who viewed the mounting homosexual pressure for full social integration as a profound threat to morality and the family. Nothing more clearly demonstrates the tenacity of this antagonism than the resistance met by efforts to enact a broad civil rights code for homosexuals in New York City.

While the *New York Times* endorsed such legislation, asserting that it "merely [sought to assure rights to] the minority of New Yorkers who in their private lives adopt a 'sexual orientation' different from that of the majority,"[7] a coalition comprised of the uniformed civil services, the New York Catholic Archdiocese, and conservative political groups were adamant in their opposition. A front-page editorial in *Catholic News*, published by the New York Diocese, stated:

[It is] imperative that every person of religious persuasion recognize the consequences that will almost surely follow the passage of this bill . . . there will be no effective way to decline to welcome into two-family dwellings homosexual "couples" nor to decline to employ homosexuals in positions of sensitive personal influence such as elementary and high school teachers and counselors and persons on staffs of organizations that provide services to children and young boys and girls. . . . Homosexuality is an increasing threat to sound family life in our city.[8]

As a result of such pressure and despite the backing of New York's liberal mayor, John Lindsay, the City Council repeatedly turned back the legislation.[9] That such a defeat could occur in New York, with its large, politically active gay community, was especially troubling.

It is in the context of this ongoing, difficult, and often frus-

trating struggle against the systematic denial of social equality
that the deletion of homosexuality from *DSM-II* took on its
significance for the gay community. While for many psychiatrists involved in the nomenclature dispute the symbolic change
represented by that diagnostic shift had great significance in
and of itself, for homosexuals it was but one important step
in the much more difficult process of rooting out of American
life a pattern of antihomosexual values and practices. Having
neutralized psychiatry as an ideological foe, many gay activists
sought to mobilize its prestige and resources to further their
sociocultural and political goals.

Hopeful that the leadership of the American Psychiatric Association would be willing to establish a formal alliance in
this new phase of the campaign for social legitimation, Bruce
Voeller of the National Gay Task Force had set an agenda
requiring a joint effort. Since psychiatry's prior diagnostic
standpoint had provided the justification for reprehensible social practices, Voeller believed it bore a special obligation to
act as an agent of change. In a letter to the APA's medical
director written only six weeks after the December 1973 nomenclature decision, he outlined an ambitious course of action
directed at grievances ranging from the most narrowly defined
problems of civil rights to issues involving the deepest cultural
values.[10] Voeller called for a joint campaign to repeal the sodomy laws; enact civil rights legislation covering employment,
housing, and public accommodations; and change federal regulations that prohibited the naturalization of known homosexuals, excluded them from military service, and barred their
access to jobs involving security clearance. Since many of the
barriers to the full economic integration of homosexuals were
based upon the assumption that they suffered from a psychiatric disorder and were therefore incapable of undertaking certain
responsibilities, it was important to emphasize the implications
of the new official diagnostic perspective. Indicative of the
more profound changes being sought was Voeller's call for
an attack on the practice of restricting custody and visitation
rights of homosexual parents in divorce cases. So too was his

insistence upon the right of gay individuals and couples to become adoptive and foster parents. Since the pathological view of homosexuality continued to affect the education of the young, Voeller noted that it was virtually impossible for adolescents with homosexual orientations to develop identities free of self-hatred. The presence of gay student groups in high schools and universities was vital to changing the situation. Yet the effort to gain official sanction for such organizations had met with the fiercest opposition on the part of school administrators. Psychiatry, which had in the recent past provided the justification for such educational policies, was now called upon to support the demands of gay students.[11] In addition, psychiatrists were urged to call for the rewriting of secondary school hygiene texts that conveyed negative views of homosexuality. Finally, turning to the psychiatric profession itself, Voeller urged an end to the pattern of antihomosexual exclusions in residency programs and demanded the adoption of textbooks consistent with a nonpathological view of homosexuality.

Though some psychiatrists expressed enthusiastic support for so ambitious an undertaking on the part of the APA and the National Gay Task Force, the executive committee of the Psychiatric Association rejected Voeller's call to action.[12] In part this decision reflected an unwillingness to be too closely identified with the gay struggle. The Association's leadership at that time was being buffeted by the vitriolic denunciations of those who had opposed the nomenclature shift and was preparing for the upcoming referendum on that issue. For the APA such an alliance was bound to have more costly consequences than December's formal commitments to gay rights required. It is clear that many elements in Voeller's program went far beyond anything the vast majority of psychiatrists would find ideologically acceptable. That was especially the case with regard to his interest in the full social legitimation of homosexuality.

Despite its demurrer, however, the APA affirmed its willingness to express support for gay rights on an ad hoc basis, issuing supportive declarations when appropriate. Indeed, on numerous occasions over the next years, the APA placed itself on record in defense of the civil rights of homosexuals. Armed with the resolutions of 1973, John Spiegel and Judd Marmor, presidents of the Association between 1974 and 1976, were able to give organizational force to their own strong commitments to gay rights.

In 1975, Spiegel issued a stinging denunciation of the refusal of many school boards to employ gay teachers. Rejecting as sheer prejudice the fear that homosexual teachers posed a threat because of either the impact they might have on students' sexual identities, or the possibility of seduction, he went on to state:

Many fine teachers, from Socrates on, have been homosexuals. There are many homosexual teachers in our school systems now, but they are forced to live in fear of being "found out"—at considerable cost to themselves and in turn to society. Others stay out of the teaching profession because they fear exposure. A teacher should be judged on the basis of professional competence, not on the basis of personal lifestyles or sexual preference.[13]

In that same year, Judd Marmor, speaking as president of the APA, extended the Association's critique of discriminatory practices against homosexuals to the armed services. Citing both the diagnostic and the civil rights resolutions of the board of trustees, he challenged the assumption that the requirements of discipline and morale in the sex-segregated services made it impossible to grant homosexuals the right to serve.

If *individual* homosexual women or men prove to be unsuited to military life by virtue of specific actions that would apply equally to heterosexuals, those individuals should be separated from the service. As a *class*, however, there is no sound psychiatric basis for treating homosexual men and women any differently from other people in the armed services. In actuality innumerable gay men and women have served in the armed forces with distinction and have received honorable discharges. The fact that they were undetected as homosexuals merely indicates that their sex life, no less than that of heterosexuals, was a private matter, as indeed it should be.[14]

Finally, in 1977 APA President Jack Weinberg protested the refusal of the United States to naturalize homosexuals as citizens.[15] Since the United States immigration law justified such exclusion by classifying homosexuals as afflicted with "[a] psychopathic personality or sexual deviation or a mental defect," he argued that new immigration policies were required to bring the law into correspondence with the deletion of homosexuality from the APA's manual of psychiatric disorders.

The mood of resistance to the advance of homosexual rights, so evident in the bitterness with which almost every effort to enact protective legislation was met, took on a disturbing new form in 1977 when a Miami referendum revealed the existence of popular support for withdrawing the protections so recently extended to homosexuals. Swayed by the demagogic appeals of those who charged homosexuals with undermining the fabric of social life, indeed with challenging the foundations of morality, Miami's voters had signaled a new phase in the gay struggle for legitimation. To those who saw in each small victory a hard-won achievement, it was now apparent that the process set in motion in the early 1970s might be reversed. Alarmed and angered by this setback, the gay community sought support for its embattled position. The APA's board was drawn into this controversy as allies of the gay struggle called upon the Association's leadership to issue a strong statement of protest. After toning down the initial drafts prepared for their consideration, the trustees ultimately approved a declaration expressing concern that the Miami vote might inspire those across the country seeking to end the extension of homosexual rights.[16] The resolution linked the prospect of such a turn to the increasingly conservative social climate, which threatened the status not only of homosexuals but of racial and ethnic minorities as well. Having taken on a reformist role during a period of social change, the APA now found itself in an environment that was indifferent, if not hostile, to such a stance.

THE STATUS OF HOMOSEXUALITY

WITHIN PSYCHIATRY

While the decision to delete homosexuality from the nomenclature as well as the adoption of a civil rights resolution
placed the APA in a reformist stance toward American society
at large, it set in motion a series of changes within the psychiatric profession that were equally significant. Perhaps the most
striking development was the emergence within the APA of
an open constituency of homosexual psychiatrists. For a number of years they had met covertly, primarily for social reasons,
during annual meetings. With the existence of a strong movement for gay self-affirmation throughout America and an apparently less restrictive atmosphere on the part of psychiatry,
a Gay, Lesbian, and Bisexual Caucus was constituted at the
May 1975 convention. The group elected a steering committee,
which included Richard Pillard of Boston, and began publishing
a mimeographed newsletter. Though its meetings were open,
a policy of informal and anonymous membership reflected the
belief that for most psychiatrists acknowledgment of their homosexuality would constitute a serious professional liability.
The discretion required of this group reveals the extent to
which a sharp disjunction existed between the APA's official
declarations and the reality of psychiatric professional relations.

In its official statement of purpose the caucus made explicit
its discontent and posed a sharp challenge to what it perceived
as the legacy of antihomosexual bias in psychiatry. Conscious
of how much the now-discredited view of homosexuality as
a form of psychopathology continued to influence the thinking
of psychiatrists and the content of training programs for mental
health workers, the caucus declared its intention to act as a
critical force. Leaving untouched the assumptions of ongoing
research and the content of journal articles and psychiatric

textbooks, after the protracted struggle to delete homosexuality from the APA's *Diagnostic and Statistical Manual,* would render the victory hollow. Further, the caucus members believed that unless the socialization of psychiatrists with regard to homosexuality were changed, the narrow consensus that had made possible its deletion from the nomenclature might well be undermined. Painfully aware of the circumstances that had required homosexual psychiatrists to hide their sexual identities, the caucus further pledged itself to the investigation of discriminatory practices in medical schools, psychiatric residency programs, and other professional settings. Only a commitment to affirmative action could redress the historical pattern of systematic exclusion of homosexuals from psychiatry. With every reason to doubt the impact of the nomenclature shift on the day-to-day practices of psychiatrists, the caucus served notice that it intended to "examine the . . . treatment of gay people and to investigate instances in which a patient has been treated in a way which denigrates him on account of his sexual preferences."[17] Finally, in order to guarantee institutional support for the searching critique of psychiatric practices, the caucus announced its intention to press the APA to establish an official Task Force on Gays, Lesbians, and Bisexuals.

Assuming that between 5 and 10 percent of the psychiatric profession was homosexual, the caucus claimed that its potential constituency numbered between 1,250 and 2,500.[18] It is therefore remarkable that its formal membership never rose much above 100.[19] Nevertheless, because of the commitment of those with the courage to join its ranks and the dedication of its leadership, the caucus was able to make its presence felt at APA conventions through the presentation of a series of panels addressing both organizational and substantive issues. In addition, despite the initial reluctance of some leaders of the APA,[20] the caucus was successful in winning approval in 1978 for a special task force. But between such institutional victories and the transformation of psychiatric theory and practice there was an enormous gulf. The social legitimation of homosexuality so eagerly sought by caucus members as well as by other gay activists remained an elusive goal.

There were indications in the period after 1973 of some changes within psychiatry of the kind called for by the caucus. Among the most noteworthy was the decision on the part of Alfred Freedman and the coeditors of the widely used *Comprehensive Textbook of Psychiatry* to replace Irving Bieber's essay[21] on homosexuality, which had appeared in the 1967 edition of their volume, with one written by Judd Marmor.[22] Though Freedman has asserted that that decision predated the vote of the APA's board of trustees to delete homosexuality from the nomenclature and that it had little to do with ideology,[23] the action represented an extraordinary about-face. It is unlikely that Freedman and his coeditors failed to appreciate the ideological significance of their move, or to anticipate the impact it might have upon the thinking of future mental health workers.

Bieber's essay was an unequivocal statement of the pathological view of homosexuality, containing his oft-repeated criticisms of those who, like Evelyn Hooker, raised questions about its designation as a psychiatric disorder. Marmor's contribution reflected his own well-known rejection of the pathological perspective as well as his belief that homosexuality represented a normal variant of human sexuality. "In the final analysis, the psychiatric categorization of the homosexual outcome as psychopathological is fundamentally a reflection of society's disapproval of that outcome, and psychiatrists are unwittingly acting as agents of social control in so labeling it."[24]

Perhaps more extraordinary than this dramatic ideological shift was the absence of any editorial comment suggesting to readers of the revised textbook that Bieber's essay existed and that its replacement with Marmor's contribution reflected a major change in psychiatric thinking about homosexuality. It was that failure which aroused the wrath of Jonas Robitscher, a psychiatrist concerned with the potential political abuses of psychiatry and a sharp critic of the decision to delete homosexuality from *DSM-II*.

Just as in a totalitarian country when a leader is deposed, the history of his period is altered to fit the new policy, the change in the official position of homosexuality has led to a rewriting of textbooks. The generation of younger psychiatrists brought up on the new official position will inevitably see Marmor's position as the "scientific" point of view and the older position if they learn about it at all as "outmoded," "old-fashioned" and "unscientific."[25]

While Robitscher's language was hyperbolic, and distorted the existence of considerable pluralism within psychiatry—falsely alluding to the shameful record of the Great Soviet Encyclopedia—it did reflect the deep concern of many psychiatrists about what they perceived as the effort to force ideological change.

A less dramatic but equally significant indication of the process of change that had begun to occur was Silvano Arieti's decision to add an essay by Richard Green to that of Charles Socarides in the newest edition of his *American Handbook of Psychiatry*. Green, like Marmor, had emerged as a vocal antagonist of the pathological view of homosexuality. This addition, rather than denying the older perspective, emphasized the unresolved nature of psychiatric thinking on this issue. Commenting on his decision, Arieti noted: "The *Handbook* does not sponsor any point of view. Psychiatry has not reached a stage of consensus about everything. Every point of view represented by *bona fide* opinion and clinical or scientific evidence is [considered]. We want to be fair to everyone."[26]

The long-term significance of such "literary" shifts will depend in large measure on the extent to which the orientation of psychiatric residency programs begins to reflect the changes in those texts. If the programs do not change, the volumes themselves will become irrelevant—the mere expressions of an official posture. In the short run, however, dramatic changes cannot be expected. Older views of homosexuality will retain their preeminent status as long as those who were trained when the pathological view was unquestioned continue to provide instruction and supervision for psychiatrists-in-training.

A survey undertaken in 1978 by the American Association of the Directors of Residency Programs[27] makes this clear. Eighty percent of the programs surveyed reported that the board of trustees' decision to delete homosexuality from *DSM-II* had had no impact on either the content of their programs or their admission standards. Nevertheless, when asked to describe the predominant view of homosexuality among both the instructional and supervisory staffs of their programs, 73 percent of the respondents agreed with the statement "Homosexuality is not necessarily an indication of psychopathology, but may be one." Twenty-three percent reported that in their programs homosexuality was always viewed as an indication of psychopathology. Finally, only 5 percent stated that in their training programs homosexuality was seen as a normal variant of human sexuality.

These data may, of course, be read to suggest that the APA's official decision to remove homosexuality from *DSM-II* had merely confirmed a major shift that had already occurred in the thinking of psychiatrists. But it is more likely that when confronted with the necessity of characterizing their own programs, directors, aware of the extreme sensitivity of the issues involved, opted for a middle position free from apparent dogmatism, and that these responses masked the extent to which the pathological view of homosexuality continued to prevail.

In sharp contrast to the claims made by the Gay Caucus and the reported experiences of many homosexual psychiatrists and other observers, not one residency program director acknowledged that the homosexual orientation of an applicant would constitute the basis for denial of admission. In only 4 percent of the cases was it asserted that homosexual applicants were individually evaluated to determine their "suitability for admission." More striking, in no case was it reported that homosexuality had been a bar to admission before 1973. Since these data are inconsistent with the reports on the ideological orientations of residency programs described above, it is fair to surmise that political considerations affected the responses on this survey question as well. With demands for equality having attained some legitimacy, it had become increasingly necessary, even among those who viewed homosexuality as pathological, to assume a public posture that denied the relevance of such a standpoint to the social and political aspirations of homosexuals.

The continued widespread opposition by America's psychiatrists to the APA's official position on homosexuality was evident in a survey conducted in 1977 by the journal *Medical Aspects of Human Sexuality*.[28] Though the APA's 1974 referendum had made clear the presence of a serious split among its membership, these new findings suggested that the leadership no longer represented the majority position. Analysis of the first 2,500 responses to a poll of 10,000 psychiatrists found that 69 percent believed that homosexuality usually represented a pathological adaptation. Only 18 percent disagreed with this proposition. Sixty percent of the respondents asserted that homosexual men were less capable of "mature, loving relationships" than their heterosexual counterparts. Finally, 70 percent supported the view that the problems experienced by homosexuals were more often the result of "personal conflicts" than of stigmatization.

In attempting to explain the differences between this survey and the vote of the APA membership in its 1974 referendum, editor Harold Lief acknowledged the possibility of a skewed response. More important was his suggestion that the earlier poll might have been affected by sociopolitical considerations, the vote to delete homosexuality having been perceived as an affirmative action on behalf of the struggle for homosexual rights. With the cooling of the reformist impulse among psychiatrists, and the emergence of a more conservative social climate in the United States, psychiatric attitudes toward homosexuality as a diagnostic entity might have begun to shift. For the leadership of the APA, the Lief study was the occasion of some embarrassment and confusion. That the concept of mental illness could be affected by the evolution of social values was compatible with a view of psychiatry as a clinical discipline; that it could reflect the more ephemeral shifts in popular mood suggested an instability that undercut claims to a scientific status for the profession. Bemused by the apparent reversal in psychiatric thinking, *Time* magazine sardonically reported the results of Lief's survey under the headline "Sick Again?"[29] Though the survey may well have overstated the dimensions of the conservative turn by psychiatrists in the United States, there was little doubt among many leaders within the APA that the direction of change had been accurately depicted. While the shift was not directly reflected in official thinking, it did provide the context within which the debate over the status of homosexuality was to occur during the drafting of the third edition of the *Diagnostic and Statistical Manual of Psychiatric Disorders (DSM-III)*.

DSM–III AND THE STATUS OF HOMOSEXUALITY:

THE POLITICS OF INTRAPROFESSIONAL CONFLICT

While gay protest had compelled the American Psychiatric Association to confront the diagnostic status of homosexuality in 1973, intraprofessional dissatisfaction with the entire structure of *DSM-II* had resulted, quite independently, in a decision to undertake a thoroughgoing revision of the *Manual*. In part because of the central role he had assumed in the homosexuality debate, Robert Spitzer was appointed chair of the APA's Task Force on Nomenclature and was assigned the responsibility of overseeing the complex process of drafting *DSM-III*.

Spitzer believed that to lend coherence to the new nomenclature, it was of crucial importance to develop a parsimonious definition of the concept "psychiatric disorder." During the 1973 dispute he had made such an effort, focusing on the twin factors of subjective distress and general impairment of social functioning. Dissatisfied with the formulation he had come to as a way of justifying the deletion of homosexuality from *DSM-II*, he now sought a definition that was both more sophisticated and more precise. In large measure the weaknesses he now recognized in his earlier effort were not dissimilar from those noted by his critics during the homosexuality debate. An insistence upon distress and generalized impairment of social functioning would have precluded the classification of forms of behavior, especially the sexual deviations,[30] which most psychiatrists agreed ought to be included in the new nosological manual. The absence of subjective distress and the circumscribed nature of the disabilities were, in fact, typical features of some of these conditions. As a result Spitzer amended his definition, expanding it so that it could encompass forms of behavior judged to be of "inherent disadvantage."[31]

From Spitzer's perspective homosexuality did not belong in the nomenclature because it did not preclude the possibility of an affectionate relationship between adult human partners. By contrast, the other behaviors classed as sexual deviations did preclude such relationships and were therefore inherently disadvantageous.[32] For those who deemed the failure to achieve an affectionate sexual relationship between human partners of the *opposite* sex an inherent disadvantage, Spitzer's formulation involved little more than an elaborate theoretical justification for his all too obvious normative assumptions.

From the outset, the effort to formulate a classificatory label reflecting the board of trustees' December 1973 decision had met with great controversy. The source of the disagreement, however, was quite different from that which had surfaced during the earlier debate, when it was the opponents of the removal of homosexuality from *DSM-II* who had argued strenuously against Spitzer and his allies. This time, proponents of the pathological view recognized the futility of reenacting the earlier bitter debate and were all but silent. What emerged instead was an intense and acrimonious conflict over the inclusion of a special category for homosexuals distressed by their sexual orientation. During this controversy, which lasted over a year and was played out through a voluminous correspondence, Spitzer was cast as a conservative defender of psychiatric orthodoxy by those who sought to delete any specific reference to homosexuality from *DSM-III*. The reformers who had attained victory in 1973 now revealed themselves to be deeply split. The cautiously constructed diagnostic label "sexual orientation disturbance" and its justification had failed to provide a basis for the continuing alliance of those who saw homosexuality as a normal variant of human sexuality and those who considered it suboptimal but less problematical than the behaviors designated as psychiatric disorders.

Because the classification "sexual orientation disturbance" coined during the 1973 debate was ambiguous about the nature of the disorder it was designed to label, Robert Spitzer developed a new term, "homodysphilia." Unlike "sexual orientation disturbance," which could, on its face, be applied to a range of sexual behaviors, homodysphilia provided the requisite element of specificity. Though an awkward neologism, it made clear that the diagnosis was meant to apply only to homosexuals distressed by their sexual orientation. Since he believed that nothing more than a shift in terminology was involved, Spitzer did not consult the members of the Task Force subgroups charged with overseeing work on sexual disorders.[33] To his surprise, the new term provoked a sharp negative reaction. The first indication of the fury that was to break loose in the next months over the issue of homosexuality came when Richard Green wrote Spitzer a bitter letter of resignation from the subgroup on sexual disorders, denouncing both the new term and what he considered the high-handed fashion in which matters of such crucial importance were being decided. Most serious was his charge that the membership of the subgroup had been altered by the addition of Spitzer's own ideological allies. By so "packing" the committee, Spitzer had been able to push through decisions in utter disregard of those who were chosen initially because of their scientific expertise on matters of sexuality.[34]

There had been some earlier rumblings about Spitzer's handling of this issue. As early as May 1975, even before "homodysphilia" made its appearance, the Gay, Lesbian and Bisexual

Caucus had expressed its dissatisfaction.[35] Spitzer was threatened with "another period of militancy" if he persisted on his course.[36] It was not, however, until March 1977, when a formal draft of *DSM-III* appeared, that the conflict became a full-blown debate. To those who had begun to suspect Spitzer of harboring an antihomosexual ideological perspective, two features of the new classification, now changed to "dyshomophilia," proved especially disturbing. The grouping of the new diagnostic term with fetishism, zoophilia, pedophilia, exhibitionism, voyeurism, and sexual sadism was interpreted as an effort to reassert the view that homosexuality itself was a perversion. That something more than a superficial issue was involved was clear from the discussion of the factors that might predispose to this disorder. "Since homosexuality predisposes to dyshomophilia, factors which predispose to homosexuality probably also predispose to dyshomophilia."[37] Those who believed that Bieber and Socarides had been defeated in 1973 were alarmed to read that dyshomophilia emerged out of family constellations in which the child's same-sexed parent was remote or a poor role model and in which the relationship with the parent of the opposite sex was disturbed. An effort to reverse the victory of 1973 was, they feared, in process.

In an attempt to thwart that regression, Richard Pillard, who had assisted in drafting the 1973 New England District Branch resolution on homosexuality, and who had emerged as a leader of the Gay Caucus, sought to mobilize opposition to the inclusion of dyshomophilia in *DSM-III*. A letter calling for concerted action was sent to potentially sympathetic psychiatrists. Included were Judd Marmor; Leon Eisenberg, who had served on the board of trustees in 1973; Marcel Saghir, coauthor of a major empirical study of male and female homosexuality; Harold Lief, editor of *Medical Aspects of Human Sexuality;* George Winokur, a leader of the nonpsychoanalytic "St. Louis Group"; and Richard Green. After outlining his profound concern over the implications of Spitzer's effort, Pillard suggested that if all attempts to have dyshomophilia deleted failed, it would be crucial to struggle for the inclusion of a parallel classification for heterosexuals distressed about their sexual orientations. If psychiatrists were concerned about dyshomophilia, certainly they should be concerned about heterodysphilia.[38]

Encouraging responses were received from all but Eisenberg and Lief. While he didn't consider dyshomophilia a very useful term, Eisenberg noted that as a board member in 1973, he had made an explicit commitment to the retention of a special category for homosexuals distressed by their sexual orientations. He rejected the proposal for heterodysphilia, noting that the only heterosexuals he had met who were distressed by their sexual orientations were schizophrenics attempting to deny all sexuality.[39] While Winokur supported Pillard's effort, he indicated that he was unwilling to become an active participant in the debate. "I do not want to argue over words . . . the creation of new words leaves us open to the epithet of 'clown.' It is unfortunate but not worth an enormous amount of time or trouble."[40] Marmor offered more enthusiastic support. Focusing on both Spitzer's new term and the more important issue of the special diagnostic category it represented, he wrote:

> My own view is that a person's sexual orientation is irrelevant to the question of whether or not there is a mental disorder present. The fact that psychiatric nomenclatures still seek to include the concept in a special diagnostic slot is archaic. If a homosexual is distressed about his orientation, the appropriate diagnosis should be the underlying psychological disorder, e.g., anxiety reaction . . . depressive reaction.[41]

Stressing the theoretical error of designating a disorder in terms of the specific source of the anxiety or depression, he noted, "To start creating separate diagnostic categories for the things about which people get disturbed would be a throwback to nineteenth century diagnostic categories with hand-washing manias, an infinite variety of phobias, etc."[42] Since homosexuality per se represented no pathology, there could be no justification for including it as the central feature of a diagnostic label. Because of his own belief that such an effort represented an "insidious attempt to preserve an anti-homosexual bias," stemming from an "unconscious homophobia which persists in so many of our generation . . . the origins of which are basically moral and judgmental rather than scientific,"[43] Marmor reluctantly supported the inclusion of heterodysphilia.[44] Only such a move could undermine the inevitable and undesirable consequences of singling out homosexuality in this regard.

Richard Green, who even before Pillard's letter had made his opposition clear to Spitzer, not only agreed to provide ideological support for the deletion of homodysphilia, but began to press members of the Task Force's sexual dysfunction and gender identity subgroups to join his effort. In one of what was to become a plethora of communications, he wrote with great urgency:

Psychiatry must move forward in the 1970s and the 1980s into the arena of scientific, objective respectability. Psychiatry, alone, stands as the last bailiwick other than some church groups plus Eastern European and Arabic countries in condemning homosexuality as a mental illness or a sin. We will live with DSM-III for a long time. I urge that we look forward and not backward and request your support.[45]

Both Pillard and Green recognized the possibility that Spitzer's views might well prevail within the Task Force on Nomenclature, and so they began to consider the appropriate strategy for overriding any unacceptable decisions it might make. Convinced that it might be necessary to appeal to the Council on Research and Development, to which the Task Force was responsible, and even to the board of trustees, they were ready, in the early stages of this battle, to broaden their constituency for the new conflict on homosexuality.[46] In part, their strategy was designed to convince Spitzer that they were willing to humiliate him at the highest levels of the American Psychiatric Association. Since Spitzer believed that his views were those of the APA hierarchy, he found their threat hollow. Of greater concern to him was the possibility that, given the new mood of conservatism among psychiatrists, a broadening of the debate might recklessly risk a reversal of the December 1973 decision to delete homosexuality itself from the nomenclature.

Though Spitzer quickly conceded the inadvisability of including dyshomophilia among the paraphilias (sexual deviations), his opponents viewed this change as merely cosmetic. To press Spitzer further, Richard Green, who believed that a majority of his colleagues on all three relevant Task Force advisory subcommittees supported his position, undertook a poll of their members.[47] Spitzer, claiming that the options provided in Green's ballot failed to reflect the range of choices being debated, and understanding the importance of asserting his own authority over such procedural matters, circulated his own referendum to the subgroups on sexuality. In support of his position, he argued that dyshomophilia was a "distinct clinical entity" which required classification for purposes of both research and "treatment assignment." In stark contrast to the views of his opponents, he noted:

The concept of dyshomophilia takes a middle position regarding the pathological status of homosexuality, even though the text clearly states that homosexuality *per se* is not regarded in *DSM-III* as a mental disorder. I believe that in our current state of ignorance this is a scientifically defensible position. I believe that if we remove dyshomophilia . . . we could be justifiably acccused of responding to political pressure.[48]

To those who had suspected that Spitzer's diagnostic category implied a questionable attitude toward homosexuality, this statement provided corroborative evidence. Marmor denounced Spitzer's position as "quite arbitrary," "unwarranted," and "a unilateral decision countervening the views of an overwhelming majority of the Board, the Assembly and the Council on Research and Development."[49]

After more than three months of protracted efforts to elicit unambiguous votes in his poll Spitzer conceded that it had been impossible to arrive at a consensus.[50] Five members, including Richard Green, Paul Gebhard of the Institute of Sex

Research at Indiana University, and John Money of Johns Hopkins University, opposed Spitzer's position. Gebhard, like Marmor, warned that "to single out homosexuality from all the numerous possible causes of distress, suggests there is something pathogenic about it."[51] For Money the real danger in Spitzer's effort was that it would in fact bring about the surreptitious readmission of homosexuality to the psychiatric nosology. "It has taken our society long enough to quit using moral indignation as a criterion of psychiatric classification, and I do not want to see a return to such practice. . . ."[52] Nine members supported Spitzer. However, even among his allies, the term dyshomophilia met with little enthusiasm. With great reluctance, but some humor, he acceded to a new term, "homosexual conflict disorder."[53]

While consensus eluded the subcommittees, it was becoming obvious that despite the threats of Pillard and Green, no one involved in the discussions wanted to see the conflict expand beyond the Task Force on Nomenclature. At its September 1977 meeting, the Council on Research and Development was exposed to a private airing of the dispute. Judd Marmor had been invited by Lester Grinspoon, its chair, to attend the meeting so that he might contest Robert Spitzer's thinking on the issue. After hearing the antagonists, the council made clear its reluctance to be embroiled in the dispute. It was the Task Force that must resolve the issue. One month later the committee established by the Assembly of District Branches to oversee work on *DSM-III* assumed a similar posture.[54] Finally, even those especially concerned with the relationship between psychiatry and the homosexual community expressed fears about the potential risks of a broad debate within the APA on this question. In a letter to Frank Kameny of the Mattachine Society, Michael Mavroidis, who had been serving as a liaison between the Task Force and the gay community, wrote:

I personally feel that it would be destructive both to the gay rights movement and to psychiatry for this issue to be publicly debated and voted on at this time. I think that the general public views official psychiatry as having decided that homosexuality *per se* is not a mental illness, and the risks of losing what the press would describe as a debate regarding homosexuality should forestall anyone from carrying this debate beyond the Task Force to the Assembly . . . or the APA general membership.[55]

Frustrated in his effort to obtain a consensus from the subgroups on sexuality, Spitzer turned to the full membership of the Task Force for a vote on whether to include a separate diagnostic category for homosexuals distressed by their sexual orientation.[56] But as in every other such effort, many of those polled refused to be limited by Spitzer's options. Instead they responded with an array of written exceptions, objections, and amendments, some of which created uncertainty even for Spitzer. And so before a tally could be taken on the vote initiated in mid-October, a new term and justification were developed. Renamed "ego-dystonic homosexuality," the new category involved a conceptual shift as well. Instead of focusing on the distress experienced by some homosexuals because of their pattern of sexual arousal, the new classification emphasized the impairment of heterosexual functioning.[57] Thus the new draft defined the essential features of "ego-dystonic homosexuality" as

A desire to acquire or increase heterosexual arousal so that heterosexual relations can be initiated or maintained and a sustained pattern of overt homosexual arousal that the individual explicitly complains is unwanted as a source of distress.[58]

For those troubled by the earlier emphasis on distress over homosexuality, because it was inconsistent with the theoretical orientation of *DSM-III*, the new classification was preferable to its predecessors. Others, who had detected in Spitzer's prior drafts an antihomosexual bias, welcomed his willingness to revise radically the discussion of predisposing factors. The first draft of *DSM-III* had failed to distinguish between the etiology of homosexuality and that of dyshomophilia. In contrast, the new discussion focused clearly on the roots of the latter.

Since homosexuality itself is not considered a mental disorder, the factors that predispose to homosexuality are not included in this section. The factors that predispose to ego-dystonic homosexuality are those negative societal attitudes towards homosexuality which have been internalized. In addition features associated with heterosexuality such as having children and socially sanctioned family life, may be viewed as desirable, and incompatible with a homosexual arousal pattern.[59]

With these revisions Spitzer had been able to gain the support of some of his most adamant critics, including Judd Marmor.[60] Others, like Richard Pillard and Richard Green, remained unalterably opposed to a separate label for distressed homosexuals. For them, the new classification revealed unambiguously that Spitzer and his allies were committed to preserving the priority of heterosexuality as a sexual preference. Yet they and the members of the Gay Caucus recognized the futility of continued debate.[61] With a final tally of the Task Force members indicating a clear majority for Spitzer's formulation, the dispute came to an end. While deep disagreements remained, not only over the appropriateness of a separate category for distressed homosexuals, but over the nature of homosexuality, they no longer could serve as the basis for fractious conflict. Exhaustion rather than agreement had resulted in at least temporary closure of the dispute.

It is remarkable that the controversy over the status of homosexuality in *DSM-III* remained throughout an intraprofessional matter. While there were some early threats to involve the gay community in the kind of militant action that had been so much a part of the dispute over *DSM-II*, they failed to materialize. Although Frank Kameny of the Washington Mattachine Society and Bruce Voeller of the National Gay Task Force were kept abreast of the dispute, they appear to have remained bystanders.[62] This shift in strategy cannot be explained in terms of either flagging militancy on the part of gay activists in general or loss of interest in the psychiatric profession's discussions of homosexuality. Indeed, militant assaults on the most vocal defenders of the pathological view continued, with lectures by Irving Bieber and Charles Socarides remaining targets of attack.

Two changes in the period after 1973 seem to explain the dramatic shift. In the first place, the dispute was perceived as involving a *narrowly* symbolic issue. After all, homosexuality per se had been deleted from the diagnostic manual as a result of the earlier struggle. A dispute about the classification of distress over homosexuality and its location in the nomenclature did not warrant a major organizational effort. Given the limited scope of this controversy, gay activists shared the perception of their allies within the profession that a full-scale struggle over "ego-dystonic homosexuality" might be counterproductive. In 1978 no one wanted to provoke a reconsideration of the original deletion decision. With the risks so high and the possible gains so marginal, a protracted encounter was not worth the effort. Finally, having emerged victorious in 1973, having witnessed the emergence of an active Gay Caucus of psychiatrists, and having pressed the APA into a supportive posture on civil rights, homosexuals could dismiss the controversy as an internal, technical, and arcane problem for psychiatrists.

CONCLUSION

For psychiatrists engaged in clinical work, the extent to which normative considerations inform contemporary definitions of mental health and illness remains largely an unexamined matter. Confronted by those whose behavior seems "grossly pathological" or who are tortured by painful conflicts, most see it as their task to restore their patients to normal functioning by eliminating incapacitating disorders or reducing the level of anxiety. But for those whose perspective is framed by more theoretical considerations, the role of values in psychiatry has become a matter of increasing attention and concern. A striking gulf has appeared between practitioners and theoreticians, with the latter engaged in discussions of how unarticulated assumptions affect the work of the former. Therapists remain, however, largely unaffected by the insights of those who seek to interpret the meaning of their practices. Only when their conventional orientations have been challenged by extraordinary occurrences have therapists been forced to assume a more self-reflective posture. The dispute over the status of homosexuality as a psychiatric disorder did just that, compelling many clinicians to confront the extent to which social values frame the most basic elements of their professional work.

Efforts on the part of psychiatrists to articulate a theory of mental health that could serve as a standard by which to evaluate behavior have been marked by unmistakably normative assertions regarding the appropriate relationship between the healthy individual and the society in which he or she lives. Karl Menninger typified this tendency when he wrote in 1930:

Let us define mental health as the adjustment of human beings to the world and to each other with a maximum of effectiveness and happiness. Not just efficiency or just contentment—or the grace of obeying the rules of the game cheerfully. It is all those together. It is the ability to maintain an even temper, an alert intelligence, socially considerate behavior and a happy disposition. This, I think, is a healthy mind.[1]

Confronted with an array of similar definitions from psychiatrists in both England and the United States, Britain's Barbara Wooton has termed the concept of mental health "value soaked" and has argued that it bears a "strong cultural stamp."[2]

While such evaluations have provided the antipsychiatrists ammunition with which to attack the "scientific pretensions" of the mental health professions, those committed to the survival of psychiatry have, with increasing frequency, been willing to acknowledge the role of normative factors in the theoretical underpinnings of their work. Melvin Sabshin, medical director of the American Psychiatric Association, has argued that normality and health "cannot be understood in the abstract, rather they depend on cultural norms, society's expectations and values, professional biases, individual differences, and the political climate of the times."[3] Sabshin's comment might be considered one notable example of the ideological success of the Szaszian critique of the objectivist tradition in psychiatry. More than two decades earlier, however, the pioneering psychoanalyst Heinz Hartmann had remarked on the centrality of "subjective valuations" in the framing of conceptions of health. For Hartmann it was these influences that accounted for the considerable variation to be found in definitions of mental health and illness among differing cultures and distinct historical periods. It was only because of the existence of shared values within cultures that the role of values tended to be masked, taking on a natural aura. "Within a uniform society these judgments will exhibit a far-reaching similarity, but that does not deprive them the least of their subjective character."⁴

More recently, Fritz Redlich, a leading academic psychiatric researcher, also underscored the powerful role of cultural influences on definitions of mental health and illness. For him, discussions of normal and abnormal behavior turn out, on closer examination, to be discussions about good and bad behavior. Bluntly acknowledging the extent to which psychiatrists were bound by such considerations, he and Daniel Friedman, Chair of Psychiatry at the University of Chicago, wrote, "The judgments of psychiatrists cannot in reality be far removed from those of the *common man,* of the societies and cultures in which psychiatrists and patients live."⁵ The symptom of disorder in one society might thus well be the sign of achievement in another.⁶

Even psychiatrists unwilling to assent to Redlich's more global propositions have been forced to acknowledge that at least with regard to the "character disorders," social values play a significant role. While these psychiatrists have assumed that in conditions marked by profound incapacitation or suffering, normative factors are at most of marginal importance, they have been compelled to note that where there is little or no subjective distress, and where the abnormality is defined primarily by an inability or unwillingness to abide by prevailing ethical and social standards of behavior, the objectivist posture is untenable.

Controversy regarding the classification of behavior as pathological is, however, a matter not only of differences between judgments about the desirable and the undesirable, but of alternative approaches within psychiatry to the question of deviance. Profound conflicts exist regarding the appropriate scope of psychiatry, its modes of explanation, and its targets of therapeutic intervention. At one extreme is the psychoanalytic tradition. With a model of appropriate psychosexual development providing the standard for the ideal state of mental health, that tradition has been able to classify a broad range of behavior as warranting clinical attention. For psychoanalysis the suboptimal is pathological. From such a perspective it has been possible to assert that health—optimal functioning—is rarely, if ever, attained. Rather than regrettable exceptions, degrees of pathology are a universal feature of the human condition. Thus Freud was able to state that "a normal ego . . . is like normality in general, an ideal fiction."[7] Ernest Jones, his early collaborator and biographer, was equally explicit: "We have no experiences of a completely normal mind."[8] In contrast to the expansive psychoanalytic perspective, there is an alternate tradition in which the classification of forms of behavior as disordered has been restricted to a much narrower range. This psychiatric orientation, until recently more dominant in Europe than in the United States, has limited the labeling of behavior as pathological to highly undesirable aberrations, those conditions associated with marked suffering and disability. Like the medical tradition after which it has modeled itself, it has tended to define pathology in terms of the *subnormal* rather than the *suboptimal*.[9]

Nothing more tellingly reveals the extent to which contemporary psychiatric theory and practice have been affected by ethical and normative concerns than the dismay expressed about the current state of affairs by those theorists who continue to hold out the possibility of a value-neutral psychiatry. Unlike the antipsychiatrists, who have asserted that the very nature of psychiatry precludes such an attainment, and have demanded that the sociopolitical functions of psychiatric practice be exposed, these critics denounce the confusion between ethics and medicine. One such critic, Christopher Boorse, a philosopher who has attempted to clarify the concepts of health and illness, has characterized the methods relied upon by most psychiatric theorists as "largely indefensible." For him the vast literature on mental health is profoundly flawed—filled with "misuses of language" or assertions that are "flatly conjectural."[10]

Central to the antipsychiatric critique of the concepts of mental health and illness is the assumption that they represent an illegitimate extension from the older and sounder notions of physical health and disease. In contrast to the value-laden concept of mental disorder, physical diseases are portrayed by the antipsychiatrists as given in nature, and therefore historically and culturally invariant entities. An assumed disjunction between the facts of the biological world and the values of the psychological-behavioral realm has been the premise of Thomas Szasz's assertion that mental illness is nothing more than a myth, a fraudulent conceptualization. The presumptions of this critical perspective have been subjected, with increasing frequency, to an attack of a rather unexpected kind. Instead of asserting that both mental and physical illnesses are objective conditions, value-free, and given in nature, the new criticism has attempted to demonstrate that *all* concepts of health and disease are informed by human values.

The foundations for this standpoint had been laid by Talcott Parsons early in the 1950s.[11] In his sociological analysis of the "sick role" Parsons had demonstrated, in regard to both physical and mental illness, that deviations from socially mandated role performances were entailed. The full implications of the Parsonian formulation gradually found expression in the work of analytic philosophers, despite the radical departure from conventional thought that was involved. By the 1970s philosophical opinion had so come to reflect the view that all diseases are culturally defined that Christopher Boorse found it necessary to argue for the objectivist position as if it were an embattled perspective.[12]

One of the most provocative and influential expressions of the newly ascendant point of view is found in Peter Sedgwick's essay "Illness—Mental and Otherwise." Starting with an appreciative evaluation of the antipsychiatrists, he credits them with having made it clear that "mental illness is a social construction," and that "psychiatry is a social institution incorporating the values and demands of its surrounding society."[13] Despite the profound insight of their critique, however, they had failed to press their analysis to its limits. For Sedgwick, both physical and mental illnesses are social constructions. "There are no illnesses or diseases in nature."[14] Only those conditions having an undesirable impact on human goals are so labeled. Not even the "blight" that strikes corn is a disease given in nature. It is only because we prefer the survival of some crops that we speak of them as being diseased. "If some plant species in which man had no interest were to be attacked by a fungus or parasite, we should speak not of disease but merely of competition between two species."[15] In nature there is no difference between a broken arm and a broken fingernail. It is only because of the importance we have attached to work and mastery over the environment that the former seems more significant than the latter. From this radically cultural perspective, Sedgwick is able to conclude:

All sickness is essentially deviancy. That is to say, no attribution of sickness to any being can be made without the expectation of some alternative state of affairs which is considered more desirable. In the absence of this normative alternative, the presence of a particular bodily or subjective state will not lead to the attribution of illness.[16]

The impact of Sedgwick's arguments and those of the philosophers and social scientists who in the past decade have torn systematically at the objectivist posture of medicine can be detected clearly in the work of a number of psychiatrists, including Robert Spitzer. In attempting to protect psychiatry from its antipsychiatric critics, he has not sought to prove that mental disorders are phenomena given in nature. Instead he has argued for the universally subjective character of all medical diseases. Psychiatry could at last present its *bona fides* as a medical subspecialty, but on foundations radically at variance with what might have been expected by those with positivist dreams.

Many fevered polemical discussions of psychiatric classification could be mercifully shortened were there a basic understanding that the concept of disease or illness is made by men. It does not reflect any intrinsic property in nature. All the variations in the human condition that exist in nature, such as left-handedness, genius, tuberculosis, schizophrenia, atherosclerosis and dwarfism, are in a sense equally natural. It is man who in his effort to improve the quality and length of his life who has developed the concept of illness to identify those conditions for which there exists a consensus that they are bad and ideally should be treated.[17]

What distinguished the mental disorders from the physical was the extent of consensus about the undesirability of the latter and the often deep disagreements that existed regarding appropriate behavioral and psychological states—differences of degree, not of logic, not of kind.

To uncover the role of values in the definition of health and disease does not, however, imply that choices in this realm are arbitrary. To assume that, as do many of the critics who recoil at the suggestion that illness and health are *merely* subjective, would be to ignore the degree to which certain deviations represent departures from profoundly held beliefs about the ends of human existence, and the appropriate functioning of humans as biosocial beings. With agreement about the latter, discussions of the meaning of certain states may be subjected to rigorous analysis and to the demands of reason. It is only when those ends become a matter of dispute that statements about disease and health appear to lose their moorings.

No remarkable achievement is involved in detecting the ways in which values have affected assumptions about health and illness in prior eras or in cultures besides our own. What is unique about the current period is that we have begun to perceive the extent to which values have played such a crucial role in our own classifications of health and disease. That change is not so much a consequence of our superior intelligence, or of the information we have accumulated from historical and cross-cultural studies. Rather, the impetus for undertaking many such studies, the very awareness of the problematical status of the concepts of health and disease, is at least in part a product of our own new-found understanding. Our new wisdom is ironically the result of what often is deemed a distressing fact of our sociocultural condition—the collapse of a sense of the naturalness, the rightness of our values regarding many of the ends of human existence. It is that collapse that has rendered transparent what for so long was opaque.

Because concepts of mental health and illness are so intimately linked to prevailing sociocultural standards of appropriate behavior, it is not surprising that in a period characterized by challenges to those standards, psychiatry would be beset by internal confusion and controversy. But it is precisely at such moments that the profession acquires a degree of relative autonomy. Freed from the strictures of hegemonic and unquestioned standards, it may side either with the still-dominant norms of behavior or with the values that inspire critical and challenging social forces. That freedom, relative independence, and power become, however, sources of grave difficulty. With the normative foundations of its work made manifest, the posture of value-neutrality becomes untenable. Psychiatry is forced to assume a partisan role.

Outside the profession, those who seek to preserve conventional standards of behavior demand that their values be those of the psychiatric profession. Those pressing for change do the same. Whatever course is chosen, criticism cannot be avoided. Within the profession those who share the dominant values of society will be accused by their colleagues of betraying scientific objectivity, placing psychiatry in the service of socially conservative interests. Those who come to agree with the challenging forces will be attacked as having sacrificed science to reformist politics. Psychiatry can live with such disagreements, disquieting as they may be. Whenever it becomes necessary for the profession to speak as a corporate entity, however, fractious debate will be inevitable and a mechanism for resolving conflicts will be required. At times the political features of the mechanism will be masked; on other occasions those features will be obvious. In the debate on homosexuality within the American Psychiatric Association the effort to attain closure was baldly political, and it was this that stunned observers.

More striking than the deep division among psychiatrists that emerged during the dispute over whether to delete homosexuality from *DSM-II* was the pace at which changes in psychiatric thinking on this issue occurred. Hendrik Ruitenbeek noted in *Homosexuality: A Changing Picture*, published in 1973, that in the ten years that had elapsed since the appearance of his earlier volume[18] on homosexuality, the dominance of the pathological view had been all but shattered. Dismissing Irving Bieber, Charles Socarides, and their followers, he claimed that there were increasing numbers of psychiatrists and psychoanalysts who believed that homosexuality was "just another form of sexual behavior," for whom heterosexuality was no longer the "preferred life style."[19] Though hardly typical of psychoanalytic writing, even in the 1970s, it would have been almost unthinkable a decade earlier to find an analyst who would argue as Robert Seidenberg did in Ruitenbeek's collection:

The homosexual culture is a valuable asset to civilization. There is already an abundant supply of heterosexuals—as our ecologists are warning us perhaps too ample a supply. We may live to see the day when those who renounce traditional family life, as homosexuals have, will become the new ecological cult heroes.[20]

In the years following the Psychiatric Association's decision to delete homosexuality from its nomenclature of disorders, views that in the past might have been greeted with official scorn were granted sympathetic, sometimes enthusiastic receptions. In 1979 Clarissa K. Wittenberg wrote a warm front-page review of Alan Bell and Martin Weinberg's *Homosexualities* for *Psychiatric News*, the APA's official newspaper. The volume under review, a study conducted under the aegis of Alfred Kinsey's Institute for Sex Research, had torn at assumptions about the pathological nature of homosexuality. For Wittenberg the work was "certain to be an instant classic," a status, she argued, it fully deserved.[21]

Nothing more dramatically illustrates the profound change in thinking about homosexuality among many mental health professionals than the recent debate over providing therapeutic assistance to homosexuals voluntarily seeking a heterosexual adjustment. Though the dispute involved primarily psychologists rather than psychiatrists, it revealed the extent to which there had been a stunning alteration in the milieu within which homosexuality was being considered. The debate was sparked by Gerald Davison's 1974 presidential address to the Association for the Advancement of Behavior Therapy, in which he argued that under prevailing conditions no request by a homosexual for sexual reorientation could be considered truly voluntary. Given the "homophobia" of contemporary society, all such requests had to be viewed as coerced. A therapist who cooperated in such therapeutic ventures was thus transformed, perhaps unwittingly, into an agent of society's antihomosexual bias.

More importantly, Davison argued that the very existence of a therapeutic posture toward those seeking more conventional sexual orientations tended to reinforce the sociocultural priority of heterosexuality. How often, he provocatively asked, would therapists agree to assist heterosexuals seeking a homosexual reorientation?[22] Putting aside the question of therapeutic efficacy, he stated that "even if we *could* effect certain changes, there is still the more important question of whether we should. I believe we should not."[23] While acknowledging that individual homosexuals might suffer if therapists were to adopt his perspective, Davison asserted that homosexuals as a class would benefit. The political standard of social justice was thus given preeminence over the clinical standard. The interest of "the homosexual" was given priority over the desires of individual homosexuals.

The mostly hostile reaction provoked by Davison's challenge makes clear that his views were shared by only a small minority. Nevertheless, his remarks were given wide exposure[24] and were considered of sufficient importance to warrant an extended professional debate. When similar arguments had first been made by homosexual activists like Frank Kameny in the 1960s, they were viewed as part of an extremist challenge to the professional therapeutic commitment of psychiatry. By the mid-1970s, in the wake of the Psychiatric Association's battle over *DSM-II*, the mental health professions had become so thoroughly engaged in the struggle for homosexual rights that they could no longer avoid an internal confrontation over the sociopolitical implications of their own clinical perspective. No longer was the benign therapeutic posture considered a guarantee against conflicts of interest between those who treated and those they sought to treat.

What can account for the speed with which so many psychiatrists and so many other allied mental health professionals have altered their thinking on homosexuality? What made the arguments of gay activists appear so credible when the work of Hooker, Kinsey, and Ford and Beach had been dismissed so readily for more than two decades? Those who have denounced the deletion of homosexuality from *DSM-II* claim that the American Psychiatric Association was intimidated into taking its action, and that despite the Association's official posture, a vast majority of psychiatrists continue to view homosexuality as a pathological condition. That the American Psychiatric Association responded to the concerted pressure of an angry, militant movement that had made full use of coercive and intimidating tactics is undeniable. To assert, however, that the decision of December 1973 represented nothing more than a capitulation in the face of force involves a great distortion. Though it is difficult to determine the precise proportion of psychiatrists who have adopted the nonpathological view, it is clear that the numbers are substantial.

Those who assumed the most central role in pressing for change within the Psychiatric Association have tended to minimize the importance to this process of the disruptive challenge by gay activists. They have preferred to characterize their motivations and concerns as preeminently professional. At best, they have been willing to acknowledge that the homosexual attack accelerated a process of rethinking that had begun *within* psychiatry. Robert Spitzer was unusual in this regard, acknowledging quite openly the importance of gay pressure. When publicly asked by Irving Bieber whether he would consider removing fetishism and voyeurism from the psychiatric nomenclature, he responded, "I haven't given much thought to [these problems] and perhaps that is because the voyeurs and the fetishists have not yet organized themselves and forced us to do that."[25] More typical of those who had pressed for change was John Spiegel's comment that "while the agitation of the gay movement quickened our sympathetic awareness of the gay concerns, the action taken was not a response to gay demands as such. It was a scientifically based decision."[26]

For those psychiatrists who were ultimately to side with the demands of the Gay Liberation groups, whatever initial opposition was provoked by the indecorous use of disruptive tactics was quickly overcome. Politically more liberal than other physicians or the general population,[27] they understood that gay activists had merely relied upon the forms of social protest then being used by the disenfranchised throughout the United States. To support demonstrations, sit-ins, and disruptions by students, racial minorities, welfare mothers, and antiwar activists, while opposing them when used against the psychiatric establishment, would have been a self-serving hypocrisy. But more important than this willingness to tolerate the discomfort produced by being the target of protest was the almost visceral recognition on the part of many psychiatrists that the list of gay grievances had substantive merit.

Psychiatrists responded with great concern to the charge that their diagnostic standpoint had become a major prop for social repression; that the stigmatization brought on by psychiatric classification was especially virulent; that, rather than a source of melioration, psychiatry had become the source of great pain and suffering. Perhaps more than any other group, homosexuals were the victims of what many academic sociologists had claimed was the inevitable consequence of "labeling" deviant behavior. In the social climate of the early 1970s, it would have been difficult for liberal psychiatrists to ignore the parallels between the discontents of racial minorities, the poor, opponents of the war in Vietnam, and the Gay Liberation movement, which had been linked by its leaders to the other movements of protest. With pressure mounting within psychiatry for the mobilization of its professional resources on behalf of social change, the demands of gay activists had an unusual force. The capacity of the orthodox psychiatric perspective on homosexuality to command allegiance began to wane.

Political liberalism alone cannot, however, explain the dramatic shift in outlook on the part of psychiatrists. Equally important was the growing confusion about the scope of the profession's concerns and the concomitant interest in the development of a narrower, less inclusive definition of mental illness. With the theoretical foundations for classifying homosexuality as a psychiatric disorder uncertain, it was possible for "extraprofessional" values to assume greater salience than otherwise might have been the case. This point is underscored by the fact that psychoanalysts, typically more liberal than other psychiatrists,[28] remained steadfastly committed to the pathological perspective. While some analysts like Judd Marmor had been at the forefront of the effort to remove homosexuality from *DSM-II*, most had opposed, often vehemently, the decision to delete it from the nomenclature. Because of their powerful professional ideology involving a highly developed theoretical orientation, psychoanalysts were protected against the pressures exerted by homosexuals. They were, in fact, able to argue that the deletion of homosexuality from *DSM-II* was against the "true interests" of those who so urgently and wrathfully pressed for change. To the most bitterly expressed complaints about the consequences of being labeled sick, psychoanalysts were able to respond that the pain felt by homosexuals was intrapsychic in origin. "We have no reason to subscribe to the superficial view which maintains that the reversal of discrimination against homosexuals—the reversal of external conflicts to whatever extent possible—would render internalized, internal conflicts nonexistent."[29] The psychoanalytic treatment of the pathology, not the removal of a diagnostic label, was what homosexuals required.

Given the expansive definition of psychopathology characteristic of psychoanalysis, and a theoretically grounded basis for the classification of homosexuality as a perversion of normal psychosexual development, it would have been extremely difficult for psychoanalysts to acknowledge the legitimacy of gay arguments without doing great damage to the coherence of their outlook.

Psychoanalysts, though the most vocal opponents of the diagnostic shift, are of course not alone. Despite the official positions of the American Psychiatric and the American Psychological Associations, significant numbers of psychiatrists and psychologists continue to view homosexuality as a pathological condition, and are able to lend professional and scientific weight to the powerful social resistance to the legitimation of the homosexual orientation. Under their aegis and with their assistance, textbooks prepared for use in schools and universities continue to reflect the pathological view. A survey of psychology texts published between 1975 and 1979 and recommended for undergraduate use in Canadian universities found that 60 percent of the books sampled discussed homosexuality under the category of "deviance," with references being made to sexual dysfunction, behavior disorders, inappropriate sex object choice, psychopathology, and maladjustment.[30] A second survey, devoted to an analysis of the textbooks used in sex education programs in the United States, found a systematic bias in favor of heterosexuality, with adult homosexuality being depicted as neither desirable nor normal.[31]

On a more popular level, homosexuality has retained its pathological status among the psychological advice-givers in the daily press. Reflecting, as well as providing support for, the popular antipathy toward deviations from the heterosexual norm, Ann Landers typifies the resistance to the newly adopted position of official psychiatry. Writing in July 1976, she stated:

I fought for the civil rights of homosexuals twenty years ago and argued that they should be regarded as full and equal citizens. However, I do not believe homosexuality is "just another life style." I believe these people suffer from a severe personality disorder. Granted some are sicker than others, but sick they are and all the fancy rhetoric of the American Psychiatric Association will not change it.[32]

With support from psychiatrists still committed to the pathological view, this influential columnist was able to dismiss the position adopted by the APA. As Abram Kardiner, a senior psychoanalytic figure and bitter opponent of the Psychiatric Association's decision, noted, "The suspicion with which middle America views homosexuality cannot be voted out of existence."[33] We have thus arrived at a remarkable juncture. The official position of American psychiatry on the pathological status of homosexuality is contested not only by dissenting professionals, but by lay people as well. To the APA's 1973 decision, those convinced of the abnormality of homosexuality respond, "These people are sick and should be treated as such."

Nothing shows more clearly the nature of the current impasse than the dispute over the appropriate policy of the Immigration and Naturalization Service toward homosexuals seeking entry into the United States. In August of 1979, more than five years after the APA had made its decision, Surgeon General Julius B. Richmond ruled that government physicians would no longer consider homosexuality a "mental disease or defect."[34] He advised the Immigration Service that its officers should end the practice of referring suspected homosexuals to the Public Health Service for examination, the required practice during the prior twenty-seven years. Though immigration officials issued a temporary order instructing their officers to admit homosexuals into the country, a Justice Department ruling in December 1979 required a reinstatement of the exclusionary policy. In explaining its decision, the department stated that when Congress had passed the Immigration and Nationality Act of 1952, it had considered homosexuality a disease. "Not a word in the statute or its history suggests a Congressional

intent that the Surgeon General be empowered in the future
to eliminate homosexuality as a ground for exclusion by declaring his disagreement with Congress's determination."[35] Thus,
in the face of a desire to treat homosexuals as unacceptable,
it was a congressional finding rather than the position of the
psychiatric profession that was the deciding factor in determining whether or not homosexuals were sick.

Having exercised the relative autonomy made possible by
prevailing sociocultural conditions in the early 1970s, psychiatry finds itself at the center of profound controversy. This
situation cannot long endure. Unlike heterodox tendencies
within the profession, the psychiatric mainstream must ultimately affirm the standards of health and disease of the society
within which it works. It cannot hold to discordant views regarding the normal and abnormal, the desirable and undesirable, and continue to perform its socially sanctioned function.
Only if American society were to change dramatically in the
next years would the 1973 decision to remove homosexuality
from the list of psychiatric disorders become securely rooted.
There is every indication that the necessary social transformation will not occur. Whatever small prospect there had been
in the recent past for the full integration of homosexuals into
American social life seems to have all but vanished. While
intense struggles on the part of Gay Liberation groups still
produce some victories, they come with great difficulty. Predic-
tions that the gay movement for social acceptance would provoke a bitter, reactionary backlash have not, however, proven
accurate. The hard-won gains of the last decade have not been
swept aside. Rather, a halt has been called to further major
advances. Modest civil rights gains could be accommodated
by American society, but not social legitimation. The homosexual movement rode the crest of social protest in the late 1960s
and early 1970s. Now, like the broader movement of which
it was part, it encounters deep resistance to change. The recent
era of major reform has come to an end in the United States.
Under these circumstances the APA's 1973 decision is bound
to become increasingly vulnerable.

In removing homosexuality from the *Diagnostic and Statistical Manual,* the Psychiatric Association symbolically deprived American society of its most important justification for refusing to grant legitimation to homosexuality. As the need for such a justification resurfaces in the current period, pressure will mount on psychiatrists to reclassify homosexuality as a disorder. Lacking a coherent theoretical orientation with which to protect itself from such pressure, psychiatry may find it exceedingly difficult to resist those demands. No more than in 1973, however, will the response of official psychiatry represent a mere capitulation to power. Rather, psychiatrists may well begin to see things differently. If necessary, the psychiatric and scientific justification for once again declaring homosexuality an illness will be found.

As America enters a period of social conservatism, fueled by concerns over dwindling resources, an unstable economy, and declining international prestige and power, the possibility of such a reversal cannot be dismissed. To diminish the likelihood of such an outcome will take powerful resistance on the part of a well-organized gay community and its psychiatric allies.

AFTERWORD

TO THE 1987 EDITION

I

In the concluding paragraphs of *Homosexuality and American Psychiatry* I noted that because the decision of the American Psychiatric Association to delete homosexuality from its official classification of mental disorders grew out of the conditions of social protest and change of the 1960s and 1970s, a conservative turn in the 1980s might well provide the cultural and social foundations for efforts to reclassify homosexuality as a psychiatric illness. It could not be known then that the most fundamental challenge to the status of gay men in America would come not from a change in the political climate but from a pathogen that would threaten the survival of male homosexuals and that would, in addition, threaten to undo the social advances that had been made by gays and lesbians in the preceding two decades. This was the striking and utterly unpredictable context within which a surprising final act in the dramatic encounter between homosexuality and American psychiatry was to be played.

Homosexuality and American Psychiatry was published in February of 1981. Just four months later the Centers for Disease

Control (CDC) began to report the appearance, in previously healthy gay men, of diseases that had been seen earlier only in individuals whose immune systems had been severely compromised.[1] In June 1981, *Morbidity and Mortality Weekly Reports*, CDC's publication, described an outcropping of five cases of pneumocystis carinii pneumonia in Los Angeles. Terming this occurrence "unusual," the *Reports* suggested the possibility of "an association between some aspect of homosexual lifestyle or disease acquired from sexual contact and pneumocystis pneumonia in this population."[2]

The next month, CDC reported that in the prior two and a half years Kaposi's sarcoma, a malignancy unusual in the United States, had been diagnosed in twenty-six gay men. Eight of those patients had died within two years of diagnosis. In each of these cases, two factors were striking: the youth of the victims—in the past, Kaposi's had been reported only in elderly Americans—and its "fulminant" course.[3]

During the next year the CDC continued to record the toll of what was now called acquired immune deficiency syndrome (AIDS). By May 28, 1982, 355 cases of Kaposi's sarcoma, pneumocystis pneumonia, and other opportunistic infections among those who had not been previously diagnosed with immune suppressed conditions had been reported. Of those afflicted, 79 percent were either gay or bisexual. Among the heterosexual patients, the dominant feature was illicit intravenous drug use. Though there was no definitive explanation of how AIDS spread, there was increasingly suggestive evidence that some factor transmitted through sexual contact and the sharing of needles by drug users was involved. Why recent immigrants from Haiti seemed to be overrepresented among the heterosexual AIDS cases was a mystery.

The population at large seemed unaffected. In July 1982, however, CDC reported AIDS in three heterosexuals with hemophilia.[4] Two had died; one was critically ill. These cases suggested that the disease could be transmitted by blood or blood products. These fears were confirmed when the case of a twenty-month-old infant with an unexplained cellular immune deficiency along with opportunistic infection was reported. The child had received multiple transfusions after birth. One of these had come from a donor who, though apparently in good health at the time of his donation, had subsequently developed the first symptoms of AIDS.[5]

The social reaction to AIDS during the first years of the epidemic was indelibly marked by the unique social distribution of the disease. With more than 90 percent of reported cases coming from those of marginal social status (gay and bisexual men, intravenous drug users, Haitians), it is hardly surprising that ultimately the fears associated with a deadly disease of unknown etiology merged with those associated with contamination from below and without.

The response of the public to AIDS was, however, slow to take form.[6] With few exceptions, there was little media interest in the unique and troubling pattern of disease that at first seemed to affect only homosexual and bisexual males, intravenous drug users, and Haitians. Silence in the press was for the gay community an indication of prevailing homophobia. It represented an unwillingness to respond to the suffering of gays, a refusal to marshal the medical and technical resources for the tasks of discovering the causes of AIDS, of developing preventive strategies, and of providing clinical interventions that could interrupt the course of the disease. But at the same time there were those in the gay community who feared the consequences of too much public discussion of a disease that was so closely identified with male homosexuals. Might not such discussion provoke fears about a "gay plague"? Might it not provoke a backlash that would threaten the very important though modest advances made in the years of social struggle and legal challenge?[7]

Fears of what form a broadened public interest might take were in fact confirmed. Anxiety about the risks of contagion and of the possible spread of the disease by casual public encounters with members of high-risk groups seized the public. Reports began to appear of the refusal of prison guards, undertakers, garbage collectors, and even health care workers to perform their duties with those suspected of having AIDS as well as with AIDS patients themselves.[8]

These reactions were punctuated by the extreme responses from those who sought to use the occasion of public controversy over AIDS to underscore their own antipathy to homosexuality and to what they viewed as the disastrous social consequences of greater social tolerance in sexual matters. The *Moral Majority Report*[9] featured a front-cover photograph of a family wearing surgical masks to introduce a story entitled "AIDS: Homosexual Disease Threatens American Families." Jerry Falwell demanded strong action against the homosexual carriers of AIDS. Invoking the image of divine retribution for sexual licentiousness, the Moral Majority leader asserted that AIDS represented a "spanking": "Herpes, AIDS, venereal disease . . . are a definite form of judgment of God upon society."[10] Patrick Buchanan, the conservative political columnist, subsequently appointed White House director of communications, invoked a naturalistic vision of the punishment of gays when he wrote in the *New York Post*, "The poor homosexuals—they have declared war on Nature, and now Nature is exacting an awful retribution."[11] In the most extreme cases, there were calls for the incarceration of homosexuals "until and unless they can be cleansed of their medical problems."[12]

What accounted for the shift from the relative silence of the first year or so of AIDS reporting to the dramatic attention of the subsequent period? Both the rise in the number of cases and the rising mortality certainly played a role. But more was clearly involved. The emergence of AIDS cases among hemophiliacs dependent upon Factor VIII—the clotting agent derived from large numbers of blood donations—and the occurrence of cases among recipients of blood transfusions—especially among infants and children—provoked a sense of dread about the spread of a deadly disease to "vulnerable" and "innocent" bystanders. In the very act of responding to the spread of AIDS the community expressed not only its fears about contagion but also its moral judgment. Gay males and

drug users were victims, but were implicated by their own behavior in the onset of the disease. Those in need of transfusions and Factor VIII were "innocents" who could do little to
protect themselves.

The debate that swirled around the necessity of developing
appropriate blood collection practices in the face of AIDS was
emblematic of the debates that were to emerge in the next
years about every dimension of public health policy and the
response to AIDS.[13] On the one hand, there was a realization.
that the welfare of the community required the development
of measures designed to inhibit the spread of AIDS. On the
other hand, gays and their political allies feared that incau-
tiously crafted policies might stigmatize the homosexual community, thus adding scientific and medical fuel to the social
antipathy directed at those who had so recently succeeded in
making strides toward social toleration, if not integration.

In early 1983, the National Hemophilia Foundation moved
to gain agreement from commercial plasma companies to ban
donations from all male homosexuals. Gay leaders, aware of
the symbolic significance of being excluded from the blood donor pool and fearful of the stigma that might well be associated
with the charge of "bad blood," urged efforts be made to dis-
courage only those homosexuals who were believed to be at
specially high risk—those who had engaged in sexual relations with many partners. However, with the increasing recognition that gays could inadvertently contaminate the blood
supply, it was only a matter of time before the Public Health
Service would issue its first exclusionary recommendations. In
March 1983, the PHS called upon members of all high-risk
groups, including "sexually active homosexual or bisexual
men with multiple partners,"[14] to refrain from blood donations. Those responsible for collecting blood were to inform all
potential donors of these federal standards. These were the
most liberal of what was to be an increasingly restrictive series
of recommendations. Eventually, virtually all homosexual
males were to be excluded from the donor pool. In its recommendations of December 1984, the PHS urged the exclusion of

"all males who have had sex with more than one male since 1979, and males whose male sex partner has had sex with more than one male since 1979."[15]

The debate over the nation's blood supply was set against the background of a far broader set of concerns within the gay community, concerns stemming from the troubling recognition that homosexuality was once again becoming the focus of medical attention, debate, scrutiny, and policy. Now, only a decade after the demedicalization of homosexuality represented by the APA's 1973 decision to delete homosexuality from *DSM-II*, the power of medicine was being brought into intimate contact with the gay community. That power was at once the sole hope for halting the spread of the disease that threatened to devastate that community and the specter threatening to subvert the achievements of the prior twenty years. There was a risk not only that medical justifications would be used to reverse the public victories won as the result of great organizational efforts, but that every dimension of private sexual expression would become the target of diagnosis and challenge.

As gays had forced psychiatry to confront itself, now medicine was compelling the gay community to examine its own behavior. Within the gay community, the early epidemiological linkage that had been suggested between "fast lane" behavior and the enhanced risk for contracting AIDS forced a reflection upon the most intimate dimensions of sexual behavior. Some suggested that AIDS might be the consequence of repeated assaults on the immune system resulting from sexual acts, including anal intercourse. Others argued that indiscriminate sexual contact with large numbers of anonymous partners simply enhanced the prospect of being exposed to an as-yet-to-be-discovered disease-bearing agent.

Joseph Sonnabend, a physician caring for many AIDS patients, emerged as the leading advocate of the immunological-overload theory. "There is such a thing as sexual excess, though to say that sounds like some throwback to Victorian morality," he asserted. "Put simply, I believe one of the biggest risks is to be exposed anally to semen from many different partners, especially in a large urban area where the risks of coming into contact with cytomegalovirus, which I think is a causative agent somehow, is very high." Sonnabend was especially critical of physicians who, because of political and social concerns, recoiled from the implications of these data: "Gay men have been poorly served by their doctors in the last decade. There was no clear and positive message about the dangers of promiscuity. We must admit that our desire to be nonjudgmental has interfered with our primary commitment to our patients."[16]

For many gay physicians, Sonnabend's unvarnished challenge passed beyond the bounds of appropriate clinical and professional discourse. Writing in the *Journal of the American Medical Association*, Neil Schram and Dennis McShane, of the American Association of Physicians for Human Rights, asserted: "It is important to note that terms such as *profound promiscuity*, when used by medical personnel to describe multiple sex partners, have a strong judgmental quality and as such are not suitable to the scientific and medical literature. Those physicians caring for homosexual males with or without AIDS have been encouraged to be supportive of their patients. It is terms like 'promiscuity' that make many homosexuals reluctant to discuss their sexual orientation with their medical care providers, even though doing so clearly improves the quality of medical care."[17]

But however the scientific issues were framed, a clear message was derived from the earliest scientific evidence. "Safe" sexual practices, sexual moderation, and caution were necessary.[18] Some gay men perceived this message as a challenge to their behavior and adopted an extremely harsh perspective on their own past activities. Calls for restraint, for the observance of "immunological Lent," and even for monogamy were not, however, always welcomed. Some viewed them as representing a thinly disguised call for a return to sexual conventionality. Once again, physicians were seeking to establish their dominance over homosexuality, a dominance that so recently had been discarded. Writing in the *Body Politic*, a Canadian gay journal, Michael Lynch stated: "Gays are once again allowing the medical profession to define, restrict, pathologize us." To follow the advice of physicians would involve renunciation of "the power to determine our own identity," and would represent "a communal betrayal of gargantuan proportions" of gay liberation, founded upon a "sexual brotherhood of promiscuity."[19] Doubting the scientific validity of data on the basis of which the cautionary advice was being profferred, another wrote: "I feel that what we are being advised to do involves all of the things I became gay to get away from. . . . So we have a disease for which supposedly the cure is to go back to all the styles that were preached at us in the first place. It will take a lot more evidence before I'm about to do that."[20] In a particularly vitriolic attack upon Jonathan Lieberson's essay on AIDS in the *New York Review of Books,* John Rechy wrote, "How eagerly do even *perhaps* 'good heterosexuals' impose grim sentences of abstinence on others."[21]

With the 1984 discovery of HIV—the retrovirus responsible for AIDS—the acrimonious dispute within the gay community about the transmissibility of the disease all but vanished, replaced by intense debates about which sexual acts posed the gravest risks of infection and about the need to respond to the threat of AIDS with a radical modification of gay culture and gay sexual practices.

By 1986 the catastrophic worldwide implications of the AIDS epidemic were becoming ever more apparent. In June of that year the Public Health Service predicted that by 1991 there would be 270,000 cases of AIDS in the United States alone, 74,000 of which would have been reported in that year alone. Upwards of 54,000 deaths from AIDS would be recorded in 1991.[22] Though the epidemiological pattern of the disease in the United States was thought to be shifting as increasing numbers of heterosexual cases were recorded, in the public's mind AIDS remained preeminently a disease of homosexuals, but one which at the same time posed grave challenges to the heterosexual majority.

Not surprisingly, public opinion polls during this period continued to reflect deep-seated social antipathy toward homosexuals. One such national survey, conducted by the *Los Angeles Times* at the end of 1985,[23] found that 79 percent of those sampled believed that sexual relations between two adults of the same sex was "always," "almost always," or "sometimes wrong." Only 15 percent declared such sexual relations "never wrong." Though there were some differences between Democrats and Republicans, those with "high" and those with "low" knowledge about AIDS and its modes of transmission, and those whose fear of AIDS was "high" and those whose fear was "low," the moral perspective on homosexuality was uniformly negative. Framed somewhat differently, the survey produced less negative responses. Fifty percent responded that they opposed homosexual relations for "everyone" while 45 percent either approved of such relations or did so for "others." What had been the contribution of AIDS to such perceptions?

A review of a number of public opinion polls by Eleanor Singer and Theresa Rogers,[24] not unexpectedly, underscored the impact of the AIDS epidemic on public attitudes towards homosexuality. The Gallup Poll showed that the proportion of respondents disagreeing with the proposition that homosexuality should be considered an "accepted alternative lifestyle" had increased from 51 to 58 percent between June 1982 and July 1983. In 1985 37 percent of a Gallup sample responded that as a result of the AIDS epidemic their attitude toward homosexuals had changed for the "worse"; 59 percent reported no change. Finally, an NBC survey of 1985 found that there had been an increase of 2 percent—to 75.3 percent—in the proportion of those interviewed who responded that homosexual relations between adults was always wrong. Though a modest shift, it was notable because it had occurred after those figures had remained unchanged for several years.

The depth of the cultural antipathy toward homosexuality, amplified by anxiety surrounding the AIDS epidemic, was reflected in the landmark Supreme Court decision of *Bowers* v.

Hardwick. Handed down on June 30, 1986, by a bitterly divided
court, the decision upheld Georgia's sodomy statute as it applied to homosexuals. Writing for the Court, Justice Byron
White rejected the claims of those who argued that the constitutional protection accorded by the courts to sexual privacy extended to homosexuals. Justice White noted that twenty-four
states and the District of Columbia "continued to provide
criminal penalties for sodomy performed in private between
consenting adults."[25] To argue therefore that a "right to engage in such conduct is 'deeply rooted in this nation's history
and tradition' or 'implicit in the concept of ordered liberty,' is
at best facetious."[26] The Court's deference to the moral standards of the community was striking. Rejecting the claim that
law must be grounded on a rational basis "other than the pre-
sumed belief of the majority of the electorate in Georgia that
homosexual sodomy is immoral and unacceptable," Justice
White argued, as had Lord Devlin in England, that notions of
morality were basic to the law. "Respondents . . . insist that
majority sentiments about the morality of homosexuality
should be declared inadequate. We do not agree and are un-
persuaded that the sodomy statute of some 25 states should be
invalidated on this basis."[27]

The force of morality and the importance of deferring to legislative judgments on how best to codify the moral perspectives of the community were underlined in a concurring opinion written by Chief Justice Warren Burger. "To hold that the
act of homosexual sodomy is somehow protected as a fundamental right would be to cast aside millennia of moral teaching." Involved was "a question of the legislative authority of
the state."[28]

For those who dissented from the Court's ruling the issue
was cast very differently. Justice Blackmun refused to place
homosexuality beyond the scope of protected privacy rights
accorded to heterosexuals or to rupture the evolving jurispru-
dence that protected intimate relations. He wrote, "This case
[is not] about a 'fundamental right to engage in homosexual
sodomy. . . .' Rather this case is about 'the most comprehen-

sive of rights and the right most valued by civilized men, namely 'the right to be left alone.' "[29] Unlike those who place the moral antipathy of millennia toward homosexuality at the center of their thinking, Blackmun stated, "I believe we must analyze the respondents' claim in light of the values that underlie the constitutional right to privacy. If that right means anything, it means that before Georgia can prosecute its citizens for making choices about the most intimate aspects of their lives, it must do more than assert that the choice they have made is an 'abominable crime not fit to be named among Christians.' "[30] The state's effort to buttress its claims by reference to the long religious tradition within which homosexuality was anathema provided no grounds for the use of secular coercive power. "The state can no more punish private behavior because of religious intolerance than it can punish such behavior because of racial animus."[31]

Whatever the ultimate fate of the Supreme Court's decision and whether or not "the court will soon reconsider its analysis and conclude that depriving individuals of the right to choose for themselves how to conduct their intimate relations poses a far greater threat to the values most deeply rooted in our nation's history than tolerance of non-conformity could ever do,"[32] *Bowers* v. *Hardwick* makes clear the extent to which powerful antihomosexual cultural traditions continue to influence American social life.

In 1981 I argued that the 1973 decision of the American Psychiatric Association to eliminate homosexuality from its list of psychiatric disorders represented a move "made possible by prevailing sociocultural conditions in the early 1970s. . . ." Instead of a pillar of convention American psychiatry had made itself an agency of cultural change regarding homosexuality. But I stressed in the first edition of this book that "unlike heterodox tendencies within the profession the psychiatric mainstream must ultimately affirm the standards of health and disease of the society within which it works. It cannot hold to discordant views regarding the normal and the abnormal and continue to perform its socially sanctioned function." I believed that the decision to remove the aura of pathology would be secured only if American attitudes toward homosexuality were to undergo fundamental changes.

It is now six years since *Homosexuality and American Psychiatry* was first published. It is clear that despite major advances in the social and legal rights of gays and lesbians and despite the apparent social legitimation of homosexuality in the more cosmopolitan centers of America, sexual relations between those of the same sex have remained morally troubling if not anathema to broad sectors of American society. The AIDS epidemic has only intensified this deeply rooted hostility. How has this sociocultural milieu affected the official psychiatric perspective on homosexuality? The answer is not what might have been expected.

II

While American psychiatry moved in the early 1970s to accommodate the challenge—both theoretical and political—of gay protests, psychoanalysis remained committed to a perspective within which homosexuality was viewed as invariably pathological. Though there were exceptions, most notably Judd Marmor, most psychoanalysts viewed the 1973 decision to delete homosexuality from *DSM-II* as a misguided, even tragic capitulation to extrascientific pressure. The struggles that emerged during the drafting of *DSM-III* between those committed to a psychodynamically oriented psychiatry and those who believed that the profession's diagnostic manual ought to be descriptive and therefore could not be founded upon the etiological assumptions derived from psychoanalytic theory deepened the fissures within American psychiatry. Though efforts at intraprofessional diplomacy sought to prevent a complete rupture, many psychoanalysts viewed the publication of *DSM-III* in 1980 as a grave defeat.[33]

In the years since the 1973 decision to remove homosexuality from the classification of psychiatric disorders, psychoanalytic thinking about homosexuality has remained fundamentally unchanged. In a recent essay published in the *Psychoanalytic Review*, Robert M. Friedman laments this state of affairs. "Psychoanalytic thinking on male homosexuality has gradually become more dogmatic, less productive, and for at least a decade now, has simply been in the doldrums. Current analytic research in this whole area is in a conspicuous crisis where the old theoretical model, and especially its theses of homosexual pathology, has to be reevaluated with frank openmindedness."[34]

Among the few psychoanalysts who have sought publicly to challenge the conception of homosexuality as pathology is Richard Isay. Like Judd Marmor before him, Isay has stressed the cultural roots of the psychoanalytic perspective on homosexuality. "The view of homosexuality as pathology and the concomitant desire to change our patient's sexual orientation is [I believe] due to the bias that only heterosexuality is normal and to our internalization of the social prejudice against homosexuals."[35] Isay's own clinical experience has led him to the conclusion that the sexual orientation of gay men is "not mutable."[36] He has therefore declared that the task of psychoanalytic treatment of gay men is to help them accept their sexual preference. With an echo of Freud's "Letter to an American Mother" Isay has urged, "As with every patient the clinical task with the homosexual is to enable him to be as free as possible of conflict that is inhibiting and self-destructive so that he can live as gratifying a life as is within his grasp."[37]

The reception which Isay has received because of his heterodox position provides little grounds for anticipating that within psychoanalysis itself major changes can be expected in the perception of homosexuality.[38] But within psychiatry the situation in the early 1980s suggested that despite the conservative social mood of America, the seeds of further change were present. The uneasy truce that had brought to a close the conflict of 1977–78 over "ego-dystonic homosexuality" in *DSM-III*, the existence of an association of openly gay and lesbian psychiatrists within the APA, as well as the official recognition of a formal committee of the Association devoted to gay, lesbian, and bisexual issues all suggested that at some point there would be a renewed conflict over the official nomenclature.

The institutional stage for such a confrontation over the status of homosexuality in the nosology of psychiatry was set in May 1983 with the appointment of the Work Group to Revise *DSM-III*, chaired by Robert Spitzer. Though the diagnostic manual had been published only in 1980 the American Psychiatric Association believed that a midcourse evaluation prior to the preparation of a diagnostic manual for the 1990s would prove useful. The mandate for the Work Group was to revise the criteria for disorders already in the manual and to add new clinical syndromes based on data accumulated since the publication of *DSM-III*. More than twenty-five advisory committees were established to assist the Work Group, including one on sexual dysfunctions.

Remarkably, the question of whether to retain the category of "ego-dystonic homosexuality" was never discussed by the advisory committee on sexual dysfunctions as work went forward to prepare a draft of a revised diagnostic manual, *DSM-III-R*. Either because of timidity or because of an inadequate appreciation of the internal functioning of the *DSM-III* review process, neither the Committee on Gay, Lesbian, and Bisexual Issues nor the Association of Gay and Lesbian Psychiatrists pressed to have the issue of "ego-dystonic homosexuality" placed on the agenda of the Committee on Sexual Dysfunctions or on that of the Work Group itself. It was only after the flare-up of controversy over diagnostic categories deemed offensive by feminist groups and the creation of an Ad Hoc Committee of the Board of Trustees and the Assembly of District Branches to review the Work Group's efforts that the issue of retaining "ego-dystonic homosexuality" emerged as a political issue in the fall of 1985.[39]

Surprisingly, the first challenge came not from the organizational representatives of gay and lesbian psychiatrists but from the chair of the Committee on Lesbian and Gay Concerns of the American Psychological Association, Alan K. Malyon.[40] In a letter to Robert Spitzer proposing the deletion of "ego-dystonic homosexuality," Malyon, like those who had opposed the diagnosis in 1977, argued that it was inconsistent with the structure of *DSM-III* "to have created a special diagnostic category based upon the designated source of dysphoric feeling." The inclusion of "ego-dystonic homosexuality" in *DSM-III* reflected a refusal to view homosexuality as a normal variant and, for Malyon, a lingering adherence to the older and more explicit pathological designation of homosexuality itself.

Spitzer's willingness, in an article published in the *American Journal of Psychiatry*,[41] to acknowledge that "ego-dystonic homosexuality" represented a nosological compromise, and perhaps more significantly his epistemological assertion that the concept of "disorder" always involved a value judgment, permitted Malyon to articulate a theme that was to appear as a *leitmotif* over the next months. "Ego-dystonic homosexuality" represented a "value judgment" and not a scientific conclusion. Because it represented a compromise between those who continued to believe that homosexuality was always pathological and those who saw it as a normal variant, it was the product of politics, not science. In making the argument, the opponents of "ego-dystonic homosexuality" thereby sought to seize the professional high ground by defending the norms of science in psychiatry against what they characterized as the value-laden efforts of Spitzer and his supporters.

Almost one month later Terry Stein, a member of the APA's Committee on Gay, Lesbian, and Bisexual Issues and past president of the Association of Gay and Lesbian Psychiatrists, addressed a lengthy challenge to Spitzer in which he sought to undercut the professional, clinical, and theoretical foundations of "ego-dystonic homosexuality."[42] In this first of what was to be a series of letters by psychiatrists opposed to the retention of the diagnostic category, Stein had to acknowledge that he wrote as an individual, since the Committee on Gay, Lesbian, and Bisexual Issues had not "had an opportunity to discuss the issue."

Challenging the Work Group to Revise *DSM-III*, because it had failed to consult with either the Committee on Gay, Lesbian, and Bisexual Issues or the members of the Association of Gay and Lesbian Psychiatrists, Stein asserted that Spitzer and his colleagues had never addressed the scientific question of the validity and utility of the diagnosis. The category was incompatible with the structure of *DSM-III*, had not served as a guide to research, had not facilitated intraprofessional communication. Most importantly, it failed to reflect an understanding of "the vast amount of psychological, sociological and historical literature that documents the fact that the wish not to have a pattern of homosexual arousal can be a normative stage for many individuals who are developing a gay or lesbian identity." Though the sources of such distress were many, the most critical, for Stein, was the "socially learned denigration of homosexuality." As such, the painful experience of one's homosexuality was but a phase that had to be traversed in the process of learning to accept one's sexual orientation. A failure to appreciate this pattern of development resulted in the erroneous labeling of "ego-dystonic homosexuality" as a disorder and could well be linked etiologically to the onset of pathology "instead of the resolution of distress." In short, "ego-dystonic homosexuality" produced an iatrogenic disorder. What was required of Spitzer and the Work Group was "a more rational process of decision making." While acknowledging that some might be offended by a decision to eliminate "ego-dystonic homosexuality" from the revised edition of *DSM-III*, Stein urged Spitzer to adhere to a "process of scientific inquiry and review . . . that would overcome any appearance of either prejudice or lack of objectivity."

While many of the subsequent letters of protest to Spitzer alluded to the ways in which the retention of "ego-dystonic homosexuality" contributed to the stigmatization of gays and lesbians, it was Robert Cabaj, president of the Association of Gay and Lesbian Psychiatrists, who stressed the ways in which refusal to delete the diagnostic category could well contribute to socially repressive policies.[43] "Needless to say with the AIDS crisis and the growing attempts by the military and insurance companies to screen out gay people, the diagnosis has very frightening potential for abuse."

The slowly evolving momentum to press for a reopening of the issue of "ego-dystonic homosexuality" was in the last month of 1985 overshadowed by the tumultuous debates surrounding three proposed diagnoses considered unacceptable by women's groups both within the American Psychiatric Association and in other clinical fields. Premenstrual Dysphoric Disorder was viewed as a classification that not only denigrated women by the application of a psychiatric label to a biological process, but could well be used as a clinical justification for discrimination; Self-Defeating Personality Disorder was deemed an attempt to medicalize the subjugation of women by abusive partners and an unresponsive social order; finally, Paraphyllic Rapism, a diagnosis that was to be applied to men who could achieve sexual pleasure only in the context of rape and coercion, was considered dangerous because it might serve to exculpate rapists in criminal proceedings.[44]

To assist in the resolution of the controversies over these proposed diagnoses, as well as over "ego-dystonic homosexuality," a meeting of the Ad Hoc Committee of the Board of Trustees and the Assembly of District Branches to review the draft of DSM-III-R was scheduled for December 4, 1985.[45] In preparation for that session, those who had started so late in the process of diagnostic revision to press for the deletion of "ego-dystonic homosexuality" began to consider a range of options, the core of which involved the elimination of the word "homosexuality" from the diagnostic manual. A new classification, "Ego-Dystonic Sexuality," was suggested to classify psychological distress relating to a range of sexual matters.[46] Included would be "confusion about preferred sexual orientation or dissatisfaction with one's sexual orientation." The adoption of such a nosological classification would achieve what had so explicitly been rejected in the 1977 debate over "ego-dystonic homosexuality." The textual priority accorded heterosexuality in psychiatry's nomenclature would vanish. As one advocate of the new classification wrote, "Ego-dystonic sexuality does not single out homosexuality as the only sexual orientation that may be distressful. . . . It removes any impression that homosexuality is basically different from other sexual orientations, a concept not substantiated by modern research."[47]

At the December 4 meeting "ego-dystonic homosexuality" was the last of the controversial diagnoses to be discussed and was indeed given less time on the agenda than those diagnoses that had aroused the wrath of women's groups. Two opponents of retention had been invited to present their views, Robert Cabaj and Bryant Welch, chair of the Board of Professional Affairs of the American Psychological Association. During the less than one hour of discussion there appeared to be some sympathy for those opposing retention. One Ad Hoc Committee member remarked: "Homosexuality used to be considered a sin. The medical profession took it out of the moral realm and made it an illness. Ego-dystonic homosexuality is the last vestige of the medical model of homosexuality. It will be dropped eventually, if not in *DSM-III-R* then certainly in *DSM-IV*." When asked why ego-dystonic sexuality was preferred to ego-dystonic homosexuality, Bryant Welch replied, "I guess a vestige of a vestige is better than a vestige."[48]

Nevertheless, in its report presented to the Board of Trustees three days after the December 4 session,[49] the Ad Hoc Committee supported the retention of "ego-dystonic homosexuality," though it urged that the revised manual include "a stronger statement about the controversial nature of the diagnosis." This decision did not, however, represent part of a broader rubber-stamping of Spitzer's position. On the bitterly fought matter of Premenstrual Dysphoric Disorder the committee rejected the inclusion of the diagnosis in *DSM-III-R* and urged instead that it be placed in an appendix as a way of "encouraging further scientific study," thus making possible "serious consideration for inclusion in *DSM-IV*." The Board of Trustees in an interim move sustained the recommendation of its Ad Hoc Committee.

In the aftermath of the board's decision Robert Spitzer wrote to those who had led the move to delete "ego-dystonic homosexuality," justifying his rejection of their demands by describing his own statement to the Ad Hoc Committee.[50] He acknowledged that the Advisory Committee on Sexual Dysfunctions had never reviewed the matter of "ego-dystonic homosexuality." Such a thorough consideration of the issues involved would have been time-consuming and not very productive, since the arguments put forth for deletion "are well known, so it would be unlikely that the members of [the Advisory Committee] would change their positions on the matter even after extensive discussion." Of the nine members of the committee, seven, Spitzer wrote, were strongly opposed to deletion of the category. Furthermore, Spitzer underscored the importance of preserving a compromise diagnosis. "To remove that category would [shatter] that achievement and would be viewed as the acceptance of the view that homosexuality is a normal variant." Finally, Spitzer noted that since the APA Task Force on the Treatment of Mental Disorders had commissioned a chapter on ego-dystonic homosexuality for a forthcoming volume, deletion of the classification would present a serious problem.

Both the tone and the argument of Spitzer's response were viewed as dismissive and insulting by those who favored deletion.[51] But in early 1986 some had begun to believe that the prospects for success in *DSM-III-R* were vanishing. The task ahead was to prepare the way for a more effective struggle for deletion in *DSM-IV*.[52] But Terry Stein, who viewed Spitzer's letter as "an embarrassment to our profession," seemed less resigned.[53] Even James Krajeski, chair of the Committee on Gay, Lesbian, and Bisexual Issues, whom some had viewed as less than aggressive in pursuing deletion, seemed to hold out hope for a reopening of the entire issue at the May 1986 meetings of the American Psychiatric Association.[54]

At a session of the Association of Gay and Lesbian Psychiatrists held during the APA's convention a unanimous vote urged the removal of ego-dystonic homosexuality. Members and other individuals were urged to write to Spitzer expressing opposition to the retention of "ego-dystonic homosexuality" and to the inclusion of the three diagnoses so opposed by women's groups.[55] The Committee on Gay, Lesbian, and Bisexual Issues, which some accused of having failed to force the matter of "ego-dystonic homosexuality," was pressed to demand a full hearing on the issue before permitting the Board of Trustees to take final action on *DSM-III-R*.[56]

This wave of opposition and protest achieved what Robert Spitzer five months earlier had declared impossible and a waste of time. On May 21, 1986, Spitzer invited Terry Stein, Robert Cabaj, James Krajeski, and Alan Malyon to meet with some members of the Advisory Committee on Psychosexual Disorders, his own Work Group, and the Ad Hoc Committee of the Board and Assembly to discuss "ego-dystonic homosexuality."[57] The meeting was held on June 24. Opposing deletion at that session were Helen Kaplan, a member of the Advisory Committee on Sexual Dysfunctions and coauthor of the chapter on the treatment of "ego-dystonic homosexuality" that was to appear in an APA-sponsored volume on the treatment of psychiatric disorders, and Dr. Mark Schwartz from the Masters and Johnson sex therapy institute.

Much of the substance of the discussion involved a recapitulation of the arguments and evidence presented in the eight months since the reopening of the debate on "ego-dystonic homosexuality." But it was clear that the weight of opinion had shifted.[58] Indeed, Robert Spitzer had gone into the meeting realizing that it would be necessary to yield on the issue of "ego-dystonic homosexuality."[59] He had come to believe that the Ad Hoc Committee of the Board and Assembly would not accept its retention and so attended the June 24 meeting prepared to offer a compromise that involved deletion of the offending classification. In a closed session following the invited presentations, the Work Group ratified Spitzer's conclusion. To meet the lingering concern of clinicians who sought a diagnostic warrant for the treatment of individuals who were distressed by their sexual orientation, an entry was to be made in *DSM-III-R* under the residual category "Sexual Disorders Not Otherwise Classified." Among those disorders was to be "persistent distress or confusion about one's sexual orientation." Spitzer's compromise was, in fact, not very different from the proposed classification of "ego-dystonic sexuality" that had been put forth months earlier by his opponents.

What was remarkable about this final curtain was the silence with which it fell. None of those who had been described six months earlier as unalterably opposed to deletion seemed to care much in the end. It was as if the struggle over words—diagnostic labels—ultimately did not matter to them, since in the "unofficial" world of clinical practice the existence of a label was viewed as of secondary importance. The virtual silence of the psychoanalytic community could well have reflected a similar conclusion, reinforced by a recognition that little was to be gained by an exhausting encounter with the American Psychiatric Association, which had demonstrated its disregard of the contributions of psychoanalysis in the fashioning of *DSM-III* itself.

The Ad Hoc Committee that had been created to contain the fractious debates over diagnosis and nosology was "delighted" by the decision.[60] With the dispute resolved the Ad Hoc Committee could recommend the deletion of "ego-dystonic homosexuality" to the APA's Board of Trustees. On June 28, 1986, that recommendation was accepted.[61]

In publicly announcing the board's decision the president of the APA, Robert Pasnau, provided empirical, clinical, and social justifications: "The diagnosis [of ego-dystonic homosexuality] which has been in the manual since 1980 is seldom used. A review of the scientific literature over the last five years revealed only thirteen references to the term. Members of the gay and lesbian community argued that the category is discriminatory because other sexual dysfunctions are not specific. Sex therapists say that the existing *DSM-III* category Psychosexual Disorders Not Otherwise Specified is sufficient."[62]

The decision to eliminate the last reference to homosexuality in the official nomenclature of psychiatry was termed by Robert Cabaj a "victory over 13 years in the making."[63] This "victory" was all the more surprising given the upsurge of concern about homosexuality in American society. But, as the 1973 decision on homosexuality demonstrated, the alignment of social, cultural, and political forces within psychiatry at any moment is not necessarily a reflection of the alignment that prevails in society more broadly. Indeed, it may be precisely because of the social anxiety produced by AIDS that American psychiatry seemed so ready to yield to those who sought to eliminate the last official "vestige" of the pathological perspective on homosexuality, a perspective that they argued only added to the social burden of those already suffering because of the AIDS epidemic.

The extent to which the American Psychiatric Association was aware of the political implications of its actions was underscored by Robert Pasnau as he explained the Board of Trustees' rejection of Work Group recommendations on two of the diagnostic categories that had so offended women, Self-Defeating Personality Disorder and Premenstrual Dysphoric Disorder. "While the initial recommendations of the Ad Hoc Committee [made in December 1985] are based primarily on the adequacy of the scientific data to support them, our final considerations must take into consideration the social and legal impact of the incorporation of these proposed additions and changes in the manual as well as their potential for abuse."[64]

Organized psychiatry having officially withdrawn at this moment from its commitment to a medical perspective on homosexuality, what remains uncertain is the form that the social response to homosexuality may take in the next years as social distress rises with the mounting toll taken by the AIDS epidemic.

NOTES

INTRODUCTION

1. Phillip Rieff, *The Triumph of the Therapeutic* (New York: Harper & Row, 1966), p. 17.

2. For Marcuse, the "performance principle" is the historically specific form taken by Freud's reality principle. "Behind the reality principle lies the fundamental fact of . . . scarcity, which means that the struggle for existence takes place in a world too poor for the satisfaction of human needs, without constant restraint, renunciation, delay. In other words, whatever satisfaction is possible necessitates *work* . . ." (Herbert Marcuse, *Eros and Civilization* [New York: Vintage Press, 1962], pp. 32–33).

3. Ibid., p. 45.

4. Ibid.

5. Repressive desublimation is deplored by Marcuse as the "release of sexuality in modes and forms which reduce and weaken erotic energy. In this process too, sexuality spreads its formerly tabooed dimension and relations. However, [here] the reality principle extends its hold over Eros" (Ibid., p. ix).

6. Vern Bullough, "Challenges to Societal Attitudes toward Homosexuality in the Late 19th and Early 20th Centuries," *Social Science Quarterly* 58 (June 1977):37.

7. Ivan Illich, "Disabling Professions" in Ivan Illich, et al. *Disabling Professions* (London: Marion Boyers Publishers, 1977).

8. Ivan Illich, *Medical Nemesis* (New York: Pantheon Books, 1975).

9. See especially Nicholas Kittrie, *The Right To Be Different* (Baltimore: Johns Hopkins Press, 1972).

10. For a discussion of the antipsychiatrists see *Anti-Psychiatry*, Robert Boyers, ed. (New York: Harper & Row, 1971).

11. Robert Stoller to Paul J. Fink (27 July, 1977).

12. *Actos Luso—Espanolas De Neurologia, Psiquiatria y Ciencias Afines* vol. 2, a Nu. 3, p. 166.

CHAPTER 1

1. D. J. West, *Homosexuality Re-Examined* (Minneapolis: University of Minnesota Press, 1977), p. 128.
2. Lev. 20:13.
3. Derrick Sherwin Bailey, *Homosexuality and the Western Christian Tradition* (London: Longmans, Green and Co., 1955), p. 73.
4. Ibid., pp. 115–16.
5. Ibid., p. 121.
6. Ibid., p. 147.
7. West, *Homosexuality Re-Examined*, p. 280.
8. Bailey, *Homosexuality and the Western Christian Tradition*, p. 148.
9. Ibid., p. 151.
10. Alexander Morison, "Outlines on Lectures on Mental Disease," cited in Richard Hunter and Ida Macalpine (eds.), *Three Hundred Years of Psychiatry 1535–1860* (London: Oxford University Press, 1963), p. 773.
11. The following discussion draws heavily upon the published and unpublished work of Vern L. Bullough. See especially, "Homosexuality and the Medical Model," *Journal of Homosexuality* (Fall 1974):99–110, *Sexual Variance in Society and History* (New York: John Wiley and Sons, 1976), and "Challenges to Societal Attitudes toward Homosexuality in the Late Nineteenth and Early Twentieth Centuries," *Social Science Quarterly* 58 (June 1977):29–44. See also Jeffrey Weeks, *Coming Out* (London: Quartet Books, 1977), chapter 2.
12. Sigmund Freud, *Three Essays on the Theory of Sexuality* (1905) (New York: Avon Books, 1962), p. 133.
13. Ibid., p. 25.
14. Sigmund Freud and Otto Rank, "Circular Letter," December 11, 1921, in *Body Politic*, May 1977, p. 9.
15. Sigmund Freud and Otto Rank, Letter, January 22, 1922, ibid.
16. Sigmund Freud, "Psychoanalytic Notes upon an Autobiographical Account of a Case of Paranoia," in *Three Case Histories* (New York: Collier Books, 1963), p. 164.
17. Otto Fenichel, *The Psychoanalytic Theory of Neurosis* (New York: Norton, 1945), p. 329.
18. Sigmund Freud, "A Child Is Being Beaten," in *Sexuality and the Psychology of Love* (New York: Collier Books, 1970), p. 131.
19. Sigmund Freud, "Analysis of a Phobia in a Five-Year-Old Boy (1909)" in *The Sexual Enlightenment of Children* (New York: Collier Books, 1971), p. 146.
20. Ibid.
21. Freud, *Three Essays*, p. 32.
22. Fenichel, *Psychoanalytic Theory*, p. 333.
23. Sigmund Freud, "The Psychogenesis of a Case of Homosexuality in a Woman," in *Sexuality and the Psychology of Love*, p. 145.
24. Sigmund Freud, "Certain Neurotic Mechanisms in Jealousy, Paranoia and Homosexuality (1922)" in ibid., p. 168.
25. Freud, *Three Essays*, p. 28.
26. Freud, "Psychogenesis of a Case of Homosexuality in a Woman," p. 157.
27. Ibid., p. 155.

Notes

28. Ibid., p. 157.
29. Ibid., pp. 137–38.
30. Ibid.
31. Quoted in Ernest Jones, *The Life and Work of Sigmund Freud*, vol. 3, *The Last Phase: 1919–1939* (New York: Basic Books, 1957), pp. 195–96.
32. Abram Kardiner, Aaron Karush, and Lionel Ovesey, "A Methodological Study of Freudian Theory III: Narcissism, Bisexuality and the Dual Instinct Theory," *Journal of Nervous and Mental Disease* 129 (September 1959):212.
33. Sandor Rado, *Psychoanalysis of Behavior II* (New York: Grune & Stratton, 1962) p. 96.
34. Ibid., p. 314.
35. Ibid., p. 206.
36. Ibid., p. 205.
37. Irving Bieber et al., *Homosexuality: A Psychoanalytic Study of Male Homosexuals* (New York: Basic Books, 1962).
38. Ibid., p. 18.
39. Ibid., p. 319.
40. Ibid., p. 220.
41. Ibid., p. 173.
42. Ibid., p. 60.
43. Ibid., pp. 79–80.
44. Ibid., p. 84.
45. Ibid., pp. 114–15.
46. Ibid., p. 172.
47. Ibid., p. 310.
48. Ibid., pp. 312–14.
49. Ibid., p. 254.
50. Ibid., p. 319.
51. Ibid.
52. Ibid., p. 278.
53. Irving Bieber, "Homosexuality," in Alfred Freedman and Harold Kaplan, *Comprehensive Textbook of Psychiatry* (Baltimore: Williams & Wilkins, 1967), p. 973.
54. Charles Socarides, "Homosexuality," in Silvano Arieti, *American Handbook of Psychiatry*, 2nd ed. (New York: Basic Books, 1974) 3:291.
55. Ibid.
56. Charles Socarides, *Beyond Sexual Freedom* (New York: Quadrangle Books, 1975), p. 11.
57. Charles Socarides, "Psychoanalytic Therapy of a Male Homosexual," *Psychoanalytic Quarterly* 38 (April 1969):173.
58. Ibid., p. 134.
59. Charles Socarides, *The Overt Homosexual* (New York: Grune and Stratton, 1968), p. 90.
60. *See*, for example, George Wiedeman, "Homosexuality, a Survey," *Journal of the American Psychoanalytic Association* 22 (1974):676.
61. Charles Socarides, "Homosexuality and Medicine," *Journal of the American Medical Association* 212 (18 May 1970):1201.
62. Socarides, *The Overt Homosexual*, p. 8.
63. Ibid.
64. Ibid., p. 7.
65. Socarides, *Beyond Sexual Freedom*, pp. 121–22.
66. Socarides, "Psychoanalytic Therapy of a Male Homosexual," pp. 188–89.

67. Socarides, "Homosexuality—Basic Concepts and Psychodynamics," *International Journal of Psychiatry*, 10 (March 1972):121.

68. For a brief description of various psychoanalytic theories of homosexuality, including those of Melanie Klein, Harry Stack Sullivan, Clara Thompson, Karen Horney, and Lionel Ovesey, *see* Bieber, "Homosexuality," pp. 6–11.

69. Great Britain Committee on Homosexual Offenses and Prostitution, *The Wolfenden Report*, authorized American edition (New York: Stein and Day, 1963). Paragraph 26 states: "There are conditions now recognized as diseases though they do not satisfy all three criteria [abnormal symptoms, a demonstrable pathological condition, some factor called the "cause"]. Our evidence suggests, however, that homosexuality does not satisfy any of these unless the terms in which they are defined are expanded beyond what could be regarded as legitimate."

70. Karl Menninger, "Introduction," ibid., p. 7.

71. American Psychiatric Association, *Diagnostic and Statistical Manual, Mental Disorders* (Washington, DC., 1952), p. 34.

72. American Psychiatric Association, *Diagnostic and Statistical Manual, DSM-II* (Washington, DC., 1968), p. 44.

CHAPTER 2

1. Alfred Kinsey et al., *Sexual Behavior in the Human Male* (Philadelphia: Saunders, 1948).

2. Paul Robinson, *The Modernization of Sex* (New York: Harper & Row, 1977).

3. Kinsey, *Sexual Behavior*, p. 625.

4. Ibid., p. 625.

5. Ibid., p. 638.

6. Dennis Altman, *Homosexual: Oppression and Liberation* (New York: Outerbridge and Dienstfrey, 1971).

7. Kinsey, *Sexual Behavior*, p. 659.

8. Ibid., p. 660.

9. Ibid.

10. Ibid., p. 637.

11. Robinson, *Modernization*, p. 69.

12. Kinsey, *Sexual Behavior*, p. 661.

13. Ibid.

14. Ibid., p. 660.

15. Ibid. It is noteworthy that both his data and his theoretical assumptions were incompatible with the views of those who argued that redirection of sexual orientation was impossible. This was in later years to become a central belief in homophile ideology.

16. Alan P. Bell and Martin S. Weinberg, *Homosexualities: A Study of Diversity Among Men and Women* (New York: Simon & Schuster, 1978), p. 14.

17. Cleland S. Ford and Frank A. Beach, *Patterns of Sexual Behavior* (New York: Harper and Brothers, 1951).

18. Ibid., p. 130.

19. Ibid., pp. 136–39.

20. Ibid., p. 143.

21. Ibid., p. 259.
22. Ibid.
23. Homophile literature in this period made repeated references to Ford and Beach's data. Later Gay Liberation literature did so also.
24. Evelyn Hooker, "Male Homosexuals and Their 'Worlds'," in Judd Marmor (ed.), *Sexual Inversion* (New York: Basic Books, 1965), p. 92. Hooker also described these events in her interview with Paul Chance in "Facts That Liberated the Gay Community," *Psychology Today,* December 1975, p. 60.
25. Evelyn Hooker, "The Adjustment of the Male Overt Homosexual," *Journal of Projective Techniques* 21 (1957):18.
26. Her methods were described in ibid., pp. 19–21.
27. Ibid., "Editor's Note," p. 18.
28. Ibid., p. 22.
29. Ibid., p. 23.
30. Ibid., p. 29.
31. Ibid., p. 30.
32. Evelyn Hooker, "Male Homosexuality in the Rorschach," *Journal of Projective Techniques* (1958):33–54 and her "What Is a Criterion?" *Journal of Projective Techniques* 23 (1959):278–81.
33. Evelyn Hooker, "Homosexuality," *International Encyclopedia of the Social Sciences* (New York: The Macmillan Company and the Free Press, 1968).
34. Hooker, "Male Homosexuals and Their 'Worlds'," pp. 95–98.
35. Evelyn Hooker, "A Preliminary Analysis of Group Behavior of Homosexuals," *Journal of Psychology* 41 (1956), p. 219.
36. National Institute of Mental Health Task Force on Homosexuality, *Final Report and Background Papers* (Washington, D.C.: Department of Health, Education and Welfare, 1972).
37. This term was suggested to me by Edward Sagarin.
38. Thomas Szasz, *Ideology and Insanity* (Garden City, New York: Anchor Books, 1970), p. 41.
39. Thomas Szasz, *The Myth of Mental Illness,* rev. ed. (New York: Harper and Row, 1974), pp. 17–80.
40. Ibid., pp. 11–12.
41. Ibid., pp. 200–01.
42. Ibid., p. 262.
43. Ibid., pp. 107–47.
44. Ibid., p. 123.
45. Szasz, *Ideology and Insanity,* p. 61.
46. Ibid., pp. 190–217.
47. Ibid., p. 212.
48. Thomas Szasz, "Legal and Moral Aspects of Homosexuality," in *Sexual Inversion,* p. 132.
49. Ibid., p. 136.
50. Ibid., p. 133.
51. Ibid., p. 136. Rather remarkably, however, Szasz asserts in the introductory remarks to this essay (p. 124) that he considers homosexuality an expression of "psychosexual immaturity." It is hard to understand the use of that expression by Szasz since it suggests a standard dictated by a "normal" goal for psychosexual development. Since he makes no further reference to that standard, it remains enigmatic.
52. Thomas Szasz, *The Manufacture of Madness* (New York: Delta Books, 1970), chapter 10.
53. Ibid., p. 170.

54. Ibid., p. 168.
55. Ibid., pp. 242–59.
56. "Healing Words for Political Madness: A Conversation with Dr. Thomas Szasz," *The Advocate*, 28 December 1977, p. 37.
57. Judd Marmor, "Introduction," in *Sexual Inversion*, pp. 9–10.
58. Ibid., p. 17.
59. Ibid., p. 5.
60. Ibid., pp. 18–21.
61. Ibid., p. 19.
62. Ibid., p. 17.
63. Ibid., pp. 17–18.
64. Judd Marmor, "Homosexuality–Mental Illness or Moral Dilemma," *International Journal of Psychiatry* 10 (March 1972):114.
65. Ibid.
66. Irving Bieber et al., *Homosexuality* (New York: Basic Books, 1962), pp. 304–6.
67. Ibid., p. 306.

CHAPTER 3

1. For a discussion of the focus on law reform by the first major movement for homosexual rights, in Germany under the leadership of Magnus Hirschfeld, *see* Jeffrey Weeks, *Coming Out* (London: Quartet Books, 1977).
2. For a discussion of Ellis, *see* Paul Robinson, *The Modernization of Sex* (New York: Harper & Row, 1977), pp. 4–9.
3. Parisex, "In Defense of Homosexuality," *A Homosexual Emancipation Miscellany 1835–1952* (New York: Arno Press, 1975), p. 286.
4. Laud Humphreys, *Out of the Closets* (Englewood Cliffs, N.J.: Prentice Hall, 1972) p. 50.
5. Donald Webster Cory, "History of the Homophile Movement," East Coast Homophile Organization Conference Brochure, p. 2.
6. Donald Webster Cory, "Address to International Committee for Sex Equality," in *One*, February 1953, pp. 10–11.
7. Mattachine Society, "The Mattachine Society Today," mimeographed (Los Angeles, 1954), pp. 3–4.
8. Ibid., p. 3.
9. *Mattachine Review*, June 1955, p. 48. In an obvious attempt to replace the concept of "deviant" with a term less pejorative in tone, Mattachine used "variant" to suggest that homosexuality was a variation on the "normal" rather than a deviation from it.
10. "Mattachine Society Today," p. 7.
11. Ibid.
12. Ibid., p. 8.
13. *Mattachine Review*, August 1956, p. 27.
14. "Mattachine Society Today," p. 8.
15. Erving Goffman has indicated that other journals of stigmatized groups also function in this way. "Often those with a particular stigma sponsor a

publication of some kind which gives voice to shared feelings, consolidating and stabilizing for the reader his sense of the realness of "his" group and his attachment to it. Here the ideology of the members is formulated—their complaints, their aspirations, their politics. The names of well-known friends and enemies of the "group" are cited, along with information to confirm the goodness or the badness of these people. Success stories are printed, tales of heroes of assimilation who have penetrated new areas of normal acceptance. Atrocity tales are recorded, recent and historic, of extreme mistreatment by normals. Exemplary moral tales are provided in biographical and autobiographical form illustrating a desirable code of conduct for the stigmatized. The publication also serves as a forum for presenting some division of opinion as to how the situation of the stigmatized person ought best to be handled. Should the individual's failing require special equipment, it is here advertised and reviewed. The readership of these publications provides a market for books and pamphlets which present a similar line." *Stigma: Notes on the Management of a Spoiled Identity,* (Englewood Cliffs, N.J.: Prentice Hall, 1963), p. 25.

16. Evelyn Hooker, "Inverts Are Not a Distinct Personality Type," *Mattachine Review,* January 1955, pp. 20–22.

17. Evelyn Hooker, "The Adjustment of the Male Overt Homosexual," *Mattachine Review,* December 1957, pp. 33–40.

18. Research Staff of *Sexology* "Enigma Under Scrutiny," *Mattachine Review,* February 1958, p. 16.

19. Norman Reider, "Sin v. Crime," *Mattachine Review,* November 1957, pp. 5–11.

20. Jack Parrish, "How Long Have You Been One?" *Mattachine Review,* October 1956, p. 33.

21. "Dr. Blanche Baker Challenges—Accept Yourself," *The Ladder,* May 1957, p. 6.

22. Luther Allen, "Homosexuality, Is It a Handicap or a Talent?" *Mattachine Review,* July–August 1955, p. 8.

23. Ibid., p. 10.

24. Luther Allen, "Homosexuality, Morality and Religion," *Mattachine Review,* February 1956, p. 25.

25. Frederick Kidder, "Review," *Mattachine Review,* January 1955, pp. 23–25. See also the review of Albert Ellis, *American Sexual Tragedy, The Ladder,* July 1957, p. 3.

26. Carl B. Harding, "Letter," *Mattachine Review,* August 1956, pp. 35–36.

27. Ken Burns, "The Homosexual Faces a Challenge," *Mattachine Review,* August 1956, p. 25.

28. Luther Allen, "Reformers Can Be Cruel," *Mattachine Review,* March–April 1955, p. 31.

29. Albert Ellis, "On the Cure of Homosexuality," *Mattachine Review,* November–December 1955, p. 7.

30. Albert Ellis, "The Use of Psychotherapy with Homosexuals," *Mattachine Review,* February 1956, p. 16.

31. Ellis, "On the Cure of Homosexuality," p. 9.

32. *Mattachine Review,* February 1956, p. 28.

33. Edmund Bergler, *Homosexuality: Disease or Way of Life?* (New York: Hill & Wang, 1956), p. 9.

34. Ibid., p. 177.

35. Ibid., p. 291.

36. Robert Phillips, "From One Degree to Another," *Mattachine Review,* May 1957, p. 11.

37. "Letter," *Mattachine Review,* February 1957, p. 14.
38. "Letter," *Mattachine Review,* May 1957, p. 9.
39. Sam Morford, *Mattachine Review,* February 1957, p. 42.
40. Ibid., p. 41.
41. Carol Hales, *The Ladder,* April 1957, p. 12.
42. "Ninth Year Ahead," *Mattachine Review,* September 1958, p. 5.
43. "Editorial," *The Ladder,* August 1964, p. 5.
44. "The Daughters of Bilitis Philosophy," *The Ladder,* June 1962, p. 7.
45. Speech to Mattachine Society of New York in Kay Tobin and Randy Wicker, *The Gay Crusaders* (New York: Arno Press, 1978), p. 98.
46. Frank Kameny, "Does Research into Homosexuality Matter?" *The Ladder,* May 1965, pp. 19–20.
47. Ibid., p. 16.
48. Ibid., p. 14.
49. Ibid.
50. Ibid.
51. Frank Kameny, "What Concrete Steps I Believe Can and Must Be Taken to Further the Homophile Movement," (Address to National Planning Conference of Homophile Organizations, August 25, 1966), mimeographed, p. 2 (on file, Institute for Sex Research, Indiana).
52. Frank Kameny, "Emphasis on Research Has Had Its Day," *The Ladder* October 1965, p. 12.
53. Donald Webster Cory, "Introduction," in Albert Ellis, *Homosexuality: Its Causes and Cure* (New York: Lyle Stuart, 1965), pp. 8–9.
54. Ibid., p. 11.
55. Ibid., p. 13.
56. "The Heterosexual Obsession," *The Ladder,* April 1965, p. 10.
57. "The DOB Convention," July 1964, p. 11.
58. "A Practical Platform," *The Ladder,* April 1965, p. 5.
59. "The Homosexual Citizen in the Great Society," *The Ladder,* February 1966, pp. 10–11.
60. Frank Kameny, Interview, 7 September 1978, Washington, D.C.
61. Files of Frank Kameny.
62. Dick Leitsch, "Campaign Statement," mimeographed (on file, Institute for Sex Research, Indiana).
63. Foster Gunneson, Jr., "The Homophile Movement in America" in Ralph Weltze (ed.), *The Same Sex* (Philadelphia: Pilgrim Press, 1968), p. 119,
64. Humphreys, in *Out of the Closets,* draws many parallels between the homosexual and Black struggles.
65. Resolutions adopted by Eastern Regional Homophile Conference, January 1968, mimeographed (on file, Institute for Sex Research, Indiana).
66. "The Homophile Community v. Dr. Charles Socarides," *The Ladder,* September 1968, pp. 29–30.
67. Columbia University Homophile League, "WE Protest the Kolb Panel," 23 April 1968, mimeographed (on file, Institute for Sex Research, Indiana).
68. Red Butterfly, "Gay Liberation," (1970), p. 3, mimeographed (on file, Institute for Sex Research, Indiana).
69. John Kyper, "Will Success Spoil Gay Lib?" *Win,* October 1971, p. 20.
70. "Statement of Purpose: GLF, Los Angeles," *Come Out,* April–May 1970, p. 11.
71. Kyper, "Success," p. 20.
72. Red Butterfly, "Gay Liberation," p. 3.

73. Ibid., p. 12.

74. Ibid., p. 13. There was deep concern with the antihomosexual attitudes of other radical forces.

75. Howard Brown, *Familiar Faces, Hidden Lives* (New York: Harcourt Brace Jovanovich, 1976).

76. Christopher Z. Hobson, "Surviving Psychotherapy," in Karla Jay and Allen Young (eds.), *Out of the Closets: Voices of Gay Liberation* (New York: Jove Books, 1972), p. 147.

77. Ibid., p. 153.

78. "Not Right On," *The Advocate* 30 September–13 October 1970.

79. Barbara Gittings, "It Was a Long, Hard Journey," in Jonathan Katz (ed.), *Gay American History* (New York: Thomas Crowell, 1976), p. 426.

80. *New York Times*, 29 June 1970, p. 1.

81. For descriptions, *see New York Times*, 28 June 1971, p. 23; *New York Times*, 26 June 1972, p. 21; *New York Times*, 25 June 1973, p. 21.)

82. The Daughters of Bilitis charged at a demonstration in front of New York's St. Patrick's Cathedral that "The Catholic Church has been one of the major oppressors of homosexuals." (*New York Times*, 23 March 1971, p. 46.)

83. Gay Activist Alliance, LaSalle College, 9 December 1971, mimeographed (on file, Institute for Sex Research, Indiana).

84. Homophile League of Philadelphia, untitled memorandum, October 1971 (on file, Institute for Sex Research, Indiana).

85. Herbert Marcuse, Barrington Moore, and Robert Paul Wolff, *Critique of Pure Tolerance* (Boston: Beacon Press, 1965).

86. "Dr. Reuben Zapped on Chicago T.V.," *Gay*, 1 March 1971, p. 3.

87. *New York Times*, 17 February 1973, p. 63. A Gay Activist Alliance flier declared "Marcus Welby is a Quack (and a Bigot)!"

88. "Psychologists Get Gay Lib Therapy," *The Advocate*, 11–28 November 1970, p. 1.

CHAPTER 4

1. Gary Alinder, "Gay Liberation Meets The Shrinks," in Karla Jay and Allen Young (eds.), *Out of the Closets: Voices of Gay Liberation* (New York: Jove Books, 1977), p. 143.

2. Ibid., p. 144.

3. Ibid.

4. Based on reports from the *Washington Post*, 15 May 1970, *Washington Star*, 24 May 1970, and the *San Francisco Chronicle*, 15 May 1970.

5. Kent Robinson, interview, 7 June 1978, Baltimore.

6. *The Advocate*, 26 May 1971, p. 3.

7. Kent Robinson, interview, 7 June 1978, Baltimore.

8. "Lifestyles of the Non-Patient Homosexual," (unofficial transcript of a panel discussion held on 6 May 1971 at the Annual Convention of the American Psychiatric Association), p. 5.

9. Ibid., p. 14.

10. Frank Kameny, "Gay, Proud and Healthy," mimeographed.

11. Ibid.

12. All citations are drawn from a tape recording of the panel discussion provided by Kent Robinson.

13. *See* chapter 2, page 64 for a discussion of this article.

14. Frank Kameny, interview. Kameny may have exaggerated. Bieber claims to have been attacked after a presentation.

15. *The Advocate*, 7 June 1972, p. 12.

16. Richard Green, "Homosexuality as a Mental Illness," *International Journal of Psychiatry* 10 (March 1972):77–98.

17. Ibid.

18. Judd Marmor, "Homosexuality—Mental Illness or Moral Dilemma," ibid.:114–17.

19. Martin Hoffman, "Philosophic, Empirical, and Ecologic Remarks," ibid.:105–7.

20. Charles Socarides. "Homosexuality—Basic Concepts and Psychodynamics," ibid.:118–25.

21. Lawrence J. Hatterer, "A Critique," ibid.:102–4.

22. American Psychiatric Association Task Force on Social Issues, "Recommendation on Homosexuality," 18 November 1971.

23. Henry Brill to Walter Barton, 11 December 1971 (on file, American Psychiatric Association, Washington, D.C.).

24. Task Force on Sexual Deviation, New York County District Branch, American Psychiatric Association, "Homosexuality in the Male," 20 March 1972, mimeographed.

25. James P. Cattell, President of the New York County District Branch to Charles Socarides, 11 August 1972.

26. Charles Socarides, interview, 29 April 1978, New York.

27. Robert Osnos, interview, 13 May 1978, New York.

28. Executive Committee, National Association for Mental Health, "Homosexuality" (adopted 17 October 1970), in *Mental Hygiene* 55 (January 1971):131.

29. San Francisco Association for Mental Health, "Position Statement on Homosexuality," 3 June 1971, mimeographed.

30. Ronald Lee, "Mental Health and Gay Liberation," April 1972, mimeographed.

31. Ronald Gold, interview, 13 September 1978 (telephone).

32. Robert Spitzer, interview, 30 May 1978, New York.

33. Bruce Voeller, interview, 13 September 1978, New York.

34. Seymour L. Halleck to Committee on Nomenclature, 1 February 1973.

35. Wardell B. Pomeroy to Committee on Nomenclature, 3 February 1973.

36. Alan P. Bell to Committee on Nomenclature, 1 February 1973.

37. These statements were taken largely from their responses to Richard Green's article in the *International Journal of Psychiatry*, cited at note 16 above.

38. The letter, which was discovered by Hendrik Ruitenbeek, is discussed in chapter 1.

39. Gay Organizations in New York City, "Memorandum to Committee on Nomenclature of the American Psychiatric Association: Should Homosexuality Be in the APA Nomenclature?" mimeographed (on file, National Gay Task Force, New York City).

40. "Statement by Charles Silverstein to the Nomenclature Committee of the American Psychiatric Association," 8 February 1973, mimeographed.

41. Interviews with Heinz Lehmann, 23 June 1978 (telephone), and Paul Wilson, 16 May 1978 (Bethesda, Maryland), members of the committee.

42. *See,* for example, "Curing the Psychiatrists," *Gay Activist,* February 1973, p. 1.
43. It was Ronald Gold who informed the *Times* of the meeting.
44. *New York Times,* 9 February 1973, p. 24.
45. Irving Bieber to Walter Barton, 9 April 1973.
46. Andre Ballard to Walter Barton, 9 April 1973.
47. Harry Gershman to Walter Barton, 18 April 1973.
48. Edward O. Joseph to Walter Barton, 5 May 1973.
49. Richard Pillard to Lawrence Hartmann, 29 December 1972.
50. *Psychiatric News,* 31 March 1973; Northern New England Psychiatric Society, *Newsletter,* May 1973, pp. 1–2.
51. *The Advocate,* 23 May 1973, p. 17.
52. Paul Wilson, interview, 16 May 1978, Bethesda, Maryland.
53. Robert Spitzer, interview, 30 May 1978, New York.
54. Among the most important studies for Spitzer was Marcel Saghir and Eli Robins, *Male and Female Homosexuality: A Comparative Investigation* (Baltimore: Williams and Wilkins, 1973).
55. Irving Bieber, "Homosexuality—An Adaptive Consequence of Disorder in Psychosexual Development," and Charles Socarides, "Findings Derived from 15 Years of Clinical Research," *Journal of the American Psychiatric Association* (November 1973), pp. 1209–11.
56. Judd Marmor, "Homosexuality and Cultural Value Systems," ibid., p. 1209.
57. Robert Stoller, "Criteria for Psychiatric Diagnoses," ibid., p. 1207.
58. Ronald Gold, "Stop It, You're Making Me Sick," ibid., pp. 1211–12.
59. *Newsweek,* 21 May 1973.
60. Ronald Gold, interview, 13 September 1978 (telephone).
61. Robert Spitzer, interview, 30 May 1978, New York.
62. Robert L. Spitzer, "A Proposal About Homosexuality and the APA Nomenclature: Homosexuality as an Irregular Form of Sexual Development, and Sexual Orientation Disturbance as a Psychiatric Disorder," mimeographed. The Symposium on Homosexuality in the *Journal of the American Psychiatric Association* (November 1973) suggests incorrectly that Spitzer's proposal was read at the May 1973 panel, which he merely moderated.
63. Henry Brill to Walter Barton, 23 June 1973.
64. Russell Monroe, interview, 20 September 1978 (telephone).
65. Henry Work to Russell Monroe, 28 June 1973.
66. Ronald Gold to members of the Council on Research and Development, undated.
67. Louis Jolyon West, interview, 31 May 1978 (telephone).
68. Louis Jolyon West to Nathaniel Ross, 28 May 1974.
69. Bruce Voeller, Jean O'Leary, and Don Goodwin to District Branch officers, 14 September 1973. On the same day a letter calling for immediate action was addressed to gay organizations around the country. They were urged to contact the presidents of APA district branches, the local Social Issues chairpersons, as well as other sympathetic psychiatrists to help win approval for the resolution. Recognizing that such a lobbying effort would require the capacity to provide psychiatric testimony about the appropriateness of a nomenclature change, all those contacted were provided with copies of Judd Marmor's speech at the Honolulu meeting.
70. "Minutes of the Assembly of District Branches," 3 November 1973.
71. Soon after Spitzer had circulated his proposal in June, Judd Marmor wrote to him urging that the phrase "homosexuality is an irregular form of sexual behavior" be replaced by "homosexuality is a variant of sexual behav-

ior." Spitzer explicity rejected that suggestion arguing that it would make homosexuality appear "too normal." (Robert Spitzer, interview, 30 May 1978, New York.)

72. "Minutes of the Reference Committee Meeting," 15–16 November 1973.

73. Confidential memorandum from Robbie Robinson to Drs. Barton, Freedman, Spiegel, Monroe, and Spitzer, 7 December 1973.

74. Memorandum from Ronald Gold to participants in APA press conference.

75. Irving Bieber, presentation to the board of trustees, "Minutes of the Board of Trustees Meeting," 15 December 1973, p. 26.

76. Charles Socarides, presentation to the board of trustees, ibid.

77. Robert McDevitt, presentation to the board of trustees, 15 December 1973, mimeographed.

78. John Spiegel, interview, 20 June 1978, Waltham, Massachusetts.

79. Leon Eisenberg, interview, 31 October 1978 (telephone).

80. John Nardini, interview, 17 January 1979 (telephone).

81. "Minutes of the Board of Trustees Meeting," 15 December 1973.

82. American Psychiatric Association, press release, 15 December 1973.

83. Ibid.

84. Ibid.

85. *Washington Post*, 16 December 1973, p. 1.

86. *Washington Star*, 16 December 1973, p. 1.

87. *New York Times*, 16 December 1973, p. 1.

88. *The Advocate*, 2 January 1973, p. 1.

89. *The Advocate*, 16 January 1973, p. 1.

90. Roger Berlin, "Letter," *Psychiatric News*, 3 April 1974, p. 2.

91. *See*, for example, Robert Weimer to Walter Barton, 18 December 1973.

92. Berlin, "Letter."

93. William J. Green, "Letter," *Psychiatric News*, 3 April 1974, p. 2.

94. Robert Goldstein, "Letter," *Psychiatric News*, 3 April 1974, p. 2.

95. Harold Voth, "Letter," *Psychiatric News*, 16 January 1974, p. 2.

96. Abram Kardiner, letter to the editor of *Psychiatric News* (unpublished).

97. Other members of the committee were: Lotham Gideo-Frank, Robert J. McDevitt, Burton L. Nackerson, Armand M. Nicholi, Nathaniel Ross, Vamik D. Volkan, and Harold M. Voth.

98. Charles Hite, "APA Task Force to Study Objections to Science Referenda," *Psychiatric News*, 3 April 1974, p. 15.

99. Irving Bieber, interview, 10 May 1978, New York.

100. Hite, "APA Task Force to Study Objections," p. 17.

101. John Spiegel, interview, 20 June 1978, Waltham, Massachusetts.

102. Hite, "APA Task Force to Study Objections," p. 15.

103. *Psychiatric News*, 6 February 1974, p. 3.

104. Bruce Voeller, interview, 13 September 1978, New York.

105. Letter to APA members, 28 February 1974.

106. In a letter dated 6 February 1974, Ronald Gold wrote to Drs. West, Marmor, and Modlin, "Please sign the enclosed letter and send it back to us as quickly as you can, since it will take some time to get it printed and mailed to the membership. . . ."

107. Letter dated 13 February 1974.

108. Bruce Voeller, interview, 13 September 1978, New York.

109. In a February 28, 1974 memorandum from Robbie Robinson, a staff member, to Walter Barton, the Association's medical director, he noted that he had called the National Gay Task Force on that date to determine the status of the mailing.

110. Charles Socarides to Walter Barton, 25 February 1974.

111. Walter Barton to Charles Socarides, 28 February 1974.
112. Harold Voth to Alfred Freedman, 13 March 1974.
113. "Referendum to Change an Action of the Board of Trustees."
114. Warren Williams, interview, 23 June 1978 (telephone).
115. Heinz Lehman, interview, 23 June 1978 (telephone).
116. Nathaniel Ross, "Letter," *Psychiatric News*, 29 April 1974.
117. Mike Royko, "Propaganda, First Class," *Chicago Daily News*, 17 May 1974, p. 3. The article also appeared in the *Philadelphia Sunday Bulletin*, 19 May 1974, sec. 4, p. 3.
118. *Psychiatric News*, 3 July 1974, p. 140.
119. *Report*, Ad Hoc Committee to Investigate the Conduct and the Referendum, Recommendations 1C and 1D.
120. Ibid., Recommendation 1E.
121. Ibid., Recommendation 4 (emphasis added).
122. Charles Socarides to APA Headquarters.
123. "Minutes of the Board of Trustees Meeting," 13–14 December 1974.

CHAPTER 5

1. Resolutions supporting gay civil rights are contained in the following: Society of Friends, "Yearly Meeting Minutes on Gay Civil Rights (1972–1974)," mimeographed; Lutheran Church in America, "Sex, Marriage and the Family," Fifth Biennial Convention (Minneapolis, June 25–July 2, 1970); Episcopal Diocese of New York, 196th Convention (May 11, 1974); National Council of Churches, "A Resolution on Civil Rights Without Discrimination as to Affectional or Sexual Preference"; National Federation of Priests' Councils, House of Delegates, March 17–21, 1974, "Resolution on Civil Rights of Homosexual Persons"; (all on file, National Gay Task Force, New York).
2. The text of the resolution was contained in a letter from the American Bar Association, office of the secretary, to Bruce Voeller (December 21, 1973).
3. American Medical Association, "Legal Restrictions to Sexual Behavior Between Consenting Adults," *Proceedings House of Delegates* (Atlantic City, N.J.: June 15–19, 1975), p. 84. This action lagged considerably behind the opinion of physicians. In 1969 a survey by *Modern Medicine* found that 67.7 percent of more than 27,000 physicians approved such a stance (*New York Times*, 3 October 1969, p. 37).
4. American Psychological Association, *News*, 24 January 1975.
5. The National Gay Task Force monitored such legislation. Its findings are contained in "Gay Rights Protections in the United States and Canada as of 1976," mimeographed (on file, National Gay Task Force, New York).
6. U.S. Civil Service Commission, *Civil Service News*, 3 July 1975.
7. *New York Times*, 3 May 1974, p. 38.
8. *New York Times*, 28 April 1974, p. 41.
9. An effort in 1971 to pass such a bill was defeated in the City Council. A similar failure in January of 1972 forced Mayor Lindsay to take executive action to protect gay municipal employees under his jurisdiction (*New York Times*, 8 February 1972, p. 35).
10. Bruce Voeller to Walter Barton, 29 January 1974.

11. Psychiatrists had often expressed opposition to official recognition of homosexual groups at universities. For example, Benson R. Snyder, a psychiatrist and dean at the Massachusetts Institute of Technology, stated that he was concerned about young students "who are uncertain about their identities getting caught in an exploitive situation." (*New York Times*, 15 December 1971, p. 47.)

12. American Psychiatric Association, "Minutes," Board of Trustees, Executive Committee (April 1974).

13. John Spiegel to Bruce Voeller, March 25, 1975.

14. Judd Marmor, open letter (June 30, 1975).

15. Jack Weinberg to Julius Richmond, Surgeon General, September 8, 1977.

16. American Psychiatric Association, press release, 1 August 1977.

17. Gay, Lesbian, and Bisexual Caucus of the American Psychiatric Association, *Newsletter*, January 1976.

18. Frank A. Rundle and James A. Paulsen (cochairpersons, Caucus of Gay Psychiatrists of the APA), Memorandum to Harold M. Visotsky, Chairperson, Council on National Affairs, "Establishment of a Task Force on Homosexual Psychiatrists," 6 December 1977.

19. Personal communication, Richard Pillard.

20. *See*, for example, Harold Visotsky to James A. Paulsen and Frank Rundle, 26 September 1977.

21. Irving Bieber, "Homosexuality," in *Comprehensive Textbook of Psychiatry*, Alfred Freedman and Harold Kaplan, eds. (Baltimore: Williams & Wilkins, 1967), pp. 963–76.

22. Judd Marmor, "Homosexuality and Sexual Orientation Disturbances," in *Comprehensive Textbook of Psychiatry*, Alfred Freedman, Harold Kaplan, and Benjamin Sadock, eds. (Baltimore: Williams & Wilkins, 1975), pp. 1510–20.

23. Alfred Freedman, interview, July 6, 1978, New York.

24. Marmor, *Textbook of Psychiatry*, p. 1517.

25. Jonas Robitscher, unpublished manuscript.

26. Silvano Arieti, personal communication.

27. American Association of Directors of Psychiatric Residency Training, *AADPRT Second Annual Questionnaire*, 31 October 1978, mimeographed.

28. "Sexual Survey #4: Current Thinking on Homosexuality," *Medical Aspects of Human Sexuality* 11 (November 1977), pp. 110–11.

29. "Sick Again?" *Time*, 20 February 1978, p. 102.

30. The psychoanalytic community was especially distressed by Spitzer's focus upon subjective distress since it precluded the possibility of diagnosing disorders in which the defense mechanisms served to deny the presence of intrapsychic conflict. Writing in the *Newsletter* of the American Psychoanalytic Association, October 1976, Oscar Legoult stated, "Aside from the absurdity which allows so many severe nosological entities to depend upon ego syntonicity and successful adaptational camouflage for their diagnosis, Dr. Spitzer's position is a serious weakening of the stance in psychiatry in the current discussions going on with respect to psychiatric benefits and of psychiatry's position under proposed National Health Insurance. The logic of the position is not so far from stating that possibly psychiatric efforts should be directed toward making any condition ego-syntonic, that social stigmatization is in fact the cause of illness and that mental disorder is a myth" (p. 4).

31. Robert Spitzer, "Memorandum to Members and Consultants of the Sex Subcommittee," 28 May 1976.

32. *Diagnostic and Statistical Manual-III*, draft, April 15, 1977, p. 210.

33. Robert Spitzer to Richard Green, 27 December 1976.

34. Richard Green to Robert Spitzer, 14 December 1976.

35. Gay, Lesbian and Bisexual Caucus, *Newsletter,* January 1976.
36. John Fryer to Robert Spitzer, 28 May 1975.
37. *DSM-III,* draft, April 15, 1977, p. L18.
38. Richard Pillard to Judd Marmor, March 1977.
39. Leon Eisenberg to Richard Pillard, 29 March 1977.
40. George Winokur to Richard Pillard, 8 April 1977.
41. Judd Marmor to Richard Pillard, 15 March 1977.
42. Ibid.; Judd Marmor to Robert Spitzer, 15 April 1977.
43. Judd Marmor to Robert Spitzer, 12 May 1977.
44. Judd Marmor to Richard Pillard, 15 March 1977.
45. Richard Green, Memorandum to Harold Lief, Diane Fordney, Paul Gebhard, 6 April 1977.
46. Richard Pillard to Richard Green, 31 March 1977.
47. Richard Green, Memorandum to DSM-III Colleagues, 27 June 1977.
48. Robert Spitzer, Memorandum to Members of the Advisory Committee on Psychosexual Disorders, 8 July 1977.
49. Judd Marmor to Robert Spitzer, 21 July 1977.
50. Robert Spitzer to Richard Green, 23 September 1977.
51. Paul Gebhard to Robert Spitzer, 3 October 1977.
52. John Money to Robert Spitzer, 8 August 1977.
53. Robert L. Spitzer, Memorandum to Members of the Advisory Committee on Psychosexual Disorders, 5 October 1977.
54. Michael Mavroidis, Memorandum to Task Force on Nomenclature and Statistics Advisory Committee on Psychosexual Disorders, Assembly Task Force on DSM-III, 31 October 1977.
55. Michael Mavroidis to Frank Kameny, 31 October 1977.
56. Robert Spitzer, Memorandum to Task Force on Nomenclature and Statistics and Advisory Committee on Psychosexual Disorders 18 October 1977.
57. Most important were the remarks from Donald Klein of Spitzer's own institution, the New York State Psychiatric Institute. It was he who recommended both a change in terminology and a shift away from a focus on distress over homosexual impulses to impairment of heterosexual functioning. Memorandum from Donald Klein to Robert Spitzer, 3 December 1977.
58. *DSM-III,* draft, December 20, 1977, L1.
59. Ibid., L2.
60. Robert Spitzer, Memorandum to Task Force, Advisory Committees, other consultants, et al., 1 February 1978.
61. Richard Green, personal communication.
62. Duplicates of several letters exchanged during the controversy were sent to both on at least two occasions. Kameny sent sharp criticisms to Spitzer, but his active involvement appears to have ended there.

CONCLUSION

1. Cited in Barbara Wooton, *Social Science and Social Pathology* (London: George Allen and Unwin, 1959), p. 211.
2. Ibid., p. 220.
3. Daniel Offer and Melvin Sabshin, *Normality: Theoretical and Clinical Concepts of Mental Health,* 2nd ed. (New York: Basic Books, 1974), p. 179.

4. Heinz Hartmann, "Psycho-Analysis and the Concept of Health," *International Journal of Psycho-Analysis* 20 (1939):309.

5. Cited in Ruth Macklin, "Mental Health and Mental Illness: Some Problems of Definition and Concept Formation," *Philosophy of Science* 39 (September 1972), p. 349.

6. Marie Jahoda, *Current Concepts of Mental Health* (New York: Basic Books, 1958), p. 12.

7. Cited in Christopher Boorse, "What a Theory of Mental Health Should Be," mimeographed, 1976, p. 25. This paper appeared subsequently in *The Journal for the Theory of Social Behavior* 6 (April 1976).

8. Ibid., p. 26.

9. Offer and Sabshin, *Normality*, p. 90.

10. Boorse, "Theory of Mental Health," p. 28.

11. Talcott Parsons, "Definitions of Health and Illness in the Light of American Values and Social Structures," in E. G. Jaco, *Patients, Physicians and Illness* (New York: Free Press, 1958), pp. 165–87.

12. Christopher Boorse, "On the Distinction Between Disease and Illness," *Philosophy and Public Affairs* 15 (Fall 1975):51.

13. Peter Sedgwick, "Illness—Mental and Otherwise," *Hastings Center Studies* 1, no. 3 (1973):27.

14. Ibid., p. 30.

15. Ibid., p. 31.

16. Ibid., p. 32.

17. Robert Spitzer and Paul Wilson, "Nosology and the Official Psychiatric Nomenclature," in Alfred Freedman, Harold Kaplan and Benjamin Sadock (eds.), *Comprehensive Textbook of Psychiatry* 2nd ed. (Baltimore: Williams & Wilkins, 1975), p. 826.

18. Hendrik Ruitenbeek, *The Problem of Homosexuality in Modern Society* (New York: Dutton, 1963).

19. Hendrik Ruitenbeek (ed.), *Homosexuality: A Changing Picture* (London: Souvenir Press, 1973), p. 13.

20. Robert Seidenberg, "Accursed Race" ibid., p. 164.

21. Clarissa K. Wittenberg, "Kinsey Report on Homosexuality," *Psychiatric News*, 16 February 1979, p. 1.

22. Gerald C. Davison, "Homosexuality: The Ethical Challenge," *Journal of Consulting and Clinical Psychology*, 44 no. 2, (1976):161.

23. Ibid., p. 162.

24. *Journal of Homosexuality* (Spring 1977), pp. 195–261.

25. *New York Times*, 23 December 1973, sec. 4, p. 5 (emphasis supplied).

26. Unpublished letter of John Spiegel to *Time*, 15 September 1975.

27. Arnold Rogow, *The Psychiatrists* (New York: Delta, 1970), pp. 118–50.

28. Ibid., p. 123.

29. George Wiedeman, "Homosexuality: A Survey," *Journal of the American Psychoanalytic Association* (1974):693.

30. "Study Indicates Anti-Homosexual Textbook Bias," *Psychiatric News*, 17 August 1979, p. 14.

31. Daniel E. Newton, "Representations of Homosexuality in Health Science Textbooks," *Journal of Homosexuality* 4 (Spring 1979) pp. 247–54.

32. Ann Landers, *New York Daily News*, 23 July 1976, p. 48.

33. Abram Kardiner, "The Social Distress Syndrome of Our Time—Part 2," *Journal of the American Academy of Psychoanalysis* 6, no. 2 (1978):218.

34. *New York Times*, 15 August 1979, p. 14.

35. *New York Times*, 27 December 1979, p. 16.

AFTERWORD TO THE 1987 EDITION

1. The discussion of the early response of the gay community to AIDS is taken from my article "AIDS and the Gay Community: Between the Specter and the Promise of Medicine," *Social Research* 52, no. 3 (Autumn 1985):581–606. Reprinted, with changes, by permission.

2. U.S. Department of Health and Human Services, *Morbidity and Mortality Weekly Reports (MMWR)*, 5 June 1981.

3. *MMWR*, 3 July 1981.

4. *MMWR*, 16 July 1982.

5. *MMWR*, 10 December 1982.

6. Harry Schwartz, "AIDS in the Media," appendix to Dorothy Nelkin, *Science in the Streets: A Background Paper* (New York: Twentieth Century Fund, 1984).

7. See, in general, Dennis Altman, "The Politicization of an Epidemic," *Socialist Review*, November/December 1984.

8. See, for example, "Morticians Balk at AIDS Victims," *Washington Post*, 18 June 1983.

9. *Moral Majority Report*, July 1983.

10. *Washington Post*, 6 July 1983.

11. *New York Post*, 24 May 1983.

12. *New York Times*, 7 August 1983.

13. Discussed in Ronald Bayer, "Gays and the Stigma of Bad Blood," *Hastings Center Report*, April 1983, pp. 5–7.

14. U.S. Department of Health and Human Services, Memorandum from the Director, Office of Biologics, National Center for Drugs and Biologics, "Recommendations to Decrease the Risk of Transmitting Acquired Immune Deficiency Syndrome from Plasma Donors," 24 March 1983.

15. U.S. Department of Health and Human Services, Memorandum from the Acting Director, Office of Biologics Research and Review, "Revised Recommendations to Decrease the Risk of Transmitting an Immunodeficiency Syndrome (AIDS) from Blood and Plasma Donors," 14 December 1984.

16. *American Medical News*, 20 January 1984, p. 3.

17. *Journal of the American Medical Association* 251 (20 January 1984):341.

18. Lawrence Mass, "The Case against Medical Panic," *New York Native*, 17–30 January 1983, p. 23.

19. Jonathan Lieberson, "Anatomy of an Epidemic," *New York Review of Books*, 18 August 1983, p. 19.

20. Ibid., 22.

21. John Rechy, letter to the *New York Review of Books*, 13 October 1983, p. 43.

22. U.S. Public Health Service,"Public Health Service Plans for the Prevention and Control of AIDS and the AIDS Virus: Report of the Coolfont Planning Conference, June 4–6,1986," mimeographed.

23. *Los Angeles Times* poll, conducted 5–12 December 1985, mimeographed.

24. Eleanor Singer and Theresa Rogers,"Public Opinion and AIDS," *AIDS and Public Policy Journal*, July 1986, pp. 11–12.

25. *Bowers* v. *Hardwick*, slip opinion, White decision, p. 6.

26. Ibid., pp. 7–8.

27. Ibid., p. 9.

28. Ibid., Burger decision, p. 2.

29. Ibid., Blackmun decision, p. 1.
30. Ibid., p. 2.
31. Ibid., p. 14.
32. Ibid., p. 16.
33. Ronald Bayer and Robert Spitzer, "Neurosis, Psychodynamics and DSM-III: A History of Controversy," *Archives of General Psychiatry*, February 1985, pp. 187–96.
34. Robert M. Friedman, "The Psychoanalytic Model of Male Homosexuality: A Historical and Theoretical Critique," *Psychoanalytic Review*, Winter 1986.
35. Richard A. Isay, "Homosexuality in Homosexual Men: Some Distinctions and Implications for Treatment," in G. Fogel, F. Lane, and R. S. Liebert (eds.), *The Psychology of Men* (New York: Basic Books, 1986), p. 278.
36. Ibid., p. 286.
37. Ibid.
38. See for example the report "Scientific Meeting of the Psychoanalytic Association of New York, May 20, 1985," *Newsletter of the New York Psychoanalytic Association*, n.d., pp. 9–12. Also Richard Isay, interview, 2 August 1986, New York.
39. Robert Spitzer, interview, 25 July 1986, New York.
40. Alan Malyon to Robert Spitzer, 4 October 1985.
41. Robert L. Spitzer, "The Diagnostic Status of Homosexuality in DSM-III: A Reformulation of the Issues," *American Journal of Psychiatry*, February 1981, pp. 210–15.
42. Terry Stein to Robert L. Spitzer, 4 November 1985.
43. Robert Paul Cabaj to Robert L. Spitzer, 26 November 1985.
44. For a brief description see "DSM-III-R: Amendment Process Frustrates Non MDs," *American Psychological Association Monitor*, February 1986, pp. 17–24.
45. Memorandum of Steven S. Sharfstein, "Meeting on December 4, 1985 Regarding DSM-III-R Controversies," 6 November 1985.
46. Alan K. Malyon to Bryant Welch, 24 November 1985, and James P. Krajeski to Robert Spitzer, 26 November 1985.
47. Stuart E. Nichols to Robert L. Spitzer, 29 November 1985.
48. Memorandum of Arnie Kahn to Alan K. Malyon and Carol Burroughs, "December 4, 1985 Meeting at the American Psychiatric Association on Ego-Dystonic Homosexuality."
49. Memorandum of Robert Pasnau to Participants and Guests Who Attended the December 4, 1985 Meeting of the Ad Hoc Committee of the Board and Assembly to Review DSM-III-R, 11 December 1985.
50. Robert L. Spitzer to Terry Stein, Robert P. Cabaj, James P. Krajeski, and Alan K. Malyon, 30 December 1985.
51. Terry Stein, telephone interview, 16 August 1985.
52. Alan K. Malyon to Bryant Welch, 25 January 1986.
53. Memorandum of Terry S. Stein to Ronald Selbst and Sarah Allison, "Comments on DSM-III-R," 23 April 1986.
54. James P. Krajeski to Robert L. Spitzer, 9 April 1986.
55. Robert Cabaj, "EDH Removed from DSM-III,R," *Newsletter of the Association of Gay and Lesbian Psychiatrists*, September 1986, p. 3, and Association of Gay and Lesbian Psychiatrists, "Important Notice," undated.
56. Robert Cabaj, interview, 4 August 1986, Boston, and Terry Stein, telephone interview, 16 August 1986.
57. Robert L. Spitzer to Terry S. Stein, Robert P. Cabaj, James P. Krajeski, and Alan K. Malyon, 21 May 1986.
58. Cabaj, "EDH Removed from DSM-III,R."
59. Robert L. Spitzer, interview, 25 July 1986, New York.

60. Robert L. Spitzer, interview, 9 February 1987, New York.
61. American Psychiatric Association, press release, 1 July 1986.
62. Ibid.
63. Robert Cabaj, "President's Column," *Newsletter of the Association of Gay and Lesbian Psychiatrists*, September 1986, p. 1.
64. American Psychiatric Association, press release, 1 July 1986.

INDEX